TREE

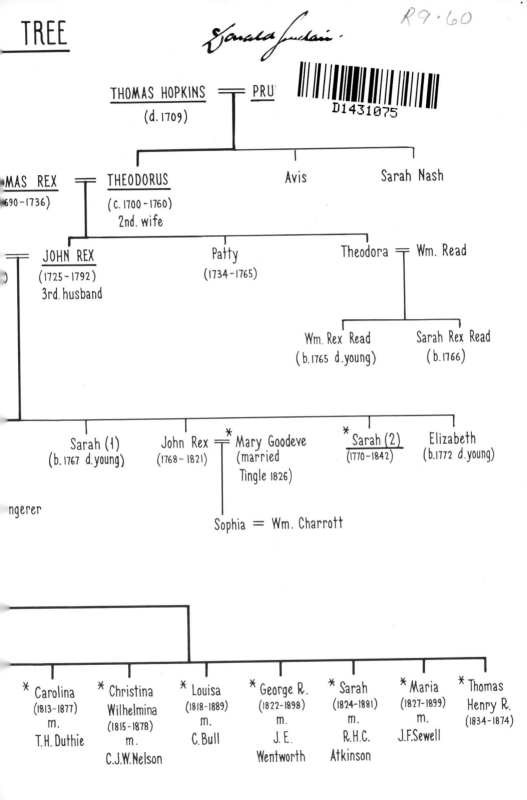

Gerald Sinclair.

R9·60

THOMAS HOPKINS (d. 1709) == PRU'

THEODORUS (c. 1700 – 1760) 2nd. wife   Avis   Sarah Nash

…MAS REX (…690 – 1736) ==

JOHN REX (1725 – 1792) 3rd. husband   Patty (1734 – 1765)   Theodora == Wm. Read

Wm. Rex Read (b. 1765 d. young)   Sarah Rex Read (b. 1766)

Sarah (1) (b. 1767 d. young)   John Rex (1768 – 1821) == *Mary Goodeve (married Tingle 1826)   *Sarah (2) (1770 – 1842)   Elizabeth (b. 1772 d. young)

…ngerer

Sophia = Wm. Charrott

* Carolina (1813 – 1877) m. T. H. Duthie

* Christina Wilhelmina (1815 – 1878) m. C. J. W. Nelson

* Louisa (1818 – 1889) m. C. Bull

* George R. (1822 – 1898) m. J. E. Wentworth

* Sarah (1824 – 1881) m. R. H. C. Atkinson

* Maria (1827 – 1899) m. J. F. Sewell

* Thomas Henry R. (1834 – 1874)

…eficiaries of her will.
… copyhold lands.

C.G.M.

GEORGE REX: DEATH OF A LEGEND

The four sovereigns of Great Britain who reigned in George Rex's lifetime: (Top left) King George III (by Ramsay). (Right) King George IV (by Lawrence). (Bottom left) King William IV (by Shee) Queen Victoria (by Hayter). Reproduced from the original portraits by gracious permission of Her Majesty Queen Elizabeth II. (Photos: A.C. Cooper, London)

GEORGE REX:
DEATH OF A LEGEND

Patricia Storrar

Patricia Storrar

M

ISBN 0 86954 017 3

First published in 1974 by
MACMILLAN SOUTH AFRICA (PUBLISHERS)
Johannesburg

Associated companies in London, New York,
Dublin, Melbourne and Madras

Phototypeset in 11/12½pt Baskerville
by Dieter Zimmermann (Pty.) Ltd., Johannesburg
Printed by Wallachs Printing Company, Pretoria

Contents

Illustrations

*'Truth hath no greater enemy than
verisimilitude and likelihood'*

Preface

There is an interesting chain of circumstance and coincidence behind the publication of this book. When I set out some time ago to gather material on Knysna and Plettenberg Bay with the idea of writing a general story of this fascinating area, I necessarily had to read, in the course of my research, a good deal about George Rex, Marshal of the Vice-Admiralty Court at the Cape during the first British occupation and founder of the little hill-ringed town of Knysna in the Cape Province. One cannot enquire, even superficially, into the history of Knysna without acquiring some information about the first man to become a substantial landowner in this area.

When I had read a dozen or so books referring wholly or in part to the legend of his having been of royal birth, and numerous accounts by early travellers of his hospitality to all comers, of his grand *ménage* at *Melkhout Kraal* and his admirably organised husbandry, I was left with the uncomfortable feeling that this was no cast-off scion of a royal house who had had everything poured into his lap by a guilty father. This was a man of brain and ambition, more than averagely well educated and possessed of a keen busines sense. The two halves of the picture did not quite fit.

Authors and historians have, however, been delving into the past for well over a century in the hope of finding the key to the puzzle of Rex's identity. Much has been written on the subject, based largely on surmise, speculation and circumstantial evidence. How was I, living almost on the scene of his achievements but hundreds of kilometres from archives and reference libraries, going to do any better? It was at this point that I heard quite coincidentally from two informed sources, that the leading authority in Britain today on the reign of George III, Rex's supposed father, was Professor Ian R.. Christie, Professor of Modern British History at University College, London. Slightly astonished at my own temerity, I cast my line and hook over nearly ten thousand kilometres of ocean.

Professor Christie, distinguished author of several scholarly works, sought-after contributor to historical journals, a senior member of a large department at one of the leading British universities, took the bait in one bite. He found it irresistible. Back came a list of books to be read, a succint summary of the character of George III as a young man, photo-copies of some of the King's letters to Lord Bute, and a suggestion that it might be worthwhile studying something of the little-known genetic disease, porphyria,* as a possible clue to a link between the royal family and the family at Knysna. While he dismissed as palpably improbable – if not impossible – the suggestion that there could have been a marriage between Prince George and Hannah Lightfoot, he listed with true scholarly thoroughness several other trails which it would be worthwhile following up.

This was towards the end of September, 1972, and it was the start of many months intensive correspondence – a correspondence stimulating and rewarding beyond my wildest dreams. Suggestions, hints, directions, questions and comparisons flew back and forth; the answers all travelling from north to south. The truly outstanding discovery of the evidence which conclusively established the genealogy of the Rex family was Professor Christie's alone. It was a brilliant display of scholarly virtuosity. With unerring skill he extracted from the ancient records four documents which establish Rex's parentage beyond all argument. Without this key discovery this book would never have seen the light of day.

Oddly enough, one of Professor Christie's own books (a book on late eighteenth century British politics, published in 1970) is entitled MYTH AND REALITY – a name which foreshadows to a certain extent the sifting of fact from fiction in which he found himself newly engaged. *Myth* has understandably been woven into the tapestry of the Rex story; to Ian Christie we owe the *reality*.

By now I was uncomfortably aware that this was too important a piece of research for the results of it to be mentioned casually in a chapter of a general history of Knysna and Plettenberg Bay. Then came another coincidence. A friend in the publishing world said, 'I hear you're writing a book on George Rex.' This was quite incorrect at the time, but the idea suddenly seemed a sound one. My travels to the archives and the libraries now began.

There is a tendency, common enough today, but of rank growth in the early years of the last century, to assume that any child of outstanding talents could only have been fathered by a man in the highest social position. When we consider, however, the material circumstances in which the majority of men and women of genius were reared, it is obvious that the reverse is more often than not the

*Appendix A

case. In Beethoven's own lifetime a rumour started that he was the illegitimate son of King Frederick William of Prussia. He was furious. The genius, whose mother was a good woman to whom he was devoted, wrote to a friend, 'I gladly leave it to you to make known to the world the honesty of my parents and of my mother in particular.'[1]

So here is the myth and the reality about George Rex, who too had a good mother. It is my sincere hope that it will not only set the record straight, but will enable readers – particularly the hundreds of Rex descendants who have played so significant a part in South Africa's story – to see the founder of Knysna in a new light, a rather more admirable light than that which was previously focussed on him. This man founded a town and a dynasty, and his descendants have every right to be proud of him.

A remarkable story it is, this story of one of South Africa's earliest, most notable settlers, who was firmly established as a prosperous colonist many years before the first substantial wave of settlers from the United Kingdom arrived in 1820.

Patricia Storrar

Plettenberg Bay, Cape Province,
South Africa.
April, 1974.

Acknowledgments

The author's sincere thanks are due to:

Her Majesty, Queen Elizabeth II, for her gracious permission to reproduce the portraits of the four British sovereigns (frontispiece) and to the Surveyor of the Queen's Pictures, Mr. Oliver Millar, of St. James's Palace, London, for his ready co-operation in having the necessary photographic copies made.

Professor Ian R. Christie, Professor of Modern British History at University College, London, not only for his discoveries which prompted the writing of this book, but for months of patient correspondence, wise advice and meticulous scrutiny of the text of those chapters relating to Rex's life in London;

Admiral John Munday, Director of the National Maritime Museum, Greenwich, for the photographs of the Oar Maces of Admiralty in the possession of the museum, and Rear-Admiral P. W. Brock, a Trustee of the National Maritime Museum, for his keen research into naval matters relating to this story and for the gift of a copy of Oar Maces of Admiralty;

The Queen's Librarian, Windsor Castle, Mr. Robert Mackworth-Young, for directing her enquiries relating to King George III into the correct channels;

Mr. Robin Reilly, of London, leading authority on Wedgwood products and author of *Wedgwood: The Portrait Medallions* (London, 1973), for much information on the work of Josiah Wedgwood and Sons and for the photographs of the Wedgwood medallions reproduced in this book;

Mr. Thomas Burr, of the National Trust, for making available for inspection the registers of births, deaths and marriages which took place in Kew Chapel in the eighteenth century;

Mr. Arthur Lloyd-Taylor, of Brighton, author of *The Taylors of Kew*, for information on Kew Chapel;

Mr. Ivon Asquith, of London, who collected much of the documentary material on which the reconstruction of George Rex's life in London has been based;

Mr. Harry Oppenheimer for permission to reproduce the sketch of *Melkhout Kraal* by Major A. C. Gregory from an album in the Oppenheimer private collection in the library of Little Brenthurst;

Professor Vernon S. Forbes for much information on the pioneer travellers in South Africa and for his great personal interest in this work;

Sir John Murray, of Plettenberg Bay, for advice on early land tenure in the Cape and on notarial practice;

Doctors G. T. Nurse and Trefor Jenkins, of the Human Sero-Genetics Unit, South African Institute for Medical Research, for information on the implications of blood group gene frequencies in the Cape;

the Reverend Arthur J. Rex Beddy and Mrs. Joan Beddy for the loan of George Rex's personal diary, for ready cooperation in all matters relating to the Rex family's history and for allowing the author to scan many family letters in their possession;

Miss Mary Gunn, of the Botanical Research Institute, Pretoria, for photographs of Rex's home, *Schoonder Zigt*, for a great deal of botanical information and for copies of extracts of unpublished diaries of Carl Drège and Thomas Miller;

Dr. Mary Alexander Cook, Curator of the Drosdty Museum, Swellendam, for valuable information on *Schoonder Zigt;*

Those authors in South Africa who have, in the best tradition of literary freemasonry, courteously volunteered information touching on several aspects of Rex's life (among them are Thelma Gutsche, Frank Bradlow, A. Gordon Brown, Vernon S. Forbes, and Marjorie Bull);

Miss Anna Smith, City Librarian of Johannesburg, for permission to reproduce John T. Serres painting of the Dutch and English squadrons in Table Bay and for her hepful interest at all times;

Mr. A. A. Telford for his skilled reconstruction in sketch form of *Schoonder Zigt* and of Rex's brig putting to sea through the Knysna Heads;

Mrs. B. Nagelgast, head of the Strange Collection, Johannesburg Public Library, and Mrs. E. Ritchie, of the Humphreys Collection, University of the Witwatersrand Library, for knowledgeable co-operation and keen research;

Dr. A. M. Lewin Robinson, Director of the South African Public Library, Cape Town, and his staff, especially Miss M. F. Cartwright, in charge of manuscripts in the Africana section, whose assistance was most valuable;

Mr. J. C. Quinton, Chief Librarian of the Library of Parliament, Cape Town, for permission to reproduce the sketch by an unknown artist of *The Drift, Knysna* and for having expeditiously had a copy of this sketch made;

Miss Joan Davies, Chief of the Cape Depot of the State Archives, and her staff for facilitating the necessary research in the Archives;

Mrs. Gillian Carter, in charge of the Knysna Public Library, for her personal interest in this work and for according the author special facilities in the library;

Mr. J. F. Reitz for skilled tracking down of documents in the Deeds Office, Cape Town, and for advice on legal matters;

Mr. Peter Crail, whose unique collection of tens of thousands of reference cards in the South African Public Library proved a valuable source of information;

the Director of the Department of Prints and Drawings, The British Museum, for permission to reproduce the engravings of *The College of Advocates, Doctors' Commons* and of *High Street, Whitechapel;*

the County Archivist, Essex Record Office, Chelmsford, for permission to reproduce the application by John Rex to be admitted to the Plaistow Marsh lands and the record of the sale of these lands in terms of Sarah Rex's will;

and, above all, her husband, Clare D. Storrar, for his assistance in research, ruthless revision of the script, inexhaustible enthusiasm and for being prepared to live for many months in the half-legendary world of George Rex for twenty-four hours a day.

1 Variations on a Theme

Legends tend to gain weight with age, especially legends with a touch of the purple to them. Such a legend is the one which has been widely accepted – and not only in South Africa – that George Rex, a lawyer who became Marshal of the Vice-Admiralty Court at the Cape of Good Hope during the first British occupation, was a legitimate or natural son of Prince George of Hanover, (afterwards King George III of Britain,) and Hannah Lightfoot, 'the fair Quaker'.

So firmly and so widely has this central theme of an involved story been believed for over a century and a half, that the author of the most authoritative biography of George Rex so far published[1] was able to paint with conviction a word picture of the last touching interview between the royal father and his putative son, before the younger man left England to go into voluntary exile at the Cape of Good Hope. His departure from England had apparently been deemed necessary for a number of reasons.

According to this biographer and to Rex family tradition, it was at this farewell interview that the King told George Rex of his decision to banish him, swore him to secrecy regarding his birth, made him promise never to marry, and personally handed him the mace of Admiralty, a small ebony staff surmounted by a silver crown, which was to be the badge of office of the Marshal in the newly-created Court of Vice-Admiralty at the Cape.

Among many other souvenirs which the King gave him were (according to his biographer) a signet ring bearing the initials GR; a Wedgwood portrait medallion of himself (the King); a gold locket in which was enclosed a lock of His Majesty's auburn hair; a cornelian seal set in gold, engraved with the words, 'Though lost to sight, to memory dear', and a massive pinchbeck watch.[2] These souvenirs are in the possession of the Rex family in South Africa today.

When one considers that the central figure in this drama at no time in his life laid claim to any connection with royalty and that Knysna, where Rex lived for thirty-five of his forty-two years in South Africa, is a relatively little-known corner of this vast continent, the amount of ink which has flowed from this romantic assumption is astonishing.

Not so surprising is the grip which the legend has taken on the public imagination, for it has all the ingredients of a rattling good story – royalty, mystery, sex and adventure.

But the remarkable story of George Rex and his rise to fame is only a part of a much more insistent and widely-circulated legend, one which has persisted for well over two centuries, although played down and sometimes even dismissed by modern historians.

The hard core of this story, of which a bewildering variety of permutations and combinations exists, is that Prince George, while still in his teens, contracted a marriage with a beautiful young Quaker woman, eight years his senior. If he did not marry her, he was supposed at least to have established some sort of liaison with her. First came hints that he had at an early age been smitten with the charms of this lovely woman and abducted her; well after his death came the bold assertion that he had actually married the object of his affections, but had put her away secretly when he decided to marry, in 1761, Princess Charlotte, daughter of the Grand Duke of Mecklenburg-Strelitz.

Later still came claims that children had been born of this *affaire de coeur*. As a result, there are scattered today in England, America, Africa and Australia families who believe, with the utmost sincerity and conviction, that their blood is almost as blue as King George IV's, King William IV's, Queen Victoria's, or that of any subsequent sovereign.

Strangely enough, although all versions of the legend were originally based on the assumption that the Prince had either seduced and/or married the Quaker, Hannah Lightfoot, and had then subsequently abandoned her when he made Princess Charlotte his Queen, there was, by and large, no hint of any real censure of this ungallant shedding of the wronged Quaker. The whole affair was regarded much as another tale of a handsome prince and his virtuous Cinderella, except that in this case the pumpkin did not turn into a coach and Cinderella, after her one crowded hour of glorious life was left in strict seclusion to look after her child (or children) in 'a large house surrounded by a high wall and garden' for the remaining few years of her life.[3]

Tracing the growth of the story chronologically necessitates a certain amount of leap-frogging in time, since many of the earliest alleged events were not publicised till many decades later. The assertion of a *marriage* between these two young people, for instance,

16

was not made categorically until after poor King George's death, some seventy years after the event had supposedly taken place.

Throwing chronology to the winds, therefore, here is the most popular and widely-accepted story of the Prince-and-the-Quaker-maid romance in its full flowering.

Hannah Lightfoot was the daughter of poor, but honest, parents, Matthew Lightfoot, a cordwainer and shoemaker, and his wife, Mary. They were both Quakers, as was Mrs. Lightfoot's brother, Henry Wheeler, who owned a linen-draper's business in London in Market Lane, St. James's. When Matthew Lightfoot died, it was in the hospitable home of this brother, Mr. Wheeler, that the widowed Mary Lightfoot and her daughter, Hannah, were invited to live. Because of this circumstance, a certain amount of confusion arose later as to whether Hannah's surname was Lightfoot or Wheeler.

Market Lane was a short street which ran between Pall Mall and Jermyn Street. The Opera House at that time had a private back entrance in Market Lane, reserved for royalty. Persistent legend has it that it was passing by this route to the back entrance of the Opera House one day in 1753 that Prince George, then aged fifteen, first caught sight of pretty Hannah, then nearly twenty-three, as she sat in the window of her uncle's shop to watch the royal party pass.

Hannah has often been described as 'the possessor of a fair and unsullied face', so it was not surprising that the Prince is said to have immediately fallen in love with her. The demure Quaker girl was naturally susceptible to the attentions of a personable young prince and the romance – it is said – prospered. After that first fateful glance, Prince George apparently found it convenient to use Pall Mall and Market Lane more and more frequently as he went about London town. But the course of true love did not run any more smoothly for the Prince and Hannah than it has done for any other of the famed lovers in history.

Prince George, according to some writers, had ideas at first of making her his mistress, but Hannah's Quaker upbringing and Quaker conscience would permit of no such arrangement. Marriage it had to be – or two marriages, if certain of these chroniclers are to be believed. In his plans to circumvent the less exciting arrangements made for him by his mother, Augusta, Dowager Princess of Wales, his governor, preceptor, tutors and, not least, his old grandfather, King George II, young George now found a willing accomplice in Elizabeth Chudleigh, lady-in-waiting to his mother.

'The Virgin Chudleigh', who later became the notorious Duchess of Kingston, was a mistress of intrigue and of several men.

Wise in the ways of the world, unscrupulous, anxious to keep in with the Dowager Princess and the aging King, but at the same time to safeguard her own position at Court when the young Prince should come to power, she was only too anxious to be of assistance, say all reports. She scented intrigue as a hound scents the fox. When she realised the extent of the consternation at court over the Prince's deep attachment to a commoner and also discovered that the virtuous Wheelers were hastily arranging to marry off Hannah to a young grocer, rather than risk her becoming further involved with the persistent prince, Elizabeth Chudleigh – so the story goes – evolved a scheme to suit all parties.

This was nothing less than ostensibly to further the marriage plans between Hannah and the young grocer, Isaac Axford, while ensuring that it was merely a mock ceremony and would immediately be followed by the bride's abduction by her royal lover.

The ceremony took place in December, 1753, in Keith's Chapel, Curzon Street, Mayfair, not far from Hyde Park corner. Alexander Keith, the presiding parson in this chapel, had earned himself an unenviable reputation as a not-too-fussy marriage broker. He was prepared to marry couples without the consent of parents or guardians, with no questions asked, no banns called and no licence required.

Hannah is said to have refused to answer the questions put to her in the course of the service, or to allow Isaac Axford to put the ring on her finger and, at the conclusion of the service, to have hastily preceded the bridegroom to the door of the Church.

Here she was promptly seized and carried off to a waiting carriage, in which sat the friendly plotter, Elizabeth Chudleigh. The carriage made off with all speed, everything giving way before it and turnpike gates being flung open at the cry of 'Royalty' to let it dash through.

The poor bridegroom was stupefied. When he recovered his wits he dashed off in hot pursuit, on a horse lent him by a spectator. By this time, however, the runaway couple had a head start, having been allowed through the turnpikes without let or hindrance, whereas Axford was stopped and had to pay his toll.[4]

There is some divergence of opinion here on subsequent events. One version given is that Axford succeeded in following the coach to Kew Palace, where he fell on his knees before the Prince, entreating the return of his lovely wife. Another is that Hannah actually lived with Axford for two or three weeks, that one evening a couple of itinerant musicians came to play outside the house and that, when they had finished, it was found that Hannah had been spirited away. Yet another is that Axford had merely agreed to act as proxy for the Prince and was handsomely rewarded for the part he played in the ceremony.*

The most commonly-accepted belief is, however, that Axford did not succeed in catching up with the royal pair, that Hannah was not seen by him, her family or friends from the day of the wedding onwards. Several reports agreed that she was kept in retreat by her royal lover from then on, but these reports varied widely in naming Kew, Tottenham Court Road, Lambeth, Hackney, Peckham, Islington, Hampstead, Knightsbridge, Isleworth, Bath or Blackheath as the site of this retreat. 'Cat-and-Mutton Fields, on the east side of Hackney Road, leading from Mile End Road' is the most specific address of the many given for the well-kept secret of her place of hiding.[5]

There is no suggestion anywhere in the copious literature on the subject that Hannah bore the prince a child, or children, before 1759, so she apparently spent the six years following her abduction in peace and continence.

This is the first widely-accepted story of the Prince and his fair Quaker. Details may vary, but the salient facts remain the same. Inevitably with such stories in circulation, the Prince's reputed bride aroused the interest of historians who succeeded, one after the other, in authenticating a number of interesting facts about her life. John Heneage Jesse, for instance, dealt in some detail with the alleged romance between Hannah and the Prince in his *Memoirs of the Life and Reign of George the Third,* published more than a century after the great love affair allegedly took place, and to him we owe much of the authentic data on Hannah's life.

Hannah Lightfoot was no myth. She was born on 12 October 1730, in the parish of St. John's, Wapping-in-the-East, and was only five years old when her father, Matthew Lightfoot, died. Her mother's maiden name was Mary Wheeler, as already reported, and Mrs Lightfoot's brother, Henry Wheeler, was in truth the linen-draper who was in business in Market Lane, opposite the rear entrance to the Opera House. The fact that Hannah married Isaac Axford (apparently without her mother's consent or knowledge) and that the marriage took place in Keith's Chapel, Curzon Street, Mayfair, has also been verified. To Heneage Jesse we owe the following documentation of the marriage, in the form of an affidavit by the Curate of St. George's Church, Hanover Square, where the

*Appendix B

19

records of the Curzon Street Chapel were preserved when it was closed down in 1754:

> This is to certify that in the register of marriages solemnised at Mayfair Chapel, which registers are preserved in the vestry to St. George's, Hanover Square, there appeared on the day 11 December, 1753, the following entry:
> *Isaac Axford of St. Martin's, Ludgate, to Hannah Lightfoot of St. James's, Westminster.*
> As witness my hand this 11th day of June, 1867,
> *Signed* James Macready, Curate at St. George's, Hanover Square.[6]

The fact that Hannah was not seen by her mother, relatives or friends from the day of the wedding onwards, was repeatedly confirmed by Lightfoot and Wheeler relatives when correspondence on the subject began to be given space in the newspapers of the day.[7]

So far the actual and the legendary details of Hannah's life correspond exactly. The actual account continues:

Both the Lightfoot and Wheeler families were members of the Society of Friends and we find that the subject of Hannah's having flaunted the rules of this Society, by being married by a priest, was in reality brought up at the monthly meeting of the Friends on New Year's Day, 1755, a little more than a year after her marriage. The progress of the action against Hannah can be traced in the minute book of the *Old Westminster Monthly Meetings* of the Friends.[8]

At the first meeting on New Year's Day it was reported that 'Hannah Lightfoot is married by the priest and since absconded from her husband . . .' Three members of the Society were appointed to visit her and give a report on their findings. The matter was raised at each successive meeting in 1755, but it was not until 3 September, that those appointed to enquire into the matter were able to report that they had seen Hannah's mother, who had confirmed that her wayward daughter had been married by a priest, but had denied all knowledge of her having absconded from her husband. It would appear that Mrs. Lightfoot genuinely knew little or nothing of her daughter's movements following her marriage to Axford.

In January, 1756, it was ordered at the monthly meeting of the Westminster branch of the Society of Friends that a *Testimony of Denial* be drawn up against Hannah. In March this testimony was read and approved. It read, in part, as follows:

> 'Whereas Hannah Lightfoot, a Person Educated under our Profession and who for Several years resided within the Com-

pass of this Meeting did then Enter into a State of Marriage by the Priest with one not of our Society which is directly repugnant to the good Rules and orders well-known to be established among us, on which this Meeting appointed Friends to visit her, who Several Endeavoured to find where she was in order to speak with her. But to no purpose nor could they obtain any Intelligence where she is . . .'

The gist of the rest of the *Testimony of Denial* is that the Society disowned her 'as one with whom we can have no fellowship until from a Penitent Mind and true Contrition of heart, she shall be induced to Signifie her unfeigned Sorrow for her Offence . . .' She apparently never reappeared to express her 'sorrow for her offence.'

Mary Lucy Pendered, who wrote a definitive book on Hannah Lightfoot early in the present century,[9] actually claimed to have been shown letters written by Hannah to her mother from an address unknown. In these letters, apparently, Hannah repeatedly urged her mother to put her trust, as her daughter had done, in a certain 'Person' who was well disposed towards them both. If they only had faith in this Person's benevolence, the girl wrote, their circumstances would shortly be greatly improved.

The probability is that, after her marriage to Axford and her subsequent desertion of him, the fair Quaker was taken into the protection of some wealthy and influential patron. The fact that her portrait was apparently painted by the great Sir Joshua Reynolds strongly suggests this. This portait of 'Miss Axford' (according to the catalogue) is in the manor house of Knole Park, the home of the Sackville family. Hannah is shown in the portrait wearing a fashionable white *décolleté* dress, trimmed with tiny satin bows, and a richly jewelled headdress.

There is also the interesting *fact* (not legend) that in 1757 one Robert Pearne (or Perryn) of Isleworth left an annuity of £40 for life to 'Mrs. Hannah Axford, for her own sole and separate disposal and for her sole use and behoof'.[10] Unfortunately, it is not known what part Pearne played in her life.

Mrs. Lightfoot, possibly shattered at her daughter's disappearance, died in May, 1760, leaving a will (proved on 4 June 1760) in which she left her property to her daughter, Hannah. She stated in the will that she was not certain whether her daughter was 'living or dead, not having heard from her since about two years past'. This confirms only that Hannah was alive in 1758.

The fact that Isaac Axford is known to have re-married in 1759, is taken by most historians who have examined the Lightfoot story critically, to indicate that Hannah was dead by this date at the latest. Only one writer puts the date of her death as late as 1764, but then he was writing more than a century after the event.[11] On the other hand, according to the known birth-date of Sarah Rex (George Rex's sister and Hannah's youngest putative child) Hannah – if her mother – must have survived at least until 1770. By this time, of course, the King had already sired four princes and three princesses by his Queen.

That, then, is the actual story of Hannah Lightfoot, a fascinating story and one which presents many lacunae which can be filled in by interesting conjecture. The fact that Hannah deserted from the Society of Friends when she made her runaway marriage and that the Quakers were in those days virtuous to the point of bigotry lent an added spice to the tale.

About the young prince who allegedly snatched Hannah away from her grocer husband, we know more than about almost any other man or woman who lived two centuries ago. Because of the tremendous significance of George III's long reign, his biographers have not been lacking and every aspect of his life and times, when the Georgian era was at its most sparkling, has been recorded and analysed in great detail. From the King's own voluminous correspondence (collected and published, it fills twelve large tomes) and from the letters and records left by his governors, ministers, diarists living on the fringe of court society and a long succession of biographers ever since his death, we probably know more about the conduct and complex character of this well-intentioned – if obstinate – king than about any other person after so great a lapse of time.

There has been an unfortunate tendency for writers of textbook histories to dismiss George III as 'the Mad King', 'the King who thought Shakespeare *sad stuff,*' or 'the King who lost England her American colonies'. Recent scholarly research has, however, resulted in a reassessment of his virtues, as well as his failings, and his total contribution to the advancement of Britain has been proved to be far greater than the sum of the popular tags which have largely done duty for biographical data in the past.

With notable authority, His Royal Higness Prince Charles has recently added his voice to those defending his much-maligned ancestor. In a well-reasoned foreword to John Brooke's masterly biography, *King George III*[12], the Prince throws light on this King's true personality and points out that, if anything, his great-great-great-great-great-grandfather was overdedicated to his duty and to the defence of the British Constitution, as he saw it. The writer discusses frankly the King's bouts of mental disturbance – 'his rather dotty behaviour' – and the probability that these were attributable to his being the victim of the rare metabolic disease, a variety of porphyria*, and not to general mental deterioration. This is a possibility recognised by some leading doctors and psychiatrists today.

Prince Charles emphasises that the monarch was perfectly sane in between attacks of his illness and that throughout his long life his first concern was always for the welfare of his people. The foreword concludes: 'Few have laboured harder at being a good King than George III. He *cared* and he was a genuine, honest person; qualities which quickly endeared the King to all classes of his subjects.'

This is the virtuous King who, from the beginning, had failed to fit into the Hanoverian family pattern, which had given the British public up till then every reason for assuming that every male member of the royal house kept a mistress – if not two. Not even the most malicious detractor of George III– and there were many – ever hinted that he strayed outside the bonds of matrimony or even cast an eye covetously at another woman from the day in 1761 when he married the Princess Charlotte of Mecklenburg-Strelitz. He has been accused of no extra-marital relationships; only one pre-marital side-step from the path of duty. If one accepts that he actually married Hannah Lightfoot, then he also stands accused of bigamy.

An honourable and virtuous middle-age does not, of course, necessarily bespeak a well-spent youth and it is with the character of George as a youth that we are primarily concerned here, since he was only fifteen when he is supposed first to have fallen victim to the charms of the fair Quaker. He was, according to all reports, unusually shy, *gauche* and backward for his age – a very young fifteen indeed.

George was only twelve years of age when the sudden death of his father, Frederick Louis, Prince of Wales, catapulted him to the centre of the stage as the Heir Apparent. His old grandfather, King George II, was then in his late sixties and not expected to live much longer (he surprised them all), so the new Prince of Wales would, in the nature of things, come to the throne before long.

His mother and all those about the throne now zealously stepped up their efforts to fit him for his elevated role. Lord Harcourt, an orthodox Whig, and Thomas Hayter, Bishop of Norwich and later of London, were appointed his governor and

*Appendix A

preceptor respectively. Not only his formal education was taken in hand – his speech, his way of standing, walking, bowing and eating were subject to constant criticism.

He was in the schoolroom by 8 a.m. and his long hours spent at his books left him little time for leisure. Comments on his progress with his studies and on his intelligence vary as much as the school reports of any boy who is not a born scholar, but were undoubtedly harsher than most because so much more was expected of the future king.

From his mathematical exercises which have survived and the seven large boxes of his essays and academic exercises in the Royal Archives, it is possible to get a fair idea of his intellectual attainments at the ages of fifteen to seventeen and to scotch for all time the rumour that he was dull, apathetic and ill-educated.

He was the first king of Britain to study science as a part of his education. An intensive study of the English language and literature was accompanied by lessons in French and German, both of which he learned to write and speak quite well. He started Latin at an early age and had an elementary knowledge of Greek. Ancient, British and European history were all required subjects for him, as were the history and doctrines of Christianity. He understood elementary physics and chemistry, a little trigonometry, and algebra and geometry up to today's school-leaving level. Drawing, military fortifications, astronomy and a course of 'natural and experimental philosophy' were other subjects thought necessary for the young Prince's education.

To this comprehensive schedule of studies was added instruction in the lighter arts of dancing, fencing, riding and music. He played both the harpsichord and the flute.[13] Not a time-table to allow much time or opportunity for dalliance, or even the ordinary pursuits of boyhood.

What little leisure time he had was spent almost entirely in the company of his brothers and sisters. The chief defect of the system of education laid down for him, in fact, was that it did not bring him into contact with other boys and girls of his own age. He was too carefully corralled off from the big, wicked world and consequently grew up shy, lonely and immature. In 1752, when Harcourt and the Bishop were doing their best with the apparently unresponsive Prince, his mother expressed the wish that 'he were a little more forward and less childish for his age.' He was then fourteen.

It was his mother, always his sternest critic, who was most to blame for his shyness and awkwardness. She frequently exhorted him: 'George, be a King!' but in the process, some maintained, did not allow him to become a man. She knew the ways of the world, deplored the morals and permissive attitudes of the young people of the day, and was determined to be the mother of a virtuous and uncontaminated King. It became an obsession with her to protect all her children, but particularly her eldest son, from the corruption which she saw at work on all sides.

Lord Waldegrave, appointed to succeed Lord Harcourt as governor to the Prince, gave his considered judgment of the boy in his *Memoirs:* 'He is strictly honest, but wants that frank and open behaviour which makes honesty appear amiable ... His religion is free from all hypocrisy, but is not of the most charitable sort ... He has spirit, but not of the active kind; and does not want resolution, but it is mixed with too much obstinacy ... He has great command of his passions, and will seldom do wrong, except when he mistakes wrong for right.'[14]

Although tall and good-looking, the young Prince continued to be unsure of himself in the presence of anyone except his brothers and sisters and other members of the immediate family. Lady Louisa Stuart, Lord Bute's daughter, described him as 'silent, modest and easily abashed'. In contemporary reports his shyness was repeatedly commented upon, always adversely, because of the elevated position he would one day be required to fill. Later writers were even more scathing. He was described as 'this poor, unripe, under-developed boy – for all practical purposes still in the nursery'.[15]

When he came of age at eighteen, his grandfather, on the advice of the cabinet, offerred Prince George his own establishment at St. James's and an allowance of £40 000 a year. George was alert enough to take the £40 000 but turned down the offer of his own *ménage,* saying firmly that he preferred to remain at Savile House next to his mother.[16] What an opportunity missed, if Hannah were still alive and he wished to provide a little love-nest for her!

George was also deeply religious (his grandfather considered him fit for nothing but to read the Bible to his mother), and in the month of his becoming King in 1760, he issued a proclamation for the encouragement of piety and virtue. Incidentally, it seems to have been accepted by most writers on this subject, that it was in this same year, 1760, that Hannah Lightfoot's first child, George Rex, was born,[17] although other dates have been mooted.

Three years before this, Lord Bute, formerly Lord of the Bedchamber in the household of George's father, had been appointed by the Princess Augusta as personal tutor to the Prince, who was then approaching seventeen. It was an appointment which was to have resounding consequences. The Prince, immature and emotionally insecure, brought to his relationship with his new tutor, who seemed to have all the graces and confidence he lacked, a total and desperate devotion.

Bute controlled not only his mind, but his heart as well. The Prince was plainly enslaved to this handsome, elegant man in his forties. He could take no decision without Lord Bute's consent, could hold no opinion and make no move of which Bute did not approve. The element of self-abnegation evident in the letters which George wrote to Lord Bute during the years 1756-'66 is almost pathetic.

It was to this idolised mentor that George wrote in the winter of 1759 (the year in which he was reported, as we shall see presently, to have gone through *two* further marriage ceremonies with Hannah Lightfoot): 'You have often accused me of growing grave and thoughtful, it is entirely due to a daily increasing admiration of the fair sex, which I am attempting with all the phylosophy and resolution I am capable of to keep under. I should be ashamed after having so long resisted the charms of these divine creatures now to become their prey . . . when I have said this you will plainly feel how strong a struggle there is between the boiling youth of twenty-one years and prudence, the last I hope will ever keep the upper hand, indeed if I can weather it but a few years, marriage will put a stop to this combat in my breast, I believe you will agree with me that application is the only aid I can give to reason, that by keeping the mind constantly employ'd is a likely means of preserving those passions in due subordination to it; Believe me I will with the greatest assiduity attempt to make all the progress which your good counsels, if properly attended to, have reason to expect.'[18]

This does not strike us today as the outpouring of a young married man, of a man who has kept a mistress in secret for six years, or – even less likely – a youth who had gone through two marriage ceremonies earlier in the year in which he is writing. The Prince had started this letter to Bute: 'I mean to lay my whole breast naked before you . . .' Those who accept the Lightfoot legends must ask themselves whether he had, in fact, done so or whether he was guilty of astonishing duplicity.

It was at this period, incidentally, that in one of his many letters to 'My Dearest Friend' (Bute) the Prince mentioned 'the tooth of malice having been employed against me.' Was he, one wonders, referring to the first of the many rumours concerning Hannah?

In another letter written in the winter of 1759, the Prince confesses to his first stirring of sexual excitement: 'I am daily grown unhappy, sleep has left me, which never was before interrupted by any reverse of fortune: I protest before God I never had any improper thought with regard to her: I don't deny having flattered myself with hopes that one day or other you would consent to my raising her to a Throne . . .' And again: 'he (Bute) has thoroughly convinced me of the impropriety of marrying a country woman; the interest of my country shall ever be my first care, my own inclinations must submit to it; I am born for the happiness or misery of a great nation, and consequently must often act contrary to my passions.'[19]

The girl who had so seriously distracted the twenty-one-year-old Prince was Lady Sarah Lennox, who was then not yet fifteen years of age. She was the young sister of the Duke of Richmond and George was obviously infatuated with her. But Bute was stern: 'Think, Sire, in the meantime, who you are, what is your birth right, what you wish to be, and prepare your mind with resolution to hear the voice of truth . . .'[20]

The truth was that the idolised and influential Bute did not consider the Lady Sarah sufficiently important to be raised to the throne of Britain.

George ascended the throne in 1760, on the death of his grandfather. Those about him, realising that he was ready for marriage, cast their eyes down the list of eligible German princesses. The King took the final decision himself and in September, 1761, married Princess Charlotte of Mecklenburg-Strelitz, whom Lord Chesterfield was later to call 'a good woman, a good wife, a tender mother, and an unmeddling Queen.' George proved himself a loyal husband and affectionate, if stern, father. From this time onwards he and his Queen led lives of staid, almost Spartan, domesticity.

The above are a few of the known facts about the young protagonist in the drama from which the legend of George Rex was to evolve.

It was in 1759, two years before his marriage to Charlotte, that the first teasing hint was dropped that there might be some connection between this serious-minded Prince and the Quaker girl. Lady Sophia Egerton, writing to her uncle William, Count Bentick, on 10 December of that year, let slip the following snippet: '. . . it has often been buzz'd that H.R.H., in spite of his reserve, was not wholly insensible to the passion of Love: and I am assured that he kept a beautiful young Quaker for some years, that she is Dead, and that One Child was the produce of that intrigue . . .'[21]

The fair Quaker dead by 1759 and one child born of the intrigue! From this first tiny seed of spite grew a beanstalk of rumour which outdid anything ever planted by Jack. Asked how and why such a rumour should have originated about such an exceptionally virtuous Prince, Professor Ian R. Christie, the eminent authority on the Georgian period, cast professorial stateliness to the winds:

'Can't you imagine the malicious little tongues clacking away as these disappointed girls chatter to each other? This Oh-so-virtuous prince, who keeps his eyes down, smiles tightly and says nothing, blushes and turns away and will not rise to the lures the young beauties of the court trail before him. He can't be so impervious as all that! There must be a girl in his life – there always is. And, of course, the Quakers are splendid targets for malice, such ostentatiously virtuous people – all humbug, of course – two young humbugs together – I expect he's got a Quaker hidden in his closet. Yes, that's it – have you heard, he keeps a Quaker in his closet!'[22]

This is as good and certainly as entertaining a reconstruction of a possible origin of the legend as we can hope to get at this point in time.

The gossip had now been put down on paper. The only surprising thing about a pointed little paragraph which appeared in *The Public Advertiser* on 7 September 1770 is the fact that no more direct reference to the alleged alliance had appeared in print any earlier than this. A comment on the case in which one of the King's brothers, the profligate Duke of Cumberland, was being called upon to defend himself for having seduced the wife of the Earl of Grosvenor, contained a reference to 'a new publication entitled *The Letters of an Elder Brother to a Fair Quaker,* which will entirely retrieve the literary fame of an illustrious family.'

Six years later, on 26 February 1776, to be exact, the first issue of the short-lived paper, *The Citizen,* carried a titillating promise of 'Court Fragments which will be published by *The Citizen* for the use, instruction and amusement of Royal Infants and Promising Young Noblemen. (I) The History and advances to Miss L. .htf. .t (The Fair Quakeress), Wherein will be faithfully portrayed some striking pictures of female constancy and princely gratitude which terminated in the untimely death of a young lady . . .'

Needless to say, no such fragments were ever published and the next allusion in print to the King and the Quaker maid was contained in *The Royal Register* for 1779 (compiled by one W. Coombe). Here the author dismissed the possibility of the King's having had an affair before his marriage, even though 'such a circumstance was reported by many, believed by some, disputed by others, but proved by none.' The writer concluded that if the

Quakers, of which the young woman in the case was a member, had not made public the proceedings of the meeting at which she was expelled from their society, the matter would have died an early death.

This is a classic example of the well-known journalistic technique of saying piously: 'We do not think for a moment that there is any truth in the rumour that . . .' while making sure that the reader misses no detail of the alleged libel. It is a technique still used today by less responsible newspapers when dealing with malicious rumours about the present royal families.

The press in the latter part of the eighteenth century was a force to be reckoned with. Revelling in its new-found power, it attacked honourable institutions, the Church, the law, Parliament and the King's ministers, but inevitably a more than fair proportion of the 'news' centred on the royal family and activities of the court. It was an era of immense curiosity – disinterested intellectual curiosity, which accounted for the many brilliant advances in the spheres of art and science, but also intensely personal, gossipy curiosity. Added to this was a compulsion to commit the findings which resulted from all this curiosity to paper. It was a period of letters, diaries, manuscripts, notes, books, journals, newspapers, and memoirs and pamphlets. According to the stamp office figures, the number of copies of newspapers in circulation increased by four times between 1760 and 1837.[23]

So a hint here, a broad wink there, a denial in another place and there, on the whole, the matter rested for many years. The King, towards the end of his life blind and senile, died in 1820, after the longest reign of any British sovereign to that time. He was sincerely mourned by his people and mercifully spared the really devastating attacks of 'the sharp tooth of malice'.

It did not take long now for certain ambitious and ill-balanced persons to move in and attempt to enhance their own status by exploiting the now ancient gossip about the royal high jinks of the previous century. In April 1821, a year after the poor old King's death, the following probe for information on his supposed *affaire* with Hannah was published in *The Monthly Magazine;* 'All the world is acquainted with the attachment of the late King to a beautiful Quakeress of the name of Wheeler. The lady disappeared on the royal marriage in a way that has always been interesting, because unexplained and mysterious. I have been told she is still alive, or was lately. As connected with the life of the late sovereign, the subject is curious and any information through your pages would doubtless be agreeable to many of your readers.'[24]

Now the cat was set among the pigeons with a vengeance. Replies began to trickle in over a long period and no two stories were identical. Each eager correspondent claimed himself to be related to the dead King and Hannah, or to know somebody who knew someone else whose best friend's cousin was an immediate descendant of the now ill-starred lovers. Much of the evidence was suspect in origin, some woolly, some concocted to fill in the tantalising gaps in the Lightfoot story, but some was supplied by good people who happened to be related to Hannah or Isaac Axford in some way and sincerely believed the stories they told. As everyone who could have verified or given the lie to all or any part of the story was by now dead, the legend tended to gain new vitality with each retelling.

Three months later a correspondent replied to this enquiry, giving details of Hannah's marriage to Axford, asserting that she had actually lived with him for six weeks but that one evening, when he was away from home, 'a coach and four came to the door, when she was conveyed into it and carried off at a gallop, no one knew whither . . . It has, however, been reported that she had three sons by her royal lover, since high in the army, that she was buried at Islington under another name . . . and even that she is still living.'[25]

Interesting discrepancies now begin to appear in the story – Hannah being carried off at a gallop from her home with Axford, not from the church door; three sons fathered by her royal lover and not the one child mentioned in the first report of 1759; Hannah being still alive in 1821, whereas Lady Sophia Egerton's report had stated that she was dead by 1759.

A correspondent in the same issue of *The Monthly Magazine*, signed *Warminsteriensis*, repeated the now well-known story of the Prince falling in love with Hannah in her uncle's linen-draper's shop at the corner of St. James's Market, the details of her marriage to Axford and the fact that Axford 'never saw Hannah more' after the marriage ceremony. An interesting elaboration of the story here was that Axford's second wife, Mary Bartlett, inherited a small estate and that her first cousin, on the report being revived that Hannah was still living, claimed this estate on the grounds of the invalidity of Axford's second marriage.[26]

In the October issue of the magazine, another letter appeared elaborating on the 'many fabulous stories' about Hannah and making the first mention in print of a gentleman by the name of Dalton who had, according to this correspondent, married a daughter of Hannah Lightfoot by the King.[27] In the December issue of this same journal a particularly malicious and audacious letter was published, in which it was asserted that the late King had 'left a very numerous left-handed issue, in the upper ranks of which may be placed a late Austrian prince, a general and a count'. It was now claimed that Hannah had borne the King no less than five children.[28]

And still they wrote and still the mystery grew. A titillating rumour such as this undoubtedly provided much of the colour and stimulation provided by the films, radio and television today. In time, not only *The Monthly Magazine*, but *The Farthing Journal*, *The Gentleman's Magazine* and *Notes and Queries* all took the matter sufficiently seriously to give space to the ensuing correspondence.

In the same year as the original request for information was published there appeared *The Public and Private Life of his late Most Excellent and Gracious George the Third: embracing its most memorable incidents as they were displayed in the important relations of Son, Husband, Father, Friend and Sovereign*. The author was one Robert Huish, whom *The Quarterly Review*, with some justice, spoke of as 'an obscure and unscrupulous scribbler'. Poor George III was hardly cold in his grave before this gentleman and others like him were busy analysing the dead King's love life in luscious prose.

'. . . His affections became enchained; he looked no more to Saxe-Gotha, nor to Brunswick for an object on which to lavish his love; he found one in the secret recesses of Hampton, whither he often repaired, concealed by the protecting shades of night, and there he experienced what seldom falls to the lot of Princes, the bliss of purest love. The object of his affections became a mother and strengthened the bond between them.'

No specific mention of the fair Quaker here, but subtle confirmation of the theory that the King had kept a mysterious mistress in some suburban retreat, this time Hampton.

In 1824, a handsomely printed pamphlet, entitled *An Historical Fragment Relative to her late Majesty Queen Caroline* (Caroline of Brunswick, who had been married to King George IV) was distributed anonymously in London. Among other seemingly intimate glimpses of life in the inner circle of the court was this curious suggestion: 'The Queen . . . fully believed that his late Majesty, George III, was married to Miss Hannah Lightfoot, the beautiful Quakeress – previous to his marriage with Queen Charlotte – and as that lady did not die until after the birth of the present King and His Royal Highness the Duke of York, her Majesty really considered the present Duke of Clarence the true heir to the throne.'[29]

John Heaneage Jesse, writing in 1867, picked up another related fragment and wrote: 'It is stated that in 1765, at the time when Queen Charlotte was in the family way with the late King William the Fourth, so alarmed was she on the secret of her consort's former engagement being revealed to her, that she insisted upon the nuptial ceremony being performed anew between them, which was accordingly done at Kew.[30]

The picture of the King ostensibly making an honest woman out of his beloved – and heavily pregnant – Charlotte, after two heirs to the throne had already been born, would have been hilarious had it not been so dastardly. In this connection, it is interesting to note 'a curious tradition, firmly believed in by the children and grandchildren of George Rex . . . that the Queen was not only aware of the connection between the King and Hannah, but that she visited the Quakeress more than once . . . and periodically sent her handsome presents of money, clothes etc.'[31]

The clergyman who was alleged in those reports to have performed this extraordinary ceremony – the repeat marriage between the King and Queen in 1765 – was the Reverend Dr. James Wilmot, a character whose story has become strangely interwoven with that of the royal family – at least in that confusing part of the tale relating to the King-and-Quaker legend. The connection between the King and the clergyman will become apparent shortly.

The legend, however, received its greatest fillip of all time when the assertion of an actual marriage between the Prince and the fair Quaker was made in those two untrustworthy publications, *Anonymous Authentic Records of the Court of England* (1831-32) and the *Secret History of the Court of England from the Accession of George III to the Death of George IV*,[32] the latter published in 1832, hot on the heels of the first book. The authenticity of these two books, which served up spicery to a credulous London society, has been sternly discounted by scholars. They do reveal an astonishing intimacy with the inside life of the court and the likelihood is that several aspirant authors, well-informed on the goings-on in court circles, each made a small and libellous contribution to the whole.

Using snippets of information on those in high places, the authors based on these flimsy foundations dramatic and often malicious stories which could not fail to titillate the *hoi polloi*. Parlour maids have always enjoyed reading about the theft of the Duchess's pearls or the dark details of a ducal divorce. George III's alleged romance, although dated nearly eighty years before the publication of these two books, was by no means considered old hat and in these two books received more elaborate treatment than ever.

In the *Authentic Records* it was stated that George and Hannah had been legally married in the Curzon Street Chapel, Mayfair

Wedgwood portrait medallions of King George III and Queen Charlotte. These are modern reproductions but were produced originally during King George III's reign and were for public sale. The original moulds still exist at the potteries. (By permission of Josiah Wedgwood & Sons)

The Chapel of St. Anne, Kew, in which George III (when Prince) was supposed to have been married to Hannah Lightfoot on 17 April, 1759. (Photo. by A. Lloyd Taylor of an engraving by Charles D'Oyley)

King George III's signature in 1766 (reproduced by permission of the British Library Board) and (right) a signature on one of the many documents produced at the Ryves Trial in 1866. (By permission of the Public Record Office, London)

The authentic signature of Lord Chatham (William Pitt) from a letter which he wrote to the Duke of Grafton on 4 March, 1767, the very day on which he was supposed to have witnessed the marriage of the Duke of Cumberland to Olive Wilmot. The signature on the right is taken from the marriage certificate (sic) of Cumberland and Olive, which was produced at the Ryves Trial. (Reproduced by kind permission of the Duke of Grafton and the County Archivist, Suffolk Record Offices, this permission having been obtained by Professor Christie.) (The forged signature reproduced by permission of the Public Record Office, London) (the one that had been closed down in 1754) in 1759. The ceremony was supposed to have taken place in the presence of the bridegroom's brother, the Duke of York, and that, subsequently the King's Ministers found some means of disposing of the fair Quakeress by inducing her to marry a person by the name of Axford; and that from this time her royal lover, notwithstanding his diligent and anxious enquiries, was never able to discover the place of her retreat.'[33]

Once again the discrepancies are worth noting. It will be remembered that Hannah married Axford in 1753 and that it was supposed to have been Axford who searched diligently for his bride after she had been snatched from him by the Prince, or the Prince's accomplices. Now Axford was reported to be in possession of the fair Quaker and it was the Prince who went a-searching.

A comparison of *The Secret History* with the first book, shows the second to have been based closely on the first and consequently most of the relevant statements on the affair appear in both. *The Secret History* added to the above story the information that 'the marriage was productive of issue', that the King's ministers, when the marriage was brought to their notice, 'immediately determined to annul it' and to this end devised the Royal Marriages Act.[34] This is, of course amusing to present-day readers. The Royal Marriages Act was not passed until thirteen years after George's supposed marriage to Hannah and would not, in any case, have had the effect of rendering the thirteen-year-old marriage illegal.

The Secret History introduced a few variations of its own to the story, one being that the King's ministers, having become aware of the King's marriage to Hannah, decided that Miss Lightfoot must be disposed of and stability given to the throne by a new marriage, this time to Princess Charlotte.

This was becoming curioser and curioser. What was the author trying to prove? What interest could he – or she – have in not only discrediting the long-dead King, but in insinuating that his children by the late Queen Charlotte were illegitimate and that their eldest son 'Prinny', should not have become King George IV? It was seventy-three years since the marriage to Hannah was alleged to have taken place. What possible purpose could lie behind this gratuitously mischievious 'evidence' about an event so far in the past?

To arrive at the answers to these questions and to understand why the faint glow of an old, dying scandal came to be fanned into a vigorous flame, one must try to probe the psychology of a woman who played the central role in one of the most extraordinary cases of *folie de grandeur* on record.

To do this it is necessary to have some knowledge of the various appeals, petitions, claims and even court cases arising out of the machinations of one Mrs. Olivia Wilmot Serres. It was she who first produced actual 'evidence' of the marriages of Prince George and Hannah. Difficult as it is for the reader to believe at this stage, her varied claims do have a direct bearing on our main story and cannot be omitted. The ingenuity and pretensions of this megalomaniacal woman were so bewildering that her story almost defies condensation.

Olivia Wilmot was born in April 1773, and her parents were, to the best of our knowledge, Robert Wilmot, reputed to be a house painter, and his wife, Anna Maria (born Burton). Olivia, who was undoubtedly a beautiful and talented young woman, studied art towards the end of the eighteenth century with John Thomas Serres, a well-known artist and contributor to the Royal Academy of Arts from 1776 to 1820. He succeeded his father, Dominic Serres, as Marine Painter to King George III and the Duke of Clarence, and became a marine draughtsman to the Admiralty. The water-colour painting of the Dutch and English squadrons at the Cape of Good Hope in 1804, reproduced on Plate 6, is typical of his best work. For a time he had a vessel at his disposal and was employed in sketching enemy coasts and harbours – an invaluable service to any government in the days before photography. His salary was £100 a month and he became more than averagely wealthy.[35]

When Olivia entered his studio as a pupil, he fell in love with her and they were married in 1791, she being then eighteen. She must have had genuine artistic talent, because she was an honorary exhibitor at the Royal Academy of Arts between 1793 and 1803, and is listed in 1806 as 'Landscape Painter to H.R.H. the Prince of Wales'.[36] It was quite possibly during this association with the court that some of her later grandiose fantasies were born.

Her extravagant ways soon reduced John Serres to penury and they were both imprisoned for debt.[37] They parted in 1804 and Olivia kept the two daughters of the marriage, the elder one being Lavinia Janetta Horton Serres, to whom we shall later refer.

Somehow Olivia Serres, with her painting and her writing (she was a compulsive writer of letters, articles, diaries, petitions, theological dissertations, newspaper paragraphs, poems, essays and even a libretto for an opera) managed to eke out a living for herself and her daughters.

Because she had been under twenty-one at the time of her marriage to John Thomas Serres, a special licence had to be signed by Robert Wilmot, the man who had brought her up, to the effect that he was her true and lawful father, and that he gave his consent to the marriage.[38] To the day of his death, he insisted that he was her father, no matter how illustrious a heritage she proceeded to claim for herself.

In 1813 she presented a petition to King George III (now, alas, blind and doddering) in which she stated that she was not Robert Wilmot's daughter after all, but the natural daughter of the Duke of Cumberland (a brother of the King) and a certain Mrs. Payne (wife of Captain William Payne).

Now Robert Wilmot had a brother, the Reverend Dr. James Wilmot, Rector of Barton-on-the-Heath, Warwickshire, who lived and died a highly respected bachelor (the same man who was supposed to have officiated at the 'repeat' royal marriage of 1765). After the death of King George III and long after her uncle's death, Olivia, in a petition to King George IV, made the startling claim that she was the *legitimate* daughter of the Duke of Cumberland, but this time by another woman.

The story this time was highly embroidered and involved her respectable bachelor uncle, Dr. James Wilmot. Far from being his niece as she had always thought, she averred, she had now discovered that she was, in fact, his granddaughter! Her mother was not Anna Maria Wilmot, so she said, but the daughter of her uncle, James Wilmot, by a beautiful Polish princess, whom he had met and secretly married while he was still up at Oxford.

This was supposedly Princess Poniatowski, the beautiful sister-in-law of the King of Poland. The Poniatowski family were all devout Roman Catholics, but Olivia took in her stride the hurdle of how this Catholic princess had come to be married to an Anglican rector.

A Princess Poniatowski had indeed visited Oxford in July 1767. Also, a mistress of the King of Poland, the Countess Dunhoff (sic) had visited London and her name had been linked romantically with that of the Duke of Cumberland, so possibly these episodes had provided Olivia's fertile imagination with the germ of the mind-boggling tale which she unfolded.

She insisted that not only had the pedant and the princess married in secret in Oxford and produced a beautiful daughter (her mother, newly-disclosed), but that this daughter had captured the attention of the Duke of Cumberland, who had succumbed to her charms and married her in secret in 1767. Olivia stated categorically that she was the daughter of this secret union, that her father was *not* the devoted Robert Wilmot, who had loved and reared her, but Henry Frederick, Duke of Cumberland.

Robert Wilmot, averred Olivia, had perjured himself when he signed her marriage certificate as he did, because he had been sworn to secrecy by his brother and had agreed to bring up the reverend gentleman's granddaughter as his own daughter. He had been able to do this because his own wife had produced a stillborn child at the exact time that the Duke's daughter (sic) had been born. The live child had been substituted for Robert Wilmot's dead one – so said the irrepressible Olivia.

She claimed that she had been kept in ignorance of her distinguished parentage until the true facts had been divulged to her by the Duke of Kent, to whom they had been imparted by the Earl of Warwick as he lay on his death-bed.

It is hardly necessary to add that all those who had featured in this fanciful episode – the brothers Wilmot, King George III and the Dukes of Kent and Cumberland – were dead; there was no one who could confirm or deny her story. She seems to have set about, from this point onwards, manufacturing a mass of circumstantial evidence, the ramifications of which were to throw doubt on the legitimacy of several members of the royal family. Her stories abounded in bigamous unions and one of them in particular was to concern directly the Rex family of Knysna.

She poured forth a torrent of letters to men and women in high places and claims of ever-increasing ingenuity followed hot on the heels of one another. Details might vary, but throughout them all she stuck doggedly to her story of being the daughter of the Duke of Cumberland and therefore entitled to call herself 'the Princess of Cumberland' and for good measure, 'Duchess of Lancaster'.

In 1821 she had herself re-christened in the Islington Parish Church as 'Olive, only daughter of the late Henry Frederick, Duke of Cumberland'. About this time she was driving round London in a carriage bearing the royal coat of arms and her attendants were dressed in royal livery. She had not the means, however, to maintain all this grandeur and in the same year she was arrested for debt. She could not be arrested, she protested, because she was of royal blood. This failed to impress the authorities.

Olivia appealed to three successive sovereigns, to the Lords and Commons in her determination to have herself recognised as the 'Princess of Cumberland'. She was once again imprisoned for debt and died in prison in 1834, believing to the end that she had been greatly wronged.

The present writer has no more conclusive evidence than any other investigator into *l'Affaire Serres* that Olivia, in her frantic attempts to establish her own legitimate connections with the House of Hanover, was the instigator of the serious charge of bigamy against the dead King, which in turn gave rise to the belief that he had sired children by Hannah Lightfoot. There are, however, certain straws in the wind which seem to point in this direction.

A key figure in the whole involved affair was Olivia's long-deceased Uncle James, the innocent Rector of Barton-on-the-Heath, who was named in *The Secret History* as the clergyman officiating at both the marriage ceremonies in 1759 in which George III and Hannah were allegedly the contracting parties. Olivia, prolific writer that she was, published a memorial in 1813 on her dead uncle, claiming that he had been the author of *The Letters of Junius* (a series of bitterly ironical and often malicious attacks on the King and his policies, the Queen and certain of the ministers of the crown, which originally appeared in *The Public Advertiser* between 1769 and 1772). It was, in fact, most unlikely that he, a country parson, would have had the intimate grasp of the inner workings of the world of politics which these scathing letters revealed. Nor was his name ever mentioned in lists of recognised authors or in collections of biographies. Only his enterprising niece claimed this distinction for him.

The Secret History gave unusual prominence to the life and achievements of the Reverend Dr. James, considering that he had been dead for a quarter of a century when the book appeared. There was one claim in this book that he had, while at Oxford, become intimately associated with Dr. Johnson, Lord Archer, Lord Plymouth and Lord North and that 'From these gentlemen the doctor imbibed his political opinions and was introduced to the first society in the Kingdom'.

Other statements were: 'He had long been the bosom friend of the King and spent all his leisure time at Court. No one therefore could be a better judge of the state of public affairs than himself . . .', and 'At the age of thirty, Dr. Wilmot was confidentially trusted with the most secret affairs of State and was also the bosom friend of the Prince of Wales, afterwards George III.'

And so on – and on. It may be said of the Serres story, as has so often been said with reference to the origins of George Rex, 'the true story will never be known', but now that it is possible to view Olivia Serres and her multifarious activities in perspective, there does seem a strong possibility that she was the source of these blatant boosts for James Wilmot, her uncle. Much more important, she was probably responsible for publicising widely through her writing proclivities the account of the marriage(s) of Wilmot's 'bosom friend', George III, to a commoner eight years his senior. As a by-product, these rumours created the climate in which it was possible for claims to descent from this romance to flourish freely.

The repeated eulogistic references in *The Secret History* to a minor cleric who never, so far as is known, rose to any particular eminence in the Church or even held an appointment in London, is interesting. It is at least credible that Mrs. Serres, prompted by her delusions of grandeur, made the maximum use of her well-educated and well-respected uncle after his death, in her persistent discrediting of the dead King and the whole royal family, in her desperate attempts to bolster up her own pretensions. She may well have hoped that by incidentally proving the secret marriage of George III to the fair Quaker, she would lend support to her own ingenious claim to descent from the Duke of Cumberland and, on the maternal side, from the daughter of the beautiful Princess Poniatowski by Dr. James Wilmot.

Nor did the wheels which Olivia Serres had set in motion come to a standstill with her death.

2 Dear Cousin . . .

At first glance there does not appear to be much connection between the Princess of Cumberland (*soi-disant*) who challenged three successive sovereigns and the legal might of Britain in her determination to have herself recognised as a member of the royal house, and George Rex of Knysna, but there is in fact a very definite connection.

When she died, the mantle of Olivia Serres fell heavily on the willing shoulders of her elder daughter, Lavinia Janetta Horton Serres, who, by the time of her mother's death, had become Mrs. Ryves. This lady, who at one stage had herself rechristened as Lavinia Janetta Hortense de Serres, inherited more than just her share of genes from her mother; she inherited a mass of doubtful documents, her claims, her pretensions to royal connections and her propensity for writing pamphlets, petitions, letters to newspapers and to those in high places.[1]

It was as a direct result of a unique trial which Lavinia Ryves initiated with the purpose of having the marriage of the Duke of Cumberland and Olivia Serres' mother legally recognised, that the first documented claim came from South Africa that George Rex was a son of King George III.

Lavinia's involved affairs are almost more difficult to condense than her mother's, but a brief flash-back on her career will put into perspective the startling development which is germane to this story.

Like her mother, Lavinia married an artist and, like her mother, she obtained a divorce from her husband. Having been born in 1797, Lavinia had, when her mother died, lived for thirty-seven years in the atmosphere of intrigue, fantasy and royal pretensions created by that remarkable lady. With her mother, she had driven round London in the coach bearing the royal arms and had had servants in their royal liveries jumping down to open doors for her. Admittedly the ephemeral glory had long since departed, but the memory of those golden days lingered on. Unlike her mother, she bore six children and how she brought up the younger ones after her divorce in 1841 is something of a mystery, because she was reported to have been left 'in great destitution.'

On her mother's death, Lavinia assumed the titles, 'Princess of Cumberland and Duchess of Lancaster'. Ten years after Olivia's death in 1834, this 'Princess of Cumberland and Duchess of Lancaster' brought a suit against the Duke of Wellington, as executor of the late King George IV's will. This was a blatant attempt to claim ownership of the £15 000 reputedly left by King George III to 'Olive, our brother of Cumberland's daughter' – in other words, Lavinia's mother. (It is interesting, by the way, to note that there were always fairly large sums of money involved in the various claims put forward by both mother and daughter.) This suit was dismissed, the Court of Chancery declaring that it had no power to dispense bequests under the terms of a will which had not been proved in the ordinary way.

In 1858, one year short of a century after the alleged marriages of George III to Hannah Lightfoot, the indomitable Lavinia Ryves published *An Appeal for Royalty; a Letter to her Most Gracious Majesty Queen Victoria from Lavinia, Princess of Cumberland and Duchess of Lancaster*.[2] Out of the mass of verbiage, the opening paragraphs are worth studying:

'After patient endurance of most cruel wrongs through a period of thirty-eight years, during which I have been plunged from a state of affluence and honour into a condition of continuous privation and almost utter destitution, from the experience of kindly regard and true friendship on the part of Your Majesty's late Royal Father, to a state of entire neglect by all those persons to whom His Royal Highness expressed his solemn wishes – even on his death-bed – that I should be protected; I am at length compelled to make this public appeal to your Majesty's sense of justice and to the loyal and honourable feelings of the people of this great Nation . . . walking in the footsteps of my late Royal and revered Mother, a worthy daughter of the House of Brunswick, I have hitherto scrupulously guarded, amidst the pressure of want and neglect, felt alike by myself personally and by my young and numerous family, the great state secret, which so deeply affects the honour of that House, and which the accident of birth threw into my keeping . . . . .

The 'great state secret' was, of course, the alleged marriage of George III to Hannah Lightfoot and the implied illegitimacy of King George IV, King William IV and, presumably, Queen Victoria herself. From that august lady the enterprising Lavinia received no change at all. The *Appeal* savoured of blackmail and the Queen ignored it.

A certain amount of sympathy for Mrs. Ryves was, however, stirred up among those who read this pamphlet, largely because she had taken the trouble to reproduce in it facsimiles of a bewildering number of documents in support of her story.

The power of the printed word is, however, tremendous. Once one has seen in black and white reproductions of documents such as the following, the temptation to believe that the originals exist is almost irresistible:

April 17, 1759

'The marriage of these parties was this day duly solemnised in Kew Chapel, according to the rites and ceremonies of the Church of England, by myself.'

J. Wilmot

'George P.
'Hannah.

'Witness to this marriage –

W. Pitt
Anne Taylor'

and secondly:

May 27th, 1759

'This is to certify that the marriage of these parties, George Prince of Wales and Hannah Lightfoot, was duly solemnised this day, according to the rites and ceremonies of the Church of England, at their residence at Peckham, by myself.'

J. Wilmot

'Witnesses to the marriage of these parties:

George Guelph   William Pitt
Hannah Lightfoot   Anne Taylor.'

Apart from the Prince and Hannah, the *dramatis personae* of these scenes are interesting. The 'J. Wilmot' who ostensibly performed both these ceremonies, but who presumably held his peace two years later when the King married Princess Charlotte, was, of course, the long-deceased Dr. James Wilmot, one-time Rector of Barton-on-the-Heath, uncle of Olivia Serres and great-uncle to Lavinia Ryves.

The combination of witnesses noted in this document is unusual too – William Pitt and Anne Taylor. The latter, a woman who had once been a servant in the Wheeler household in Market Lane, was assumed to have left the house with Hannah when she left to marry Isaac Axford. The thought of the mighty William Pitt, whom the King detested and on occasion called 'that mad Pitt' and 'a true snake in the grass', jeopardising his whole political career by conspiring at the secret marriage of the Prince to a commoner, is hard to entertain.

In the early days of Lord Bute's control at Leicester House, the warmest relations appeared to exist between Bute and Pitt and the Prince, in consequence, held Pitt in the highest regard. Sharp differences of opinion over policy, however, led to a rapid deterioration in the relationship and by December, 1758, Prince George was writing to Bute: 'He treats both you and me with no more regard than he would a parcel of children, he seems to forget that the day will come when he must expect to be treated according to his deserts.'[3] In May, 1760, the twenty-two-year-old Prince felt so strongly about Pitt that he confided to Bute: '. . . he has shown himself the most ungrateful and in my mind the most dishonourable of men, I can never bear to see him in any future Ministry'.[4]

By the time the King married Charlotte in 1761, there is no doubt that Pitt would have been only too eager to make use of any knowledge he might have had of so discreditable an event as the King's secret marriage to a Quaker maid.

Then, to back up these two 'marriage certificates', was reproduced in *The Appeal* a document purporting to be the 'Last Will and Testament of Hannah Lightfoot':

Hampstead, July 7th, 1762

'Provided I depart this life, I commend my two sons and my daughter to the kind protection of their Royal Father, my husband, His Majesty King George III, bequeathing whatever property I die possessed of to such dear off-spring of my ill-fated marriage. In case of the death of each of my children, I give and bequeath to Olive Wilmot, the daughter of my best friend, Dr. Wilmot, whatever property I am entitled to or am possessed of at the time of my death.

(Signed) Hannah Regina'

Witnesses:

J. Dunning
William Pitt

Hannah Lightfoot's signature, in contrast to the text of this document, is unconvincingly shaky; the outline deliberately erratic to the most untrained eye. Even in this will, one cannot help noticing, there is tucked away a hopeful claim for Olive Wilmot (and presumably her daughter, Olivia Serres and her granddaughter, Lavinia Ryves) to inherit Hannah's property in the event of the death of her 'royal' children. Unfortunately mercenary motives were only too evident in the wording of a number of these documents.

Facsimiles of a great many other documents were reproduced in this pamphlet, including one ostensibly signed by George III, in which he expressed his wish that Olivia should be acknowledged, 'after our death', as the Duke of Cumberland's daughter, but as all of them – and more, – were produced in open court eight years after *The Appeal for Royalty* appeared, they need not be examined here.

On the whole *The Appeal* created little stir. Queen Victoria ignored it and even the Press of the day paid little attention to it.

Unfortunately for the success of her later assumptions, Lavinia Ryves had to file, in 1861, a petition to establish the legality of her mother's marriage to John Thomas Serres and thus her own legitimacy. Temporarily, for legal reasons it seems, she had to abandon her claim to royal descent and, as she was successful in this petition, she inevitably weakened her case in the unique trial which she initiated five years later. This was to be one of the most extraordinary trials in history. The papers connected with it were impounded at the conclusion of the trial, were held secret for one hundred years and then released for examination in 1967.[5]

It is from these papers, which are in the Public Record Office, London, that the following details of the trial have been taken.

In 1866 Mrs. Ryves found two shrewd outer barristers ready to take up her cause, their eyes possibly fixed on the handsome fees likely to accrue to them in the course of a lengthy trial. In this year the case, *Ryves and Ryves versus Attorney General*, was heard in Her Majesty's Court for Divorce and Matrimonial Causes. Mr. Henry N. Capel, a solicitor of 9, Lincoln's Inn Fields, appeared for the petitioners, Lavinia Janetta Horton Ryves and her son, William Henry Ryves.

The case was heard before the Right Honourable Sir Alexander James Edmund Cockburn, Lord Chief Justice of Her Majesty's Court of Queen's Bench, the Right Honorable Sir Frederick Pollock, Lord Chief Baron of Her Majesty's Court of Exchequer, and the Right Honorable Sir James Plaisted Wilde, Judge of Her Majesty's Court of Probate and Judge Ordinary of the Court for Divorce and Matrimonial Causes. An impressive assembly of legal luminaries indeed.

The court was asked to hear a plea for recognition of the legitimacy of the Duke of Cumberland's alleged daughter, Olivia Serres, and – by implication – of Olivia's daughter, who was presenting the case. If successful, of course, the right of Lavinia Ryves to call herself the 'Princess of Cumberland' might be proved and, more important, she might then hope to inherit some of the large sums of money which had been mentioned in the various documents in her possession.

It was during this trial that documents of an explosive nature and having a direct bearing on the history of the Knysna family, were produced. The nature of the great state secret, which Mrs. Ryves claimed had been entrusted to her keeping, was revealed when she produced, *on the back of* the certificates purporting to be those legalising the marriage of Olivia's mother and the Duke of Cumberland, the two 'marriage certificates' of George III and Hannah Lightfoot. These were, of course, the originals of the 'certificates' which had been reproduced in facsimile in the *Appeal for Royalty* eight years earlier. They were ostensibly the records of the two marriages in 1759, one in Kew Chapel on 17 April and the other 'at their residence at Peckham' on 27 May.

The production in court of two scraps of paper with alleged certifications of the marriages of George and Hannah on the backs of those of the Duke of Cumberland and Olivia Serres' mother caused no small sensation. The Lord Chief Justice, startled, exclaimed, 'You say that the King, as well as his brother, committed bigamy!' Unfortunately for her own case, the petitioner, instead of embarking upon a plea for her own legitimacy as soon as she took the witness stand, started an involved exposition of the Hannah Lightfoot scandal. She was stopped and the Lord Chief Justice intervened: 'The Court is, as I understand, asked solemnly to declare, on the strength of two certificates, coming I know not whence, written on two scraps of paper, that the marriage, the *only* marriage of George III which the world believes to have taken place, between His Majesty and Queen Charlotte, an invalid marriage, and consequently that all the sovereigns that have sat on the throne of England since his death, including her present Majesty (Queen Victoria) were not entitled to sit on the throne. This is the conclusion that this Court is asked to come to, upon these two rubbishy bits of paper, one signed George P. and the other George Guelph. I believe them to be rank and gross forgeries.'

There were seventy documents produced in all – forty-three of them ostensibly bearing the signatures of Dr. James Wilmot, thirty-six those of Lord Chatham (William Pitt), twelve of George III, twelve of John Dunning, thirty-two of Lord Warwick and eighteen of the Duke of Kent, apart from others less important.

There were documents in plenty relating to the alleged secret marriage of the Duke of Cumberland to Olivia's mother, several 'bequests' to Olivia from various members of the royal family, a decree granting her permission to use the title of the Duchess of Lancaster, an odd reference to *The Letters of Junius,* and so on – and on. One of the oddest was this (Paper 12): 'Olive, my dearest grandchild, I solemnly request you to seek the children that His Majesty had first born to him in lawful wedlock, two sons and a daughter, such being lawfully begotten on the Princess Hannah of Wales, His Majesty's first Consort, whose marriage it was my misfortune to solemnize. April 17th, 1759.

Witness,

J. Wilmot.'

Sometimes documents having a bearing on the same issue contradicted each other and the inconsistencies were too numerous to mention. It is only necessary to extract from this tangled mass and two other documents which have a direct bearing on the story of George Rex. These were:

'This is to solemnly certify that I married George, Prince of Wales, to Princess Hannah, his first consort, April 17, 1759, and that two princes and a princess were the issue of that marriage.

J. Wilmot'

London, April 2nd, 176-

and

'This is to certify to all it may concern that I lawfully married George, Prince of Wales, to Hannah Lightfoot, April 17, 1759, and that two sons and a daughter are their issue by such marriage.

J. Wilmot

Chatham
J. Dunning

Here are the Earl of Chatham and John Dunning again, this time concerned with proving that the King had not only married Hannah, but had sired three children (unnamed) by her and that all the children which Queen Charlotte had borne him were therefore illegitimate.

The 'mighty Cause' was now indeed clear. The Attorney General said, 'I do not disguise from myself that this is nothing less than a claim to the Throne.' At one stage the Lord Chief Baron declared: 'In my opinion it is indecent to go on with the enquiry into such matters, unless it is absolutely necessary for the purposes of justice,' to which the Attorney General replied, 'Of course, if this could be seriously called an enquiry, it would be a very important one . . . I am bound to tell your Lordship that I shall treat it as a case of fraud, fabrication, and imposture from beginning to end. It is comfortable to believe that the guilt of the fraud may be excused by the insanity of one of the Persons principally concerned.'

This last dig has been taken as a not-too-veiled allusion to Mrs. Ryves' mental state, but it was more likely a reference to her dead mother, from whom she had received the story centring round the Duke of Cumberland and the documents to support it.

One of the many fascinating questions raised by this case is that of the impulse which prompted Lavinia Ryves so patently to prejudice her own cause (the hoped-for establishment of the legality of the Cumberland-Wilmot marriage) by producing such a plethora of papers and copies of documents, ostensibly of an official nature, written mostly on odd scraps of paper and many of them primarily concerned with the George-Hannah alliance. One would suppose that the petitioner had a difficult enough task on her hands in trying to prove the Duke's alleged marriage to her grandmother, without jeopardising her case by introducing the story of George III's marriage to the fair Quaker. Possibly she hoped that by discrediting the dead King and his family, she would make Cumberland's alleged defection more credible.

In spite of the evidence of a handwriting expert, who pronounced the signatures of the King and Dr. Wilmot to be genuine, but expressed himself less sure about the many signatures of Chatham, Warwick, and John Dunning, the jury came to the conclusion that all the documents were foolish forgeries. It was a lengthy summing up, the court dismissed the case and the judge ordered that all the documents, pronounced forgeries, be impounded.

It was asked by two or three writers who took up the cause of the aging woman (she was now sixty-nine) why, if she were guilty of fraud, libel and forgery, 'she was yet permitted to walk out of that Court unintimidated, free to spread her libels on the Royal Family far and wide, without let or hindrance . . . .' The answer was, of course, simply that the court had been asked to hear an action for legitimacy and the finding was that she, Lavinia Ryves, was the legitimate daughter of Olivia and John Thomas Serres. The court had no power to prosecute her. It was made clear that no deliberate deception had been intended on Mrs. Ryves' part; she had simply inherited the documents from her mother, she believed implicitly in their genuineness and regarded the pursuance of her mother's claims as a sacred trust.

Shortly after this, a pamphlet – almost certainly written by Lavinia Ryves herself – was published. Entitled *Was Justice Done?* it went over the case in some detail and made it clear that, in the writer's view, justice had certainly not been done and that the petitioner had been deprived of the documents on which her claims depended.

Lavinia Ryves, strangely enough, won a certain amount of sympathy from compassionate friends. In that intrigue-ridden society, avid for sensation, particularly when it concerned the royal family, this was too good a story to be allowed to die down immediately.

This trial is often referred to glancingly in works dealing with the George III-Hannah Lightfoot romance, but its original significance is often passed over. It is the 'certificates of marriage' of George and Hannah, which were produced in court and later impounded, that are seized on by one writer after another as the starting point for a further romantic development and as 'proof' of the validity of certain claims to Hanoverian connections. But no attempt was made in any of the documents whatsoever to identify any of the issue of this alliance.

The importance of this trial in the context of this book is that, in the first place, it provided 'evidence' of the Prince having married Hannah Lightfoot and, secondly, that it led to the first really substantial link being forged in the chain of circumstantial evidence which has so firmly connected Hannah Lightfoot's and George Rex's names ever since.

Buoyed up by the sympathy shown her by a large circle of friends, the lively Lavinia next adopted a technique which had been employed by her mother, and made, very soon after the trial, a public appeal for any information on the George-Hannah romance which knowledgeable readers might be able to give her. Unlike her mother she did not resort to anonymity, but published her name and address on her enquiry, and not long afterwards received the following letter from Christina Nelson, one of George Rex's daughters:

My address is, Mrs. Nelson,
c/o George Rex Esq.,
Knysna, Cape of Good Hope.

Rexford,
Knysna,
Cape of Good Hope,
Dec. 10, 1866

Dear Madam,

Having observed in the *English News* of June 29, 1866, a letter published by the *Standard* in which you seemed anxious to know whether any descendant of Hannah Lightfoot is still living – I beg to inform you that I am a daughter of George Rex, the son of Hannah Lightfoot. My Father came to this Colony in 1796 and held the appointment of Marshal of the Vice-Admiralty Court here for ten years and died in 1839 at a good old age, as you will perceive by the **death notice** enclosed. My Father left a brother and sister, in England. John Rex was married but left no children and his sister, Sarah, died unmarried – since I do not see why there should be any doubt about the veracity of your statement concerning the marriage of Hannah with George III – or any of the documents you might have put forth on that trial – I am, dear Madam,

Your obedient servant,
C. Nelson.[6]

Apart from a couple of minor errors, such as the incorrect date being given for George Rex's arrival at the Cape and the length of his service in the Vice-Admiralty Court being given as ten, instead of six years, this letter has the ring of authority about it. This was no pretender, feeling her way and unsure of her ground; this woman was obviously confident of the validity of the central, simple statement in her letter. The posts were, of course, infuriatingly slow, but by February 1867, Lavinia Ryves was joyfully penning the following verbose and enthusiastic reply:

Hampstead Road,
England
Feb. 4, 1867

Dear Mrs. Nelson,

It is with much pleasure I hasten to acknowledge the safe arrival of your truly *welcome letter*, and its valuable information fully *corroborative* of all the facts and certificates to be equally of impor-

The College of Advocates, Doctors' Commons, Godliman Street, in 1854, little changed, except for gas lighting and the dress of the passers-by, from the days when George Rex was a proctor in Doctors' Commons. (From the Grace Collection, reproduced by permission of the British Museum)

St. Paul's Cathedral seen from Godliman Street, where George Rex once lived. Doctors' Commons stood to the south of the Cathedral. (Photo: Robert Storrar)

(Left) The mace of the first Vice-Admiralty Court at the Cape of Good Hope, used by George Rex in his position as Marshal and Sergeant-at-Mace. The hardwood staff is surmounted by an open silver crown. The traditional silver oar, which may have been screwed into the hollow shaft, is missing.

(Middle) A mace of the same type as that used by George Rex, except that the shaft is of metal as well as the open crown. Inscribed **Evan Jones, Marshal of the High Court of Admiralty of England, 1850.** *Marks: London 1797–'95, MB goldsmith. (Photo: National Maritime Museum, Greenwich)*

(Right) The top half of the shaft is fluted. The lower half, has a globular terminal button which unscrews to reveal a miniature gilt oar inscribed **Admiralty of England.** *Marks: London 1819–'20, Crespin Fuller, Goldsmith. (Photo: National Maritime Museum, Greenwich)*

tance to your family and myself, and which are one and all genuine, they have been preserved and conscientiously acted upon *by all* concerned who sacredly fulfilled and guarded the Documents or Certificates of *Marriages and Births truly legitimate* as also the Rights and Properties appertaining thereto and to which the surviving Descendants are justly entitled. Neither can any stigma be any longer cast upon the memory of your injured Grandmother and her Descendants. With us has rested the vindication of the position and wrongs, and the trust has not been abused, and I am proud to assert neither dishonour or immorality ever existed in the families of either you or myself, who indeed are of the same Relationship in blood, as your late lamented Father and my dear Mother, Olive, Princess of Cumberland *(for such she was)* were Mothers children, and *we are the Grandchildren. What can be nearer* and therefore cousins also, equally persecuted and wronged, but I will hope for better prospects and the establishment of the Truth and rectitude of all concerned . . .

. . . and I was in the Witness Box for *10 hours* the which I did not *fear the more* as I was *protecting the honour and Integrity of my late Mother and all concerned now no more* and it is my intention to go again *legally forward* and am preparing to do so, and shall never rest until I have finished the task I have undertaken if I am spared being 70 on the 16 of March next, with possession of all my faculties and activity. Having heard from you I shall communicate all that transpires henceforth . . . The *Will* of Hannah Lightfoot is dated from Hampstead and their residences are known in such vicinity I shall feel anxious to hear from you by the next Mail after this letter's arrival at the Cape I have not time to say all I have to communicate of moment to us as immediately concerned and I wish that any of you were in England at this time, or were coming over – I have seen Mr. Bulls letters to the worthy Mr. Carter whom I like and can place every confidence in . . . I read the account of your dear Fathers death with emotions of painful but proud feelings and a tear rose in my eyes while so doing. Have you any photographs of him wife and all of you they would be prized by all in England, there is a warm interest manifested in our behalf and I shall die happy in the knowledge I have sacredly acted up to the injunctions of the dead who were overwhelmed with persecution and robbed of the inheritance our just due but God has watched over all of us who will bring every falsehood and injury to light . . . Is George Rex the Post Master at the Cape your brother or cousin, or nephew I will now say adieu for the present and look for a letter as soon as you can send one and may God still preserve bless and protect you all is the fervent petition to the Almighty of my dear Mrs. Nelson, your ever affectionate cousin–

Lavinia Janetta H. Ryves.[7]

Mrs. Ryves's letter is strangely poignant. Discouraged, impoverished, nearly seventy years old, she still displays a rare tenacity of purpose. She is obviously overjoyed to find an 'affectionate cousin', although living some 10 000 kilometres away, who will – she hopes – make common cause with her. Some commentators were saying that the rumour about the marriage of George III and Hannah Lightfoot had 'died a sudden death in the antiseptic air of a British Court of Justice' but in Lavinia Janetta Ryves' mind the dream lived on.

The recorded statement that descendants of Hannah Lightfoot were living at the Cape was joyfully received by the woman who had staked her all on proving her own royal connections. One may be certain, from the examples given here of her compelling *cacoethes scribendi*, that this knowledge would not for long remain locked in her fevered bosom. Like her mother, she was a compulsive letter-writer, inclined to garrulity and boasting a large circle of friends. The story of the Rex family living at the Cape of Good Hope would, one can be fairly certain, have been added to Mrs. Ryves' extensive repertoire of those who, like herself, had been deprived of their birthright.

Mrs. Ryves, described as 'an active little old lady in black', died at her humble residence on Haverstock Hill in December 1871.

If the evidence of the Ryves Trial, widely reported in the newspapers, and the subsequent editorial comment on it had not assured Hannah Lightfoot her place in literature, then John Heneage Jesse's *Memoirs of the Life and Reign of George the Third*, certainly did. Obviously inclined to the belief that 'where there's smoke there's fire', he gave a detailed and intriguing dissertation on the legend, leaving the authenticity of the actual marriage of George and Hannah, of course, open to question, a course since followed by several other writers.[8]

Up till 1867, the year in which Jesse's *Memoirs* were published, there had been sporadic statements on Hannah's supposed fate (prompted by the original request for information in the *Monthly Magazine* of 1821) put forward in odd magazines from time to time. Her children became increasingly important in each succeeding reference.

Several of the letters published on this subject, dealt with one

Catherine Augusta Ritso (or Ritzau), who claimed to be a daughter of Hannah Lightfoot' by George III.[9]

The correspondence had obviously still been on the go in 1861, when the following letter appeared in *Notes and Queries* on 10 February, profferring information on a visit which the writer, William Harrison, had paid to South Africa some thirty-one years earlier*: 'With respect to the son born of this marriage (George and Hannah's) and said to be still living at the Cape of Good Hope, I think there must be some mistake (as to dates . . . .) I was at the Cape of Good Hope in 1830, and spent some time at Mr. George Rex's hospitable residence at the Knysna. I understood from him that he had been thirty-four years in the Colony, and should suppose he was about sixty-eight years of age, of a strong, robust appearance, and the exact resemblance in features to George III . . . On Mr. Rex's first arrival in the Colony he occupied a high situation in the Colonial Government, and received an extensive grant of land at the Knysna. He retired there and made most extensive improvements . . .'[10]

This is probably the most important single piece of evidence in existence relating to George Rex's possible descent from the alliance of George III and the Quaker girl – although it refers only to a likeness and makes no statement about any relationship; firstly, because it was written by a well-respected man who had actually met Rex, and secondly because it was written within three decades of the encounter described, only twenty-two years after Rex's death. It is a milestone in the Rex saga, because this is the first time that the association of George Rex's name with that of the royal family appears unequivocally documented in a widely-read publication (excepting, for reasons which will be mentioned later, a statement made in 1939 by John Lindsey, author of *The Lovely Quaker*, to the effect that Rex's relationship to George III had caused comment as early as 1801).

Carl Drège, a German apothecary visited Knysna in 1831, a year after William Harrison and not only commented in his private diary on the resemblance between George III and George Rex, saying that the latter was 'short and stocky, with a full, rounded face', but stated categorically:' George Rex is the son of King George III, also a step-brother of George IV and of William IV.'[11] There was no doubt about the relationship in Mr. Drège's mind.

In 1899 another allusion to George Rex's being a Lightfoot child appeared in print. The latter-day chronicler wrote: 'One of

*Appendix C

her (Hannah's) two sons became demented and committed suicide; the other, who took the name of George Rex, emigrated to the Cape of Good Hope, where he held a high official position, and was said to be the very image of his royal father.'[12]

But it was from the turn of the present century that Hannah Lightfoot and her putative descendants began to feature ever more significantly in literature. Instead of a brief response in answer to a query, or a sly dig of a line or two in odd magazines and sensational newspapers, the Quaker and her children began to provide the theme for an article, a monograph, a chapter of a book and finally several full-length books, one of them a highly-coloured novel.

Many assertions about happenings concerning Hannah and her offspring appeared in print a century or more after these were supposed to have taken place. Because some accounts of the earliest events were the last to appear in print, it will perhaps be minimally confusing for the reader if the main works on the Hannah-and-her-descendants theme are listed in the order in which these appeared in print, rather than an attempt made to marshal the events in chronological sequence.

In 1910 Mary Pendered wrote the first full-length book devoted to Hannah Lightfoot[13], having interviewed or corresponded with a great number of people who were either convinced of their descent from the Quaker girl, or knew some acknowledged descendants. She found out, for instance, a great deal more about the Catherine Augusta Ritso, mentioned in *Notes and Queries* as early as 1854 as being a daughter of Hannah Lightfoot and having married a James Dalton. This Catherine Ritso, curiously enough, was, after her death, stated in Burke's *General Armory* to have been the daughter of Henry Frederick, Duke of Cumberland![14]

Miss Pendered also had information from a Mrs. Permelia Corey Thomson who stated that 'Hannah's and George's first-born was denied recognition and the family name, and was christened by the name of Parks, after the beautiful parks nearby. When older he was induced to renounce all claim to the throne and was sent to America for his home . . .'[15]

America was the home of another claimant, Mrs. Aline Shane-Devin, whose story was quoted by Miss Pendered as follows: 'My father's mother was Hannah Lightfoot Rex, and her father was a son of the third George of the Hanoverian line and of Hannah Lightfoot, the Quakeress. My great-grandfather, George Rex, came to America during the Revolutionary war, and was from first to last, a devoted Royalist . . . The origin of the family has always been known and accepted by its members, though the circumstances connected with it were felt to be of so discreditable a nature to both sides that it was seldom mentioned.'[16] This reference to another George Rex, this time in America, is interesting.

All told, Miss Pendered came across seventeen families claiming to be descended from the union of George III and Hannah, their names being Lightfoot, Wheeler, Ritso, Rex, Dalton, Wheatstone, Brown, Thompson, Parks, Shane-Devin, Buxton-Lawn, Walker, Christie, Fitzgeorge, Linton, Fry and Mackelcan.

She knew, of course, all about the George Rex who had landed in South Africa a hundred and thirteen years before she wrote her book. An anonymous correspondent who had lived at Knysna some years prior to 1910, supplied her with the following summary of Rex's history as handed down by word of mouth. (Nothing substantial had been written about him to this date.)

'It is common knowledge that George Rex was George the Third's son by Hannah Lightfoot. He went out to South Africa between 1810 and 1820, with an Admiral Nourse and Sir (sic) Charles Somerset, then Governor, went up country with him and the Admiral to see about getting the land. He, Rex, was given the huge tract of land called the Knysna on two considerations; that he should not marry, and should not return to England. He was getting on for sixty when he went, and he kept his promise about not marrying; but he entered into morganatic relations out there and founded a family. The lands given him were of the best and most beautiful in the whole Colony, and he kept up an almost regal state, with white footmen and other men-servants, contrary to the custom out there.

'He entertained magnificently, and went every year to Cape Town in grand style with a wagon, fine team of oxen and a big retinue. His family maintained the same regal state for many years after his death . . .

'The late Duke of Edinburgh, when visiting the Colony, stayed with the head of the family, and on leaving, presented him with a gold watch. But Mr. Rex was exceedingly annoyed on finding his name inside engraved as 'Recks', which he took to be an intentional error and insult. The story goes that Hannah Lightfoot went out to South Africa with her two sons, but probably this is mere gossip.'[17]

The theory that Hannah Lightfoot at some stage visited South Africa has, incidentally, a certain measure of popular support. The most commonly accepted version of this is that she and her younger son were planning to visit George Rex on their way either to or from India, but that they were drowned when their ship was wrecked on the beach when trying to land at Plettenberg Bay, which lies about thirty kilometres east of Knysna. There are persons living in Plettenberg Bay today who will point out with confidence the exact site of the graves in which Hannah and her son are supposedly buried.

Mary Pendered obviously accepted the tradition that George III had sired children by Hannah – among them George Rex – but doubted whether a marriage between them had ever taken place.

In 1939 came John Lindsey's book, *The Lovely Quaker*,[18] Mr. Lindsey accepted unreservedly the theory that a marriage had taken place between George and Hannah and, furthermore, was convinced that George Rex of Knysna had been their eldest son and was consequently the legitimate heir to the throne of Britain. Mr. Lindsey had corresponded with certain persons in South Africa, been told of a number of relics in their possession, and been provided with a great deal of anecdotal evidence supporting his conclusions. He devoted a section of his book to a theory, which has also been widely accepted, that George Rex's younger brother, John, had taken the name of Mackelcan and become a distinguished general in the British army. Lindsey stated categorically, 'The King treated one son, John Mackelcan, with the greatest kindness, and the other, George Rex, with the greatest generosity.'

Among other fascinating points in Mr. Lindsey's book are the following: that Mr. Rex threatened the King with exposure unless the King saw he was well provided for; that George Rex was presented with the whole of the lands of the Knysna; that he lived in terrific and bewildering style; that his neighbours called his house a palace; that in addition to scores of slaves and coloured servants 'George Rex was served by a white butler, white footmen and white maid servants;' that he used silver crested with the coat of arms of the royal house of England; that George and Mrs. Rex made an annual journey to Cape Town where the worthy citizens and Government officials turned out to welcome them and do them honour; that the aristocracy of the Colony showed themselves proud and honoured when his children married into their families; that Rex received an unusual allowance from England; that he was singled out to be the host of the Duke of Edinburgh when he visited South Africa and that 'the Duke stayed with him for some months and treated him with the courtesy due to a relation.'[19]

Lending weight to the assertion that stories about George Rex's royal antecedents had begun to circulate shortly after his arrival at the Cape, Lindsey describes an unusual protest made in 1801, he says, by a Mr. Twistle ('who was some kind of Government servant') about the fact that 'Mr. Rex, had, almost on arrival, been presented

54

with one of the best posts in the Colony.' Twistle's argument, quoted by Lindsey, was that this preferment could be accounted for by the fact that Rex was not only the son, 'but the legitimate heir of our King, for his mother, the Quaker, and King George were joined in marriage before ever Queen Charlotte was thought of.'[20]

This complaint, according to Lindsey, was voiced in a letter which Twistle wrote to *The Cape Post,* but which the editor refused to publish.

Both Lindsey's and Mary Pendered's books were published in England and were read by comparatively few in South Africa, mainly by those with personal reasons for being interested.

In 1939, the same year as Lindsey's *The Lovely Quaker* appeared, a book dealing with Olivia Serres' fantastic claim to be the Duke of Cumberland's daughter was published. This was *Princess or Pretender?*, written by the same Mary L. Pendered who was the author of *The Fair Quaker,* but this time she worked in collaboration with Justinian Mallet.

Although the central topic of the book was the machinations of Olivia Serres and the subsequent Ryves Trial initiated by her daughter, there is a brief chapter about the alleged descendants of Hannah Lightfoot, among them, of course, George Rex.

Having sketched the outline of Rex's career in South Africa, the authors state: 'It has been believed and it is still believed throughout South Africa generally that he was the son of George III and Hannah Lightfoot', but they go on to query this belief themselves and to put forward an alternative line of descent for Rex. They did not establish conclusively which of the genealogies was the correct one, one of their major stumbling blocks being the fact that the date of Rex's birth given by the family at Knysna was 1760, while that of 'the other Mr. Rex' was 1765. The absence of any birthdate on George Rex's tombstone at Knysna has repeatedly served to deepen the mystery surrounding the central character in our present story.

A great deal of original work and painstaking research went into *Princess or Pretender?* and, although George Rex was only incidental to the authors' main them, tucked away in the appendices at the back of the book is some vital information on Rex, the importance of which will become apparent as this present story unfolds.

A monograph by Harold Napier Devitt, entitled *George, Prince of Wales, Hannah Lightfoot and George Rex,* did little to advance the search for truth. The author went over the George III-Hannah Lightfoot romance, mentioned several of the putative descendants, quoted freely from Pendered and Mallett, and listed in detail the relics in the possession of the Rex descendants in South Africa which seem to point to the royal descent of the family.[21]

It should be emphasised, incidentally, that only the major works dealing with the Rex legend are being mentioned here and that at least a score of South African writers have made use of George Rex one way or another in historical, quasi-historical and general descriptive works on the George-Knysna-Plettenberg Bay area. The already dramatic story of the Rex family was raised to new heights, for instance, in a fanciful, garbled article which appeared in an East London newspaper many years ago:[22]

'At Knysna there are several families who of course know the whole history. By them George Rex is always referred to as Admiral Rex, and I have myself seen his admiral's baton of black ebony with silver mounts with an inscription on it. When he came out from England on a frigate the Cape Government were ordered to grant him an estate of 100 000 acres, and he selected at the beautiful Knysna lagoon, where he received a very considerable grant of land and was made a magistrate or a special J.P.

'Admiral Rex bore a great resemblance to his Royal father, and moreover was one of the King's favourite sons, and for this reason the British Government, fearing a future pretender to the throne, determined that both he and his brother should be kept well away from England. His brother was sent out to India under the care of Wellesley (afterwards the Duke of Wellington) and ultimately died there. Admiral Rex was told that he was never to contract a legal marriage, so that the line of descent would be broken. He, however, had two successive wives and several children. At Knysna he lived in considerable state, and was always respected as the principal man in those parts. His descendants at the present time possess numerous most interesting relics, showing clearly the close connection between him and his Royal father.

'Not long ago it is said that one of our Princesses was shown some of these, and told the history, in which she was much interested, saying more than once, 'When I get back I shall tell Mary (then the Queen). We have talked about it before, but she always says it is a myth and that there was never any such thing . . .' '

Prompted possibly by an impulse to counteract some of the more far-fetched speculative writing on the subject, a great granddaughter of George Rex, Sanni Metelerkamp, began work in the thirties on the book which is still today the only serious compilation of a family history and biographical sketch of the remarkable founder of the Rex dynasty. This was *George Rex of Knysna: The Authentic Story*, which was published posthumously in 1955[23]. Miss

Metelerkamp was one of the first woman journalists in South Africa, skilled in the craft of writing, and she made a sincere and protracted attempt to find the facts hidden at the centre of the labyrinth of rumour, speculation and mystery which had, up till then, done duty for history of Rex's life, his possible relationship to George III, his life in England and his early years in South Africa. She did a monumental job in collecting and collating material from many points of the compass.

This was almost an act of faith on Miss Metelerkamp's part and her book is, to this day, the credo of those who accept the royal parentage of George Rex without question – and this includes a large number of South Africans and thousands of visitors from over the seas who have visited the Eastern Province and inevitably become interested in the story of a descendant of the royal house of Britain who settled at the fair Knysna and founded a settlement where none had existed before. The author conscientiously stresses over and over again that 'not a scrap of evidence exists', that 'everything concerning George Rex before he came out is silence and secrecy' and that 'all vital documents have been destroyed.' She points out that there is 'a welter of legend and mystery' and that 'the mystery will never be solved.'

But this is an emotionally charged subject. It was inevitable that, being herself a descendant of Rex, she should tend to lean subjectively towards the more romantic conclusions that could be drawn from the mass of circumstantial evidence which she accumulated. She takes the very lack of evidence as proof for certain of her conclusions and accepts 'family tradition' as gospel.

The four firm corner-stones of the story as believed and told by Miss Metelerkamp are (I) that George Rex, after taking farewell of his royal father, (as described on the first page of this book) 'sailed under sealed orders . . . to go into voluntary exile'; (2) that 'two promises were demanded of him before he left England; one, that he would never return and two, that he would never marry;' (3) that he was appointed Marshal of the newly-created Vice-Admiralty Court in return for 'some special services by which George Rex had earned the Royal gratitude' and (4) that 'before George Rex left England, King George III gave him permission to go to any part of his (the King's) possessions and choose for himself a property extending 'as far as the eye could reach.'

George Rex of Knysna presents very readably a great deal of authentic material on Rex's life in South Africa and the book represents the quitesssence of the generally accepted beliefs on the origins of this mysterious man.

In 1961 came Winifred Tapson's popular book, *Timber and Tides, the Story of Knysna and Plettenberg Bay*.[24] The Rex legend formed the theme of the second chapter, in which the now fairly familiar story of George *père* (the King) and George *fils* (the Marshal of the Vice-Admiralty Court at the Cape) was outlined. In the revised editions of the book, however, a chapter was added towards the end, in which an alternative genealogy, on the lines of that suggested by Pendered and Mallett, was put forward for Rex. The reader was left to decide which of the suggested versions of George Rex's life story was the more convincing.

Perhaps the most scholarly and meticulous piece of investigation carried out so far into Rex's personal history, but not into his origins, is Arthur J. Rex Beddy's well-documented *Genealogy of the Rex Family*, published in 1971.[25] In the introduction much is made clear about a side of Rex's domestic life which was previously shrouded in mystery, or ignored, and from the genealogy itself one gets a good idea of the ramifications of the family of nearly one and a half thousand men and women descended from the founder of Knysna. Some have become members of Parliament, farmers or business men, some have entered the Church, others have become lawyers, engineers, or have been successful in commerce or industry, and all have given something to the country which their renowned ancestor adopted so whole-heartedly at the turn of the nineteenth century.

It is by now obvious that George Rex's origins and life-story have been probed, mulled over and minutely examined more thoroughly than most families would care to have their ancestors' lives investigated.

And yet Rex remains an image in shadow. The time has come to conjure out of the past the figure of this man, to see his smile, his features, his broad shoulders and his dwelling, to meet his family, understand his aspirations, to grope our way, if possible, into his mind and, in so doing, to deduce something of his whole way of life at the Cape in the early years of the last century.

His is a far from prosaic story.

58

3 Life in London

Who was this man who caused such a stir and set in train – apparently unwittingly – a succession of rumours, counter-rumours and claims that have persisted for well over a century and a half?

Although the story of his early life has until now been a gap which sensation-loving journalists, novelists and well-intentioned biographers have rushed to fill, there is, considering that George Rex was born more than two hundred years ago, a surprising amount of documentation on his professional life available. Which of us knows, for instance, in what career our great-great-great-great-grandfathers were engaged or, for that matter, at what age they started work. And yet, here we are, able to give this precise information about young Rex thanks to two old documents which have now been added for the first time to the mass of papers, applications for appointments, letters patent of an appointment, official correspondence, notices of sale of houses, receipts for rents paid, diaries, ledgers and family letters, which have already been sifted through by chroniclers seeking to establish the life pattern of this 'mystery man'.

George Rex became articled, when roughly fifteen years of age, to one Edward Cooper, a notary public, in whose office he was to work for the next seven years and who enabled him to emerge at the end of that period as a fully-qualified notary public himself. From descriptions of George as a fully-grown man, handed down in travellers' diaries or in the Rex family through five generations, he was apparently of stocky build, with a round face, fresh complexion, blue eyes and hair tending to auburn. As the child is father of the man, it is not difficult therefore to picture this fair-faced, blue-eyed, sturdy youth – probably a little nervous – taking his place on a high stool in Edward Cooper's office in Doctors' Commons.

We are able to define this turning-point in George's young life with this astonishing accuracy thanks to his 'humble petition' in 1787 'To the Most Reverend Father in God John by Divine Providence Lord Archbishop of Canterbury Primate of all England and Metropolitan' to be admitted as a proctor in Doctors' Commons![1] In this document, which necessitates a mental leap forward for the reader and which will be referred to in greater detail later in the story, George Rex declares solemnly that he has served 'Edward Cooper, one of the Procurators General of Your Grace's Arches Court of Canterbury as his Clerk in his Office' from the 29th July, 1780, for the full Term of seven Years which expired on 29 July in this present Year of our Lord one thousand seven hundred and eighty seven . . .'

This establishes 1780 as the year in which he started work as a clerk. The fact that he was roughly fifteen years of age at this stage is deduced from a declaration signed by Edward Cooper, his employer, and Jas. Heseltine, also a notary public, on 10 November 1786, to the effect that 'George Rex of Doctors Commons London . . . . . Gentleman *of the Age of twenty-one Years and upwards,* to us well known, born in the Diocese of London, was and is a person of sober Life and conversation, conformable to the Doctrine and Discipline of the Church of England by Law established, well affected to his present Majesty King George the Third and to the present Administration both in Church and State . . .' This testimony to his character was in support of the application to be created a notary public.[2]

So much of the controversy and mystery surrounding George Rex has centred on this question of his birth-date, 'family tradition' having asserted over and over again that he was born in 1760 (the year in which King George III succeeded to the throne), that perhaps it would be unwise to assert too positively at this stage that the above document *proves* that he was twenty-one years of age in 1786.

This does, of course, bring his birth-date to 1765 and, for the purposes of this narrative, this is the year from which his age will be measured. The 1760 school of thought, however, will prefer to accept the phrase 'of the age of twenty-one years *and upwards*' as meaning that he was at least twenty-one in 1786, but could in fact have been twenty-six.

For the privilege of his being taken on as an articled clerk, George Rex's parents would have had to pay heavy premiums and he would in all probability have had to continue living at home, not being in receipt of any salary. He was fortunate indeed in having parents prepared to assist him to qualify as a professional man.

What unfortunately is not recorded is the type of schooling which young George had received prior to starting work in Edward Cooper's office. This can only be a matter for conjecture, for the present. It is quite possible that some investigator of the future, building on the concrete facts now accumulated, may one day find George's childish signature in an old text book or an entry in the attendance register of some London school and then be able to piece together the jigsaw with more accuracy. There are, for instance, four old law books of his – *William Blackstone's Commentaries on the Laws of England* – boasting his bold adult signature on the inside cover or fly-leaf, already on display in Millwood House, Knysna's little museum.

In these days of compulsory education, sending a child to school is such a simple matter. In the eighteenth century the great mass of the population was desperate for even the rudiments of an education for their children. Even parents of the middle class would probably have had their ingenuity and their purse taxed in order to ensure that their sons and daughters became acquainted with the three R's. That George Rex's parents succeeded admirably is patent.

Somewhere, somehow, George obtained an excellent grounding in the usual school subjects and a more-than-nodding acquaintance with such subjects as geography, mechanics, botany and economics, as will be seen in some of his latter-day activities and interests.

Nor would George's life have been all study in his early teens. London was an enthralling city in the second half of the eighteenth century, when this youngster's mind would have been awakening to its fullest interest in the cosmopolitan crowds, the political factions, the pleasure gardens, the costermongers, cherry girls, the bells of barrow boys, the hucksters, the fairs, the shows on street corners, the rich in their sedan chairs, the footpads in the ill-lit streets – the whole bewilderingly rich pageantry of London life at that time.

He would possibly have joined in the normal boyhood diversions of football or cricket; possibly enjoyed picnics in the country fields bordering so closely on the city, and possibly spent hours idling along the banks of the great river on which London depended for her very existence. Here was a colourful, ever-changing scene, the water alive with craft of every nation, from the tall, stately ships and the East Indiamen to the lighters, barges and small craft all bustling about their business. Here, in all probability, he thought the long, long thoughts of youth, his imagination ranging out to those distant ports from which some of the vessels had set sail.

London could be a dangerous city too, often seething with discontent, breeding clashes between classes and explosions of violence. In 1780, the year in which George entered Edward Cooper's office as a clerk, the infamous Gordon Riots broke out. One can imagine vividly the mingling of horror and excitement with which the fifteen-year-old onlooker would have seen the dogs of war let slip in the streets. He, like teenage boys the world over, would have been exhilarated rather than frightened and would probably have dashed from point to point as each fresh outbreak of violence was reported. For sheet destructive fury and range, the Gordon Riots exceeded anything in London's riot-riddled history.

Reconstructing the picture of our young man perched on a high stool, painstakingly driving his quill over sheet after sheet of legal documents, one's mind turns irresistibly to the graphic description by Charles Lamb of himself as a young man similarly engaged. But Lamb, who was born in the Temple in 1775, and was thus ten years George Rex's junior, was (at the stage he was describing) filling in the dreary years in a counting house in nearby Mincing Lance with his 'co-brothers of the quill' until he could fulfil his true ambition, which was to write.[3] George, on the other hand, had his foot firmly planted on the first rung of the legal ladder which was to lead him to a prestigious job as a notary public. For him, buoyed up by his young man's dreams, the days could hardly have been long enough.

A Notary Public is defined as 'a public official authorised to attest the legality of contracts, affidavits, declarations and deeds'. Notaries also protest bills of exchange and notes that have been dishonoured, draw up protests after receiving affidavits of mariners and masters of ships, and administer oaths. In work of this kind, before the days of photocopying and duplicating machines – or even typewriters – the emphasis in a notary's office was on what must have seemed to the novice like a never-ending stream of notes, affidavits, bills and contracts, all of which had to be copied laboriously in a good, clear hand. George's assured and legible handwriting of later years must have taken shape during this period.

That he used his time well, fulfilled his duties conscientiously and was given increasing responsibility is evidenced by the fact that at the age of twenty-one he qualified as a notary public. The application for him to be granted this privilege, as already mentioned, is addressed 'To the Right Reverend Father in God Samuel by Divine Permission Lord Bishop of Gloucester – Commissary or Master of the Faculties or to his Surrogate'. Having testified that George Rex was a person of sober habits and well-disposed towards the King and State, Cooper's and Heseltine's declaration continues: 'And we do further certify that the said George Rex is a person of known Probity and well skilled in Affairs of Notarial Concern. Wherefore we conceive the said George Rex fitly qualified to be created a Notary Public. In Witness whereof we have hereunto set our Hands the sixth Day of November in the Year of our Lord, one thousand seven hundred and eighty six.'

A note in the margin of this document reads '10th Nov. 1786 – Let a Faculty pass, the said George Rex having taken the usual Oaths before me – Wm. Scott, Surrogate.'

George Rex was now a notary. The document actually granting him his English Patent and bearing the seal of 'The Faculty Office, Doctors Commons' was issued the following day. It is a curious one to present-day eyes, bearing as it does the seal of the Archbishop of Canterbury, which was in fact routine. One must remember that from the day Doctors' Commons was formed in 1511 as an 'association of doctors of Law and of the advocates of the church of Christ at Canterbury' until its dissolution in 1857, the *Archbishop of Canterbury retained final and absolute authority over this corporate body.*

The Archbishop of Canterbury's control over the admission of advocates, proctors and notaries to courts other than the ecclesiastical courts was an unexpected result of the Reformation. In the middle ages the all-powerful Church authorities regulated admission to the ecclesiastical courts. Practice in these courts, which deal with marriage, divorce and other semi-ecclesiastical matters, was one of the most profitable branches in the practice of the law, so advocates in other courts were naturally anxious to be admitted to them.[4] They were admitted in due course, but only under the complete jurisdiction of the archbishop.

So this document, which is headed 'FACULTY granted to GEORGE REX to practise as a Notary Public' and is dated, 11 November 1786, naturally bears the seal of the Archbishop of Canterbury.[5] It opens with this greeting from the Primate: 'John by Divine Providence Archbishop of Canterbury Primate of all England and Metropolitan by Authority of Parliament lawfully empowered for the purposes herein written – To our beloved in Christ George Rex a literate person born in the Diocese of London Health and Grace. We being willing by reason of your merits to confer on you some suitable title of promotion do create you a *Publick Notary* previous examination and the other requisites to be herein observed having been had . . . and so out of our favour towards you admit you into the number and society of other Notaries . . . . .' and so on.

George Rex, having sworn allegiance to the King and support for the Protestant regime, goes on to declare, 'I will faithfully exercise the office of a Notary Public and I will faithfully make Contracts wherein the Consent of parties is required by adding or diminishing nothing without the will of such parties that may alter the substance of the fact . . .' The rest of this clause enumerates variations of the theme of the duties of a notary. One can imagine the rejoicing in George Rex's family the day this portentous document was brought home.

Continuing his determined way upwards, George, the following year, humbly petitioned the Archbishop of Canterbury to admit him as a proctor in Doctors Commons. He declares that 'Your Petitioner has been created a Notary Publick and hath constantly attended your Grace's Arches and other Ecclesiastical Courts and exercised himself in and been conversant with the Practice thereof.'

If looks as if Doctor's Commons must have had, however, its full complement of thirty-four proctors at that time, because a note in the margin of this petition reads briefly: 'October 29. 1787. Let him be admitted a Supernumerary, J. Canter-'. He served for two years as a supernumerary because George Rex's name first appears in the Law List as a fully-fledged Proctor of Doctors' Commons in 1789.[6]

By now he was twenty-four years old, no longer a youth, but a young gentleman about town. His new professional status entitled him to be called 'Esquire', a privilege extended to solicitors in an Act of Parliament of the reign of King Henry IV. Previous to this, barristers were one of the few groups of men, other than the landed gentry, which enjoyed the right to 'Esquire' by immemorial common law.

While it is almost certain that he had continued to live at home while still articled to Edward Cooper, the young proctor now joined his bachelor *confrères* in law and his address for the next eight years is shown alternatively as:

1789	George Rex	Gent. Paul's Chain
1790	George Rex	Godliman Street
1795-96	George Rex	Paul's Chain
1797	George Rex	Godliman Street[7]

Paul's Chain and Godliman Street were, in fact, two sections of the same street, Paul's Chain being the section nearer St. Paul's Cathedral and Godliman Street the section nearer the river. Godliman Street is today a short street connecting St. Paul's with Queen Victoria Street which, of course, did not exist in George Rex's day. Faraday House, the huge telecommunications centre, stands today on the site of the old Doctors' Commons and a ceramic plaque, let into the wall facing Queen Victoria Street, commemmorates this fact.

To get into perspective the considerable achievement of George Rex in graduating to a proctorship, it is important to understand something of the nature and function of that unique institution, Doctors' Commons, which was already almost three centuries old when his name first appeared on the Law lists.

The Encyclopaedia Britannica gives the following definition of it: 'DOCTORS COMMONS The common table and dining-hall of the Association of College of Doctors of Civil Law in London, hence the name of the buildings occupied by them as an incorporated society and now the name of the site of these, to the south of St. Paul's Cathedral. The Society was formed in 1509 by civilians entitled to plead in the Court of Arches. In 1786 they were incorporated under the name of the College of Doctors of Laws ... In the buildings of Doctors' Commons were held five courts, the Court of Arches, Prerogative Court of Canterbury, Consistory Court, Court of Faculties or Dispensations and the High Court of Admiralty.'

The 'Doctors of Civil Law' referred to were the advocates and to become an advocate a candidate must have obtained the degree of Doctor of Civil Law at Oxford or Cambridge; he must have obtained a rescript (official edict) or fiat from the Archbishop of Canterbury and must then have been admitted during term time by the Dean of the Arches, and have attended court for a year.[8]

The proctors were competent to advise clients and prepare cases for barristers, but not to appear as advocates, except in certain lower courts. When Doctors' Commons was dissolved in the mid-nineteenth century and the exclusive privileges of advocates and proctors abolished, the advocates took the rank of barristers and the proctors that of solicitors.

It has been stated that Doctors' Commons 'secured for itself a very bad name for fleecing the public'[9], but this was by no means peculiar in those days of sinecure and traditional privilege, especially when the layman, who regarded the law as esoteric as well as assinine, was swamped in a deluge of archaic legal verbiage, most of which was totally incomprehensible to him. It was easy for him to be taken for a ride.

On the positive side, Doctors' Commons gave a new status to the profession of the civil lawyer. It was 'an organised body of civilians who, from that time forward, filled an important position in the state'.[10]

Because of the multiplicity of courts within Doctors' Commons, the almost Gilbertian situation arose in which practitioners in the ecclesiastical court might suddenly appear as experts in other litigious cases, including those of Admiralty – a situation which is wittily parodied by Charles Dickens in his semi-autobiographical masterpiece, *David Copperfield*. Dickens was not a lawyer, but he was a shrewd and penetrating observer of the foibles of the society in which he lived and it is illuminating that his entertaining word pictures of young Copperfield's life in Doctors' Commons are quoted in all seriousness in scholarly legal works, such as W.S. Holdsworth's *A History of the English Law,* as being the best record of Doctors' Commons available. It is a situation with an ironic twist which Dickens himself would have been the first to enjoy.

'What *is* a proctor, Steerforth?' David asked his great friend when his aunt had suggested a proctorship as a possible career. 'Why he is a sort of monkish attorney,' replied Steerforth. 'He is, to some faded courts held in Doctors' Commons – a lazy old nook near St. Paul's Churchyard – what solicitors are to the courts of law and equity . . .'[11]

The actual buildings of Doctors' Commons, which had been entirely re-built after the Great Fire of London, consisted of two quadrangles. One entered the larger of these from Knightrider Street (intersecting Godliman Street) through a low archway and opposite this was a second archway leading into the second quadrangle and the garden. Besides the dwellings of the advocates, the buildings included a hall, dining-room and well-stocked library. It also housed the prerogative office, where the original wills of all who died in the province of Canterbury were insecurely housed.[12] Dickens had some biting comments to make upon the haphazard manner in which these wills were housed in 'an accidental building, never designed for the purpose' and not even fire-proofed. The wills were apparently crammed in here anyhow and anywhere.

For a description of the hall in which George Rex must have appeared many a time as clerk and proctor, W.S. Holdsworth again resorts to *David Copperfield:* 'Mr. Spenlow conducted me through a paved courtyard formed of grave brick houses, which I inferred, from the Doctors' names upon the doors, to be the official biding places of the learned advocates . . . ; and into a large dull room, not unlike a chapel to my thinking, on the left hand. The upper part of the room was fenced off from the rest; and there on two sides of a raised platform of horseshoe form, sitting on easy old-fashioned dining-room chairs, were sundry gentlemen in red gowns and grey wigs whom I found to be the Doctors aforesaid.'

After describing the presiding judge 'whom I should certainly have taken for an owl' and the advocates in their black gowns trimmed with white, David's report continues 'The languid stillness of the place was broken by the chirping of this fire and the voice of one of the Doctors, who was wandering slowly through a perfect library of evidence, and stopping from time to time, at little roadside inns of argument on the journey. Altogether, I have never, on any occasion, made one at such a cosey, dosey, old-fashioned, time-forgotten, sleepy-headed, little family party in all my life, and I felt that it would be quite a soothing opiate to belong to it in any character – except perhaps as a suitor.'

Scholars of today, while admitting that this is a substantially true picture of life in one of the courts, remind us that it was at these 'cosey, dosey, time-forgotten little family parties' that the foundations were laid of modern Admiralty law, that modern prize law was created, that much international law was made and many of the principles of our modern probate and divorce law were worked out.[13]

It is here, striding through the paved quadrangles, working in an office in one of those grave brick houses, interviewing clients, attending sessions in the solemn courts, discussing cases with a colleague in Child's coffee shop in St. Paul's Churchyard, that the bewigged and begowned figure of George Rex emerges with greater clarity than at any other time before his arrival in South Africa. What stimulating years these would have been for him and what a wonderfully exuberant world London was to be relished by the promising young lawyer.

There was, at this time, something in London to suit every pocket and taste. There were riches and squalor, exquisite sophistication and shocking displays of violence. Diversions included grand balls and assemblies, masquerades and festinos, concerts, waxworks, puppet shows and freak shows, all of which were enthusiastically patronised. Even more popular entertainment was provided by the fairs, the taverns, gambling houses, billiard rooms, bowling alleys, cock-fighting and bear-baiting dens. Out of doors, one could choose betwen shooting and archery, football matches and regattas. There were even balloon ascents, such as Mr. Lunardi's in May 1785.[14]

And quite possibly George Rex patronised the Ranelagh Gardens in Chelsea, or the Vauxhall Gardens on the South bank of the river, two of the most extravagant of the pleasure gardens which proliferated in London in that diverting age.

A short walk in the evenings would have taken him into the world of the playhouses, flourishing now as they had never flourished in the reigns of the first two Georges. The new Drury Lane Theatre, re-opened in all its glittering splendour in 1791 on the site of the original Theatre Royal, would have attracted the young blades in Doctors' Commons, among others, and the theatres of the Haymarket and Covent Garden were offering a wide variety of plays and musical fare, as well as some outstanding acting talent. There were well over five hundred playwrights at work in England between 1750 and 1800, including Sheridan and Goldsmith.[15]

But there was poverty and unrest in London too. There were riots caused by hunger and shortages and the new ideas of Liberty, Equality, Fraternity were catching on. The French Revolution burst out in all its idealistic fervour in 1789, the year in which George Rex entered Doctors' Commons as a proctor. Doubtless he watched the changing face of life at home and abroad, acutely aware of the war and of colonial expansion, and wondered where his prospects as a qualified lawyer were most promising. His mind now ranged far beyond the shores of England.

1795 was a momentous year on the world front. Following the establishment of a Republic in France in 1792 and the revolutionary wars which had started the following year, France had overrun the Austrian Netherlands and then invaded Holland towards the end of 1794. The Stadtholder, the Prince of Orange, fled to England while Holland (now named the Batavian Republic) made peace with France. The Prince, living in exile in Kew Palace, asked the British Government to protect the Cape of Good Hope until such time as he should regain his throne.

The Cape was, of course, of great strategic value as a half-way house on the prized sea-route to India and Britain too was mightily interested in seeing that it did not fall into the hands of France. In response to the Prince of Orange's request and on the understanding that the occupation would be a temporary measure, Britain agreed to mount an expedition. Early in April 1795, nine vessels, with a military force on board 1600 strong, commanded by Major-General James Craig, sailed for the Cape under the command of Admiral Sir George Keith Elphinstone and Commodore Blankett.[16]

The Stadtholder's instructions were delivered to the Commissioner General of the Cape, Abraham Sluijsken, and to Colonel Gordon, Commander of the Dutch East India Company's forces there*. These men were as a result placed in an unenviable dilemma. Although supporters of the house of Orange, they finally decided against surrendering their territory as the Prince of Orange ordered, on the grounds that the Prince was no longer at the head of the Dutch government and the rebellious burghers, particularly of Swellendam and Graaff-Reinet, were strongly in sympathy with the new Republican party in Holland. When Sluijsken heard that the newly-created Batavian Republic had allied itself with France and

*Appendix D

was consequently now an enemy of Britain, he smartly broke off all negotiations with the British. Craig landed his force on the shores of False Bay and successfully engaged the motley collection of Dutch gunners, German mercenaries and Coloured troops at Muizenberg, but then ran into trouble nearer Cape Town. It was no walk-over.

An SOS had already been despatched to Major-General Sir Alured Clarke, who was awaiting developments at a Brazilian port. He sailed at once and reached the Cape on 3 September, bringing with him 5 000 men and a generous supply of artillery. This decided the issue and the British, having overrun the Company's troops at Wynberg, marched on Cape Town.

The capitulation was signed at Rustenburg on 16 September, 1795, bringing to an end a hundred and forty three years of the Dutch East India Company's rule. In November Admiral Sir George Elphinstone (who was to return to the Cape in May 1796) sailed for the Isle of France, leaving Major-General James Craig acting as Commandant of the Settlement of the Cape of Good Hope – a not altogether enviable bequest. There were troubles aplenty ashore and the constant threat of attack by sea.

In October 1796, Admiral Elphinstone handed over command of His Majesty's ships at the Cape to Admiral Thomas Pringle, whose first action was to advise the Admiralty that a Court of Admiralty, already mooted, should be established forthwith for, among other things, 'the more effectual suppression of piracy'. It came into being on 6 January 1797, with a good deal of pomp and circumstance.[17]

Few persons in London would have been more aware than George Rex – a member of the professional group which had regular business in the High Court of Admiralty – of these dramatic developments in the faraway tip of the Dark Continent. Well qualified, thoroughly versed by now in all aspects of Admiralty law, adventurous and reliable, he was eminently suited for this type of promotion. He either applied for the post of Marshal to the court about to be created, or was recommended for the post by some Judge or other influential person. In either case, the suggestion was accepted and Rex's appointment to the post of Marshal by the Board of Admiralty followed.

The Board directed the Judge, Sir James Marriot 'to cause' the usual letters Patent to be issued by Registrar Arden, in the King's name, under the Great Seal of the High Court of Admiralty.[18] This was a normal step in view of Rex's experience and excellent qualifications for the job.

So George Rex exchanged his proctorial gown for the regalia of a Marshal and Sergeant-at-Mace of the Vice-Admiralty Court at the Cape of Good Hope. He wrote to their Lordships of the Admiralty informing them that he desired a passage on an Indiaman to the Cape of Good Hope. The Admiralty order for his passage is dated 15 March 1797.[19]

4 Of Ships and Sealing Wax

The Admiralty might issue an order for Mr. Rex's passage to the Cape, but for him actually to arrive in Table Bay was another matter. The wheels of officialdom turn slowly at the best of times; the journey itself took anything up to eleven weeks and he, no doubt, had private and business affairs to wind up. Britain being engaged in a period of almost unprecedented naval activity, the Lords of the Admiralty were hard pressed to control all their ships of war, at sea, organise the convoying of merchantmen, and sift the mass of rumour and counter-rumour about the movement of the enemy, so that the despatch of personnel to distant ports had to be fitted in accordingly.

The French have a saying, 'To part is to die a little.' If George Rex sailed from England with the intention of severing all familiar ties and making his future in the little-known land, South Africa, then indeed a small part of him must have died. He left behind his family and his legal colleagues, some of them undoubtedly friends through the seventeen years he had been in Doctors' Commons. But in view of the fact that Britain had arranged to hold the Cape under martial law on behalf of Holland – and in the process to secure the gateway to her own Eastern empire – and that most naval, military and civil officials were sent out to undertake a spell of duty for a defined period, it is more than likely that he merely accepted the promotion as welcome and the whole move as a rewarding and exciting interlude.

The climate, the warmth of the people, the economic possibilities of the settlement and the sheer beauty of that corner of it in which he chose to put down his roots, were obviously to influence his later choice and determine the pattern of his life for the next four decades.

Whatever the reasons for the delay, Rex did not leave England for several months after the order for his passage was issued. Although most ships in these war-torn years sailed in convoy, he almost certainly voyaged in *The Queen* (this name another twig of fuel to the flame of the legend?), which was the only ship to arrive at

71

the Cape from England in the month of October 1797.[1] We find him presenting his credentials to Lord Macartney, then Governor of the Cape of Good Hope, on the 30th of that month, nine months after his formal appointment as Marshal to the Vice-Admiralty Court.[2] The relevant entry in the Governor's Day Book of the Castle of Good Hope reads: 'Mr. George Rex this day presented his credentials or patent of appointment as notary public, dated London, 11th November, 1786.'

The choice of Lord Macartney, a wise and experienced diplomat of great integrity and strong principles, to command the faction-torn southern Colony during this difficult transition period, was a shrewd one. Rex must have counted himself fortunate to be officiating in his new post under a nobleman of Macartney's calibre. Widely travelled, having served England faithfully in several countries – including Russia, China and India – Macartney was by now, however, in his sixties, a martyr to gout and had agreed to accept the command of the Cape of Good Hope only on condition that he would be allowed to return to England should his health fail further. He received a warm and grateful message from the King agreeing to this condition, so it was evident he had no intention of remaining at the Cape indefinitely.[3] His wife (who was, incidentally, the second daughter of the Earl of Bute) detested foreign travel and had refused to accompany him to the rough-and-ready colony.

The Right Honourable Henry Dundas, later Viscount Melville, then Secretary of State for War, conceived the double-purposed plan of appointing Andrew Barnard, reliable, conscientious and fervently anxious to make good, as Secretary of the Colony; at the same time indicating to Lady Anne, Barnard's wife, that she would be expected to entertain on the Governor's behalf and generally act as First Lady of the Colony. Nothing could have suited the witty and ambitious Lady Anne Barnard better.

A close friendship and understanding had existed between Anne and Henry Dundas ever since he, then aged twenty-four and recently appointed Solicitor-General for Scotland, had first met this vivacious and attractive daughter of the old Earl of Balcarres, the last Lindsay of Edzell. It was probably as much to please Anne and to make the maximum use of her sparkling attributes as to secure a hard-working secretary for the newly occupied colony, that Dundas had recommended this appointment.[4] If anyone could be relied upon to smooth over gritty situations, to resolve problems of precedence and protocol, and to reconcile the Dutch and England elements in the half-formed society of the Cape at that time, it was Lady Anne.

Her place in history has been won for her, however, not so much by her diplomatic achievements – remarkable though these were – as by the preservation of her sketch books, the large collection of letters which she wrote from the Cape and the entertaining journal in which she wittily recorded the day-by-day goings-on in the *mélange* of a society into which she had been plunged. Almost no detail of life in the rather raw society, no minutiae of dress, deportment, furnishings or manners, escaped her perspicacious eye and keen ear. Her penetrating observations illuminate the scene for us as no official records could do and it is mainly thanks to her sketches, letters and journal that we are able to reconstruct the picture of the daily life at the Cape in the last few years of the eighteenth century with such excellent definition.

Many of the impressions recorded by Lady Anne Barnard must have been the same as the impressions received most vividly by the newly-arrived George Rex, for the Barnards had landed only five months before him, in May 1797. As the Governor and the Barnards had travelled in convoy, the former in *H.M.S. Trusty* and the latter in the Indiaman, *Sir Edward Hughes*, Lord Macartney had taken every opportunity of becoming better acquainted with this right-hand man, the Colonial Secretary, and there was much visiting between the two ships in the course of the ten-week voyage out.[5]

We do not need to rely on Lady Anne, however, to imagine the tense expectation with which George Rex would have caught his first sight of Table Bay and the majestic sentinel guarding it. Any traveller experiences a catch in the throat, a quickening of the pulse, at the sight of an unknown land and this particular destination, the beauty of which countless writers and artists have sought for centuries to capture with pen or paint, is more breath-taking than the approaches to many other lovely lands.

The haphazard collection of little white houses – for all the world like the houses built by a child with a pack of cards, according to Lady Anne – nestling in the green foothill- the brilliant light ricocheting off the white-washed walls; the spectacular back-drop of the rugged mountain, now deep-etched against the ultra-clear African sky, now smothered in its famous 'table-cloth'; the white sails of the ships of several nations against the blue of the bay – the magic of all this must have reached out to him even before he set foot on the little wooden jetty.

Apart from the initial impact of the grandeur of the setting, what other aspects of the town-in-embryo would have struck the thirty-two-year old Londoner, used to overcrowded, jostling streets, impatient, noisy traffic, and – in many parts of London – endless ribbons of uniform houses?

In the first place, it was not an overcrowded town he had come to. The area of the whole Colony was half as large again as England and Wales, while the total population consisted of 16 000 Europeans, 17 000 slaves, of whom 80 per cent resided in the Cape Peninsula and Stellenbosch district, and of some 15 000 Hottentots. The population of Cape Town, in 1795, was 15 000, of whom only one third were Europeans.[6]

Facing him as he left the jetty was the wide Heerengracht, main street of the town, lined with oak trees under which ran a small canal of clear, brandy-coloured water. It was springtime in this southern land and the oaks would be clothed in their first tender green. There were several low, flat-roofed white houses, nearly all shuttered against the sun and all featuring a wide stoep, on which the burgher owner and his family would sit and watch the world go by. Some of the bigger houses boasted heavy brass-studded doors. On his left, facing the mountain, were the reassuring stone bastions of the Castle, administrative centre of the Cape, and adjoining it, the dusty and often hot Parade Ground on which 'the Scarlet Coats and Blue' were regularly drilled.

Strangest of all to George Rex's English eyes and senses, must have been the presence in the streets of 'the far distant classes among human creatures' – the slaves,[7] some leaving a heavy trail of musk-scented oil on the air as they passed, some emanating an unmistakable body odour. Some were bent under heavy loads, others walked upright holding an umbrella against the sun over the heads of their masters or their mistresses, yet others bore the sedan chairs in which the women went shopping or paying their social calls.

From the time of Governor Van Riebeeck slaves had been imported to the Cape to do specialised work, the indigenous Hottentot population having at this time little inclination to learn the skills of the White man. Almost a century and a half later, slaves from the Isle of France (Mauritius) and the Far East, from Mozambique and from Malabar, from Java and Ceylon; slaves of every shade of skin from tawny amber to blackest ebony, were irrevocably interwoven into the colourful pattern of Cape society and over the decades countless permutations and combinations of colour had been added by a steady process of miscegenation and union with indigenous peoples.

At the end of the eighteenth century in the Cape the average number of slaves per household was of the order of thirty. The

Malays, with their light skins, quaint conical hats and clacketting wooden sandals, provided an exotic and exciting thread in the skein. Nearly all the men from the East were excellent artisans and many of the women skilled in needlework and lace-making; all possessed an inborn musical talent. Motherly 'ayahs' from India, a few 'coolies' from China, powerfully-muscled labourers from Mozambique and sturdy house-servants, cooks, gardeners and menial workers from many lands were all here – and here to stay. Many of the half-caste girls, with their flashing teeth, their dark, lanquid eyes and supple bodies, showed unmistakable traces of their oriental origin.

There is no record of where George Rex stayed for the first three years he was in Cape Town, so our reconstruction of his personal life during this period is necessarily speculative and fragmentary. As every second burgher household took in lodgers, accommodation was not really a serious problem, although it very often left plenty to be desired. In January 1798, some three months after George's landing, Lord Mornington, who had just been appointed Governor General of India, and his brother, Henry Wellesley (brothers of Colonel Arthur Wellesley, later the Duke of Wellington) arrived in transit to India and spent just on six weeks at the Cape. The story goes that they were given lodgings in the house of a family by the name of Bergh, but Lord Mornington arrived at the Castle early next morning begging to be given accommodation there, having been attacked by bugs in the abode he went to.[8] There was as yet no hotel proper in Cape Town.

The charge of Britain's administration of the Cape at this period was no sinecure: the confusion and uncertainty was almost indescribable. Reports of movements of enemy ships at sea would reach Cape Town and long anxious weeks would pass before they could be confirmed or denied. Swellendam and Graaff-Reinet, having revolted against the Dutch East India Company's rule and set up their own Republics, were continuing to present the British government with perplexing problems and communication between the authorities and the up-country districts in general was at its nadir. Political intrigue was rife.

In addition to the very natural resentment on the part of the Dutch colonists against the presence of the British occupying forces, there was hardly political unanimity among the burghers themselves. They were uncertain about the extent of the authority of the two-year-old Batavian Republic, some were devout Orangemen, others had pronounced Jacobin tendencies and others were for 'peace at any price'. The Dutch East India Company had, after a century of deep-rooted mismanagement, official corruption and private trading by its employees, declared its last dividend in 1782 and had left the Cape virtually bankrupt when it departed.[9]

In spite of the fact that the presence of a garrison and the frequent calling of British ships was helping to revive trade, increased expenditure in maintaining an occupying force, increased demands on the part of the burghers, allied to a disastrous harvest, had resulted in a crucial shortage of coin and corn. Lord Macartney, stout-hearted though he was, wrote to Governor Brooke, of St. Helena, in August 1797, 'Our distresses are inconceivable, and how to relieve them unless specie soon arrives from Europe, I am totally at a loss. Therefore I request you will send us by return Ships of War any sum, however trifling, that you can possibly spare . . . . .'[10]

Macartney nevertheless, as his predecessor Major-General James Craig had done before him, adopted a vigorous policy of expansion and optimistic exploration of the Colony's resources, wisely anticipating that new ports, new products, new materials for trade and hiterto unexploited parts of the country capable of supporting new crops would, in the long run, be the answer to the settlement's problems. Two expeditions, prompted by this far-seeing policy and which were, indirectly, to exert a considerable influence on George Rex's future plans, had been instigated shortly before his landing in Cape Town. The one was almost solely concerned with exploring the possibilities of Plettenberg Bay as a port; in the course of the other this bay was just one of many parts of the eastern districts of the Colony visited with a view to expanding the trade and the prosperity of the Cape as a whole.

Plettenberg Bay, which was to feature in Rex's future plans in that it was the only harbour of any kind within comparatively easy reach of Knysna, lies about thirty kilometres east of the latter. Mossel Bay, a safe and more sheltered point of anchorage, still left a traveller to Knysna with a hazardous and appallingly rough over-land journey of nearly one hundred and thirty kilometres to face after landing.

It is not suggested that Rex, recently arrived in Cape Town and busy getting the measure of his new job, was at this stage seriously interested in the possibilities of Plettenberg Bay, Knysna or any other part of Outeniqualand, but detailed reports on these two expeditions were bound to have come his way and possibly have formed the springboard from which he was in due course to launch his ambitious takeover of the Knysna lagoon and all the surrounding country. Viewed from this distance in time, it seems that there was almost an element of portent in the timing of these expeditions so far as Rex was concerned. Both started out in July 1797, three months before his arrival.

The first and major expedition started with Lord Macartney summoning his young private secretary, John Barrow, who had accompanied him on his mission to China in 1792 and in whom he had total confidence. He briefed him on a journey which he wanted him to undertake primarily with the intention of making certain confidential political enquiries. He was to travel in company with F. R. Bresler, the Landdrost of Graaff-Reinet, one of the two seriously disaffected areas. The detailed list of items on which Barrow (who incidentally was born one year before George Rex) would be expected to furnish information was contained in a letter written to him by Lord Macartney a few weeks before he left, and makes formidable reading.[11]

Apart from making general observations on the country through which they might pass, and noting the latitude and longtitude of the parts visited, he was to note any timber or naval stores he might find, any hemp, flax or tar (or substitutes for them), any convenient ports, 'particularly of the Bay or Harbour said to be formed where the Swartkops River falls into the sea (Algoa Bay), prevailing winds, depths of water, advantages and disadvantages of this bay, whether any fishing was carried on, what vessels frequented the coast, what mines had been discovered, what possibility of other mines being discovered, what commerce 'might with safety be carried on with the Hottentots, Caffres or other savage nations on our Boundary' and to discover 'whether the Caffer country abounds, as it is said, with Ivory, Gold dust and other valuable articles of trade'.

Previous expeditions with identical purposes had, of course, been undertaken during the rule of the Dutch East India Company, but the amount of information available from this period was minute.

Barrow's assignment was one which might have deterred a lesser man, but he was to fulfil with distinction the demands of not only this expedition but of two more similar ones in the following two years. 'Equipped with alert intelligence, well-stored mind and vigorous body, this young man in his thirties travelled in that spirit of scientific enquiry which was to distinguish the next century.'[12] His report was exhaustive and extraordinarily accurate considering the almost blank canvas on which he had to draw his outlines. He not only fulfilled the Governor's requirements, but added his opinions on a wide range of subjects not included in his brief and, although his harsh views on the colonists are to be deplored, his observations were for the most part objective, accurate and scientifically valuable. His report on the possibilities and characteristics of Plettenberg Bay and Knysna must have made fascinating reading for Rex.

In the same month as Barrow set out, Leiutenant William McPherson Rice, an officer of *H.M.S. Trusty* sailed in the Brig, *Hope*, with instructions from Admiral Thomas Pringle, by then in command of naval forces at the Cape, 'to explore and get information on the almost totally unknown coast of Africa to the Eastward of the Cape',[13] but his report is confined to Plettenberg Bay and its environs. Having described the forest to the north-west of the landing place and the generally wooded appearance of the coast westwards, he comments on the supply of timber, lack of water, the landing place, 'a wild stringy plant the bark of which the Inhabitants make their fishing and small lines,' Cape Seal (Robberg) and the general navigability of the bay. He notes that no fishing was carried on, 'though in the months of July, August and part of September, the bay abounds with Whales'. No mines or minerals had been discovered near the bay and there does not seem to have been any traffic or communication with the Hottentots 'or other Savage nations'. His nautical observations were accurate and all of this information was to be most useful to Rex when his eye and attention began to turn eastwards. The Knysna lagoon, of course, had received scant attention as a possible harbour, because of the dangerous rocky bar lying between The Heads which guard the entrance to the estuary of the Knysna River.

Rice returned to Cape Town in August and would probably have met Rex but Barrow, who did not return until January 1798, was still away when the Marshal and Sergeant-at-Mace took up his duties in the Vice-Admiralty Court. If information on Rex's private life is scanty for this period (unfortunately, there is no mention of him in Lady Anne Barnard's letters or journal and none of his personal letters have survived from these years), it is not difficult to get a fairly well-defined impression of the nature of his working life, mainly from official documents and records.

When the Court of Vice-Admiralty came into being early in 1797, its jurisdiction extended from Cape Negro on the West coast of Africa to Cape Corrientes on the east. It was judicially independent of the colonial government, but the document (6 January 1797) in which King George III vests the authority of the Vice-Admiralty Court in 'our right Trusty and well beloved Cousin and Councillor, George Earl of Macartney', makes it clear that, failing him, the authority would be vested successively in Major General Francis Dundas, Lieutenant Governor of the said Colony, ... Andrew

Barnard Esquire, Secretary of the said Colony . . . Admiral the Honourable Sir George Keith Elphinstone, Knight, Commander in Chief of our Naval Forces at the Station . . . and 'all Admirals, Vice-Admirals, Rear-Admirals, Captains and Commanders of any of our Ships of War'.

It is a long-winded document recalling, rather whimsically, that under an act of parliament passed in the reign of King William III for the more effectual suppression of piracy, 'it is among other things enacted that all Piracies, Felonies and Robberies committed in or upon the Sea or in any Haven, River, Creek or place where the Admiral and Admirals have power authority or Jurisdiction, may be examined enquired or tryed heard and determined and adjudged according to the directions of the said Act . . .'[14]

The first Judge of the Vice-Admiralty Court was John Holland, the Registrar was John Harrison (both appointed 9 January 1797) and the Marshal was George Rex (appointed 27 January 1797).[15]*

The original document of the Letters Patent of Rex's appointment,[16] although badly discoloured and mutilated, is in the possession of one of his descendants, the Reverend Arthur J. Rex Beddy (who, it should be mentioned, is the meticulous recorder of *The Genealogy of the Rex Family).*[17] The wording in this document, 'Know ye that We for and in consideration of the Good and Faithful Service already performed and which shall hereafter be performed to us by George Rex Gentleman and for certain other good and lawful causes . . .', has been commented upon by more than one Rex chronicler and endowed with mysterious and special significance as referring indirectly to the link between George of the Cape and George of Hanover. Sanni Metelerkamp says that in the Rex family the special service mentioned has 'been taken to refer to his self-effacement and 'voluntary exile'. This somewhat effusive wording was, in fact, typical of certain Official documents of the time. When the Hon. Henry Barrington, for instance (who was many years later to buy Portland, part of Rex's vast estate) was appointed in 1824 to the 'Office of Keeper of our . . . Woods within our Bishopric of Durham', the following wording appears in his official document of appointment: ' . . . our Beloved the Hon. Henry Frederick Francis Adair Barrington of Sedgfield in the County of Durham and for the good and Faithful Services to be hereafter performed by the said Hon. Henry Frederick Francis Adair Barrington to us and our Successors . . ."

The duties of a Marshal were largely administrative – carrying

*Appendix E

out the decisions of the court relating to the impressment of ships and of seamen, to embargo and reprisals, to wrecks and to prizes; also serving warrants on ships which were seized either as enemy vessels or for compounding any act of 'piracy, felony or disobedience'. If such a vessel, when seized, had to be sold as a prize, the Marshal took charge of it, made the necessary arrangements and gave notice of the sale. The Vice-Admiralty Court at the Cape, as elsewhere in time of war, also acted as a Prize Court.

Rex's main ceremonial function as Marshal and Sergeant-at-Mace, however, was to walk, bearing the Oar Mace of Admiralty, before the Judge as he proceeded into the court. Not until the mace was in position on the table in front of the judge – now seated – was the court properly constituted.

Any mace, large or miniature, whether borne before the Speaker, judge, mayor or chief magistrate, is one of the most ancient and powerful symbols of law and authority. In Parliament, it is carried before the Speaker by the Sergeant-at-Arms in the ceremonial progress into the House. The House is not properly constituted until the mace is in its position on the table before the Speaker. In England, in less law-abiding times, attempts were actually made to prevent the House from sitting by hiding the mace. When the old Cape House of Assembly held its one and only session in Grahamstown in 1864, 'the Sergeant-at-Arms lugubriously packed up the mace' in its French-polished oak case, while being pestered by newspaper reporters.[18]

The history of the evolution of the mace as a symbol of authority is a fascinating one.[19] As early as the twelfth century the battle-mace – a glorified knobkierie – was a formidable weapon of iron with a heavy head capable of crushing armour.

It is mentioned as an item in the equipment of the heavily armed sergeants-at-arms, a corps instituted by Richard I. 'The duty of these Sergeants originally was to watch round the King's tent in complete armour, with a mace, a bow, arrows and a sword, and occasionally to arrest traitors and other offenders about the court, for which the mace was deemed a sufficient authority.'

By the mid-thirteenth century maces were encased in silver for ceremonial purposes. Today institutions, colleges, councils, faculties, livery companies, water-bailiffs and professional bodies all use maces as instruments of authority.

When the President of the Probate, Divorce and Admiralty Division of the High Court in London walks in procession with all the judges at the beginning of the legal year in October, he is preceded by the Admiralty Marshal shouldering a Silver Oar . . . . .

When the President is sitting in Admiralty, the Oar rests in supporting brackets before him on the bench.

The Silver Oar of Admiralty is analogous to the mace as a symbol of authority in naval courts. But it does not necessarily have to take the form of a blade or oar. In the case of marshals or their deputies, a small crowned staff such as the one used by George Rex, seems to have been in use at least from the time of George II. The name of the office-bearer was often engraved on it.

In an informative booklet on this subject published by the National Maritime Museum, Greenwich, out of more than sixty illustrations of Oar Maces, thirteen are of small staffs surmounted by a crown. To compensate, as it were, for the break with the traditional oar, some have a small oar attached at the lower end of the staff or the terminal cap of the staff unscrews to reveal a small silver oar which fits into the hollow shaft. Of the Vice-Admiralty Courts overseas, all had their oar maces and of these Bermuda's is the oldest.

When the British left the Cape in 1803, George Rex retained the Marshal's mace, which is now in the possession of a Rex descendant in Knysna. Another Vice-Admiralty mace, used during the second British occupation of the Cape, is in the collection of the Honourable John Maurice de Villiers, a grandson of the first Baron de Villiers (the first colonial-born Chief Justice appointed in 1878 and first Chief Justice of the Union of South Africa). The duties of the Vice-Admiralty Court in 1828 had been taken over by the Chief Justice.[20] Unlike Rex's crowned staff, the de Villiers' mace is a traditional silver blade, engraved with the royal arms (1801-1816), the eagle and thunderbolt of Zeus, within a wreath the foul anchor, dolphins entwined on crossed tridents and, within a wreath of oak leaves, a medallion head – possibly of George III.

It has been variously claimed by writers dealing with the 'mystery' of George Rex that he had a large private fortune, that he received a salary of £1 000 a year or that he received a Crown grant of £1 000 a year. The writer has not been able to find documentary evidence of the amount of the Marshal's salary in the Vice-Admiralty Court, but it is possible that his emoluments were based on similar principles and subject to the same conditions as that of the judge at that time, Judge John Holland, who had arrived with his wife in the *Belvidere* on 3 February 1798, 'to judge on Prizes' according to Lady Anne Barnard. He was also appointed Post-Master General and given an office in the Castle. Lady Anne was delighted at Mrs Holland's arrival – an English woman of good class – and invited the couple to dinner.[21] The Judge's salary, however, gave rise to a slightly acrimonious correspondence between him and the Governor, and repercussions between the Governor and London.

The shortage of qualified legal men in the Cape during the first British occupation was acute but this was no new situation. The Colony's Courts of Justice were causing Lord Macartney many headaches at this time and in writing to Henry Dundas on 26 July 1797, he pointed out that 'none of the present members of the Court are professional men, but chosen out of the principal burghers of the town . . .', a none too satisfactory state of affairs in a small but complex community.

The number of judges had been reduced from thirteen to nine – and of these only seven were able to serve effectively – but Macartney earnestly advocated the appointment of only three or four *properly qualified* men to be chosen from among 'the able Jurisconsults or professors of the Universities of Leyden, Utrecht or Groningen, who were well versed in the Roman law tradition of the Cape.' He felt that such jurists might be induced to come to the Cape by an offer of a salary of 5 000 rix dollars (£1 000) a year. At the time of his writing, only the President of the Courts of Justice, Mr. Olaf de Wet, received this amount, the remaining members receiving between 1 000 rix dollars (£200) and 500 rix dollars (£100).[22]

The first reference to the salary of Judge Holland of the Vice-Admiralty Court is found in another letter from Macartney to Henry Dundas, written on 28 February, 1798, from which it is clear that poor Mr. Holland was not receiving anything like his approved salary owing to the instructions issued by the Council in London that his salary should be paid out of the penalties, fines and forfeitures resulting from the seizure of contraband goods. Lord Macartney is rightly concerned about this situation and wishes the salary to be paid *in toto* from the Treasury of the Navy 'because from the present regulations of the Customs House and perhaps from the increased caution and adroitness of the Smuggler, I do not imagine that so many seizures are likely to occur in future as that a moiety of the King's part would produce the £600 intended as a provision for the Judge of the Court of Vice-Admiralty's salary'.[23] So Judge Holland had come to South Africa on the understanding that his salary would amount to £600 a year. It is hardly likely that George Rex fared any better.

The acute shortage of men with adequate legal training to cope with the work of both the Courts of Justice and the Vice-Admiralty Court, has been commented upon. It was only shortly before 1797 that the Dutch East India Company allowed attornies to practise and in matters of official precedence they were, sad to relate, poorly graded.[24] George Rex, with his proctorship and his many years of experience in the Courts of Doctors' Commons, which sometimes dealt, *inter alia*, with problems of Roman Dutch Law, was no doubt seized upon with alacrity by Governor Macartney.

Upon taking up his duties as Marshal, he was immediately appointed Registrar of the Courts Martial, for trying cases of 'piracy, felony and disobedience' as well as cases of 'treason, desertion and espionage'. Two and a half months later, in January 1798, he was also appointed Advocate for the Crown.[25] It is even possible that he was permitted to take on private legal work, because on 2 August of the same year, Andrew Barnard wrote to the President of the Court of Justice advising him that 'Messrs. Rex and Wittenoon, two Gentlemen of the Law, who had qualified in London and taken the Oaths of the Colony', were to be allowed to practise as notaries from then on. Rex held the position of Registrar for over three years, relinquishing it at the end of March, 1801, when 'he prayed the Court to dispense with his further attendance on account of his official position as Marshal of the Vice-Admiralty Court, his personal attendance being required daily at that Court'.[26]

His duties in his original office had obviously increased to the point where he could no longer handle a third post, although the income from these three official positions held simultaneously, must have added up to quite a substantial figure – possibly £1 000 a year – and it was very likely during these three-and-a-half lucrative years that he laid the foundations of a bank balance which was to enable him to buy first one large property and then later his vast estates in Knysna.

On the broader canvas of the war front in Europe, the picture emerging was one which had dark overtones for Britain. At the Cape Lady Anne Barnard reported that bets were being placed among the colonists at five to one on 'peace by Christmas'.[27] In Britain the odds would have been longer. At war with France and Spain, threatened with unrest at home and the possibility of invasion from abroad (in February 1797, fifteen thousand Frenchmen actually succeeded in landing at Cardigan Bay, Pembrokeshire, but were repulsed by the local militia without a shot being loosed), her resources were strained to the maximum. The Directory of France was calling on Dutch help, Spanish help and the support of malcontents in Ireland. A letter from the War Office, written to Lord Macartney on 10 October that year, contained the warning that 'His Majesty's earnest endeavours to procure the restoration of peace have not been attended with success . . . this unfortunate circumstance will consequently call for the utmost vigilance to guard against any possible attempt by the Enemy on the Cape of Good Hope.'[28]

From this atmosphere of tension Rex came into the midst of a situation of crisis at the Cape – not least as far as His Majesty's ships were concerned. No one could seriously have blamed him if, when he had had time to take stock of the situation, he had packed his bags and left on the first ship sailing for home.

Apparently encouraged by rumours of the mutiny which had broken out a few months earlier in the fleet at Portsmouth and the Nore, the crews of the squadron at the Cape organised a general mutiny of serious proportions which erupted early in October, the month of George's landing. The ships involved were the *Tremendous, Trusty, Imperieuse, Braave, Rattlesnake, Chichester, Star* and *Euphrosyne* – the others being at sea.[29]

It all started, aptly enough, with the *Rattlesnake*. On 5 October a letter 'Signed all as one Mann, *Rattlesnake*', was addressed to the 'Gentlemen and Brothers' of the other ships, setting out the reasons for the discontent. 'We the loyal Subjects of our Country . . . have felt so much the Scourge of unlawful Treatment Almost to Dreadfull for Human Heart to Vent or to put in Execution against any Individual . . . we are likewise Resolved Not to Bear under the Affliction any longer their have Been so Mutch Whiping and Starting at the Will of Arbitrary command Whitch is Not Good Discipline . . .'

The men on board the *Tremendous* reacted swiftly to the report of 'Bad Usage which we as Brothers are very sorry for to hear. We on Board of the *Tremendous* Hath no Right to Complain But never The Less for that if you have Bad Usage We one and all will see you Righted as Far as we can Dare to procede in Defence of our King Country and Laws . . .'

The grievances were pooled and a general statement on their nature was delivered to Admiral Pringle. Four days after the start of the mutiny he wrote a detailed and patient account of the difficulties being experienced by the various contractors supplying liquor and foodstuffs to the Navy and of stringent enquiries being made about the poor quality of certain items. He promised immediate stoppage of pay of any purser found guilty of using short weights and measures, and exploded only in the last paragraph: 'I wish to God the different Ships Companies in this Squadron had with patience awaited the Arrival of such information from England (re increases in pay and provisions) and not taken the Steps they have already done in turning several of their Officers on Shore . . .'

On 12 October Pringle, 'Rear-Admiral of the Red and Commander in Chief of His Majesty's ships and vessels . . .' issued a proclamation pardoning such seamen and marines of the squadron at Simon's and Table Bays as had been concerned in the mutiny and had now returned to order. The Royal Standard was hoisted and the men returned to their duties.

The following day Macartney wrote a sanguine account of the quelling of the mutiny to London and ended his letter by saying that he was happy to report that the inhabitants of Graaff-Reinet had also returned to a proper sense of duty. It was to be several years, however, before the disorders at Graaff-Reinet were to be brought under control and it was only a matter of weeks before mutiny again broke out at the Cape, following the return of certain ships from St. Helena.

Admiral Pringle had done his best. He had given orders that the crews of the ships under his command were to be put on full allowances of all provisions and had taken stern measures with the agent victuallers who had been delivering poor quality goods. This mutiny had lasted from 26 October to 10 November, when Pringle lost patience and gave the *Crescent,* the last ship in a state of mutiny, one hour after the reading of his proclamation in which to deliver up the 'Promoters of the Present disturbance' otherwise he would 'act upon her in consequence'. Guns on shore were trained on the ship and no one had any doubt that the sorely-tried Commander in Chief would use them if necessary. Fortunately the occasion did not arise and the inflamed fleet seems to have simmered down after this firm action, the cooling off process hastened no doubt by the fact that a Court Martial condemned two of the insurgents from the *Sceptre* to death and one to eighteen months imprisonment.

George Rex in his position as Registrar of the Courts Martial, would have been directly concerned with these developments, even though the mutiny and riot were not within the province of the Vice-Admiralty Court.

A small episode will often bring a person or event from history sharply into focus and it would have helped us considerably in sketching the outline of Rex as a man and even filling it in with personality, had we known where and with whom he spent his first Christmas in Cape Town. Possibly Judge and Mrs. Holland would have invited members of the staff to Christmas dinner; possibly it was eaten with the burgher family with whom Rex was lodging. He, a personable and eligible young man from England, would certainly not have been left to eat it alone in this land whose hospitality was renowned even then. Wherever he celebrated his first sunny

Christmas, he must have been struck – as every visitor from Europe is struck to this day – by the absurdity of sitting down to the traditional fare of hot poultry and flaming plum-pudding, with all the accompanying vegetables, side dishes, pastries, sauces and sweetmeats, when the scorching summer heat was bouncing off the whitewashed walls outside.

In contrast with the scarcities and high prices which had prevailed during the last years of the Company's rule, the New Year brought with it unparalleled prosperity for the merchants of Cape Town, thanks mainly to the presence of a large garrison and the putting into port of numbers of British ships on their way to or from India. Many of the passing ships had distinguished visitors on board, so that in August 1798, Lady Anne wrote, 'Never saw I such a succession of Governors – the sea has been quite covered with them for the last six months.'[30] On the frontier, however, all was far from well and reports from Graaff-Reinet showed that Lord Macartney had indeed been premature in supposing the burghers there to be submitting cheerfully to governmental authority.

Macartney who, as Governor, had inherited an inadequate amount of both coin and money, was to leave the Colony in infinitely better financial shape than he had found it.[31] He had been forced to draw on the East India Company for civil expenditure and on the home government for pay for the troops, but the balance of payments was almost satisfactorily settled by the time he was to embark for England. He had petitioned the King some months previously to allow him to withdraw on account of his failing health and, with many expressions of regret on all sides, the date of his departure was fixed for 21 November 1798. Rear-Admiral Sir Hugh Clobbery Christian – also a sick man – had by then replaced Thomas Pringle as naval Commander-in-Chief of the station.

On 19 November Macartney issued a proclamation calling on all the principal military officers, all corporations, public bodies and all persons in the civil service in Cape Town to assemble at Government House in the Garden at eleven o'clock on the day ensuing his departure, to witness the formal taking of the oaths of office by Major-General Francis Dundas as acting Governor.[32] On the twentieth, Macartney boarded the man-of-war, *Stately*, lying at anchor in the Bay, and sailed the following day.

An unusual event had occurred four days before his departure, when hundreds of citizens of the town, George Rex surely among them, rushed to the shore to see a strange sight, news of which had spread through the town like wildfire – a great silvery mass of

86

strange exotic fish washed up on the beaches.[33] There was much talk of dire portents and other strange phenomena.

On the night (22-23) of the day following Macartney's departure, at about eleven o'clock, a serious fire broke out in the stables occupied by the horses of the Dragoons.[34] The tongues of flame, fanned by a strong South-easter, leaped with terrifying rapidity to the adjoining storehouses (one containing valuable merchandise from the East) which were destroyed within a matter of minutes. The whole town was alerted and civilians, fearing for their homes and families, joined the garrison in frantic attempts to subdue the blaze. About four o'clock the next morning the fire was finally brought under control, but by then one soldier had lost his life and more than a hundred screaming horses had died in the flames.

Everything pointed to the conflagration having been the work of saboteurs, but the Court of Enquiry which was immediately set up, decided that some scraps of wadding from the evening gun had accidentally caught fire and the strong south-easterly wind had carried the sparks to ignite the stables and result in the wholesale blaze.[35] A month later, however, 'a most wicked and diabolical attempt was made . . . to set fire to the barracks' and this time there was no doubt at all that this had been an act of sabotage. Fortunately the fire had been detected early and little damage resulted. A reward of three thousand rix dollars (£600) was offered for any information leading to the arrest of the incendiarists and, if a slave were to be the bearer of the information, he would receive the same award, be offered his liberty and conveyance out of the Colony, if he should wish it. A curfew was imposed and a most uneasy peace prevailed over Christmas.

Early in the New Year, Dundas issued a proclamation announcing new regulations relating to fire, the appointment of fire-wardens, examination of engines, the sweeping of chimneys, care of thatch and so on, including the appointment of a *College of Brandmeesters* of fifty-five persons.[36] The next day the harrassed Lieutenant-Governor must have been reassured to receive a letter from 'the Gentlemen of the Civil Department together with the principal English inhabitants of this place', making him a public offer of their services in the event of any attack on 'this valuable Colony'. Among the more than sixty signatures attached are those of Andrew Barnard, Judge Holland, George Rex, John Barrow, William Menzies and Robert Semple.[37] The last-named was within a short time to visit and eulogise the home which Rex was to move to nearly six years later. William Menzies was probably an uncle of the man of the same name who was to become a distinguished judge and firm friend of George Rex.

So tense was the situation in the modest town at the foot of the mountain, that even the Concordia Club, a social club formed by the burghers to promote 'friendship and harmony' and to which the entrance subscription was forty rix dollars and (for the support of the cellar) twenty-five bottles, came under grave suspicion.[38]

A glimpse of the difficulties under which the Vice-Admiralty Court operated during the first British Occupation is afforded by a long-distance exchange of conflicting views sixteen months later between Judge Holland, Henry Dundas, Secretary of State for Home Affairs, and the War Office. Major-General Francis Dundas was, as already mentioned, acting Governor by now. To Henry Dundas in London, the Judge wrote announcing that a sharp difference of opinion had now arisen between himself and the acting Governor over the cargo of the *Angelique,* a ship which had been seized somewhere east of the Cape and brought in as a prize.

The acting Governor maintained that, under an order of the Council of 1796, no cargoes taken to the east-ward of the Cape could be sold as prize goods. The Judge was indignant. He had already been placed in an invidious position because of his salary having to be paid out of prize money – sometimes insufficient to meet it – and now the acting Governor was disputing his authority to take in a ship with a large cargo of prize goods. More than that, there was in the Bay, he asserted, roughly £100 000 worth of property taken under similar circumstances which would inevitably perish if not landed and sold while litigation was dragging on.[39]

He enclosed with this letter, his correspondence on the subject with the acting Governor, copies of the relevant minutes of the Vice-Admiralty Court, the Marshal's certificate, copies of Lord Macartney's letters to Sir Hugh Christian on a similar point which had arisen previously, and the Marshal's (George Rex's) letters to the Custom House officials. Four months later a communication from the War Office to the acting Governor (it could not have arrived before November) stated categorically that 'it is His Majesty's pleasure that no Prize Goods the produce of any Country Eastward of the Cape of Good Hope should be sold at that Settlement for the consumption thereof, except such as are strictly of a perishable nature.'[40] If the *Angelique's* cargo were of a perishable nature, it had certainly perished long since. More serious, the Judge of the Vice-Admiralty Court had been overruled by the acting Governor. His job was no sinecure.

Naturally George Rex must have been aware, during the closing years of the century, that a good deal of official correspondence was concerned with the shortage of timber for building and naval purposes. So acute was it that the War Office gave instructions that wood should be imported from the East Indies, from New South Wales and from other areas where timber was abundant.[41] This need, neatly filed away at the back of his mind, may easily have tipped the balance when the opportunity arose later to buy land in the richly-forested area of Knysna.

Francis Dundas handed over at the end of 1799 to the new Governor, Sir George Yonge, retired Master of the Mint, 'a very, very weak old soul'. After all Lord Macartney's earnest strivings to put the Colony on a sound financial footing, Yonge embarked on a programme of reckless 'generosity' with public funds. It is worth noting that the first theatre in South Africa was built and the first semblance of a newspaper was published in 1800, during his term of office. A number of extravagant functions were held too. His pretensions and posturings made him easy game and Lady Anne Barnard's account of the grand ball which he gave in 1800 to celebrate Queen Charlotte's birthday, is spiced with her own inimitable wit. Sir George, who apparantly fancied that he bore a resemblance to George III, 'endeavoured as much as he could to talk, stand, think and look like His Majesty.'[42] This ill-advised and tactless governor was recalled in April 1801.

During 1799 and 1800 the situation in the Swellendam and Graaff-Reinet districts and throughout the whole of the eastern part of the Colony steadily worsened. It was not only a case of continuing insurrection among 'the seditious and turbulent' farmers of the two recognised trouble centres, Swellendam and Graaff-Reinet, but of the Third Frontier War breaking out and also of alarming reports coming in from the Lange Kloof, Bruintjies Hoogte, Outeniqualand, the Zuurveld and the Sundays River area near Algoa Bay; of raids on farms, murders and stocklifting. The marauding Bushmen were the most tiresome offenders as cattle thieves, but the Hottentots were for the first time combining with the Kaffirs to wreak havoc among the scattered and poorly protected colonists and present a new and terrifying threat to the White man. The attacks of the encroaching Xhosa tribesmen from the eastern banks of the Fish River also increased. Francis Dundas himself left for the field in August 1799 and after weeks and months of hardships and headaches managed to bring about an uneasy peace in what was a virtually insoluble situation.[43] It was a clash of interests far too complicated to be discussed in detail here and the repercussions from it were to be felt for many a decade.

The events of history sometimes highlight decisions made by individuals. George Rex had been only three years at the Cape, three years packed with trauma, tension and threat of danger from several fronts, but he had nevertheless decided as the century drew to a close that his future lay in South Africa. He had landed in October 1797; in November 1800, he bought from the Widow C. A. Freislich, *Schoonder Zigt*,[44] one of the ten most conspicuous homesteads of Cape Town at that time, the others being *Bellevue, De Hope, Leeuwenhof, Nooitgedacht, Oranjezicht, Rheezicht, Rust-en-Vreugde, Saasveld* and *Welgemeend*.[45]

He was never to leave these shores again.

5 Striking Roots

Anyone who has visited Cape Town will be able to visualise *Schoonder Zigt* nestling on the lower slopes of Table Mountain, not far below Platteklip Gorge. It overlooked the little town, which appeared spread below, rather like a living map, and from the broad flagged stoep of the homestead, one's eye would be drawn to the blue folds of the Blouberg hills on the far side of the bay and to the more dramatic outline of the Hottentots Holland mountains beyond. The town, better known as that time as the Caabse Vlek than as Cape Town, stopped abruptly at the top of the Company's garden, so there were few other dwellings near the main house and outbuildings of Rex's home. A handful only of substantial homesteads were scattered over the slopes, and trees, gardens and orchards, with the backdrop of the brooding mountain, provided the setting for them. Only the track along the Capel sloot passed nearby *Schoonder Zigt*, a fact which may well have influenced George Rex in his purchase of this property, because the water from this stream was known to be 'sweet' water, not *brak*.

Schoonder Street, then merely a farm track serving the property, came into being officially only in 1820, taking its name from the *Tuin Schoonder Zigt*, as the estate was called.[1] The estate had first been granted in 1735 to Jacob Theo. Hoefman of Koningberg, an apothecary in the Dutch East India Company's hospital.[2] The house itself was built between 1785 and 1787 for Jean de Bonnaire, who must have appreciated the French Renaissance influence evident in the rounded pillars, unusual gable (a type not commonly seen at the Cape) and certain details in ornamentation of the building.

Monsieur de Bonnaire, however, did not enjoy his lovely new home for long. He had sold during his lifetime 'Zeeker stuk Thuynlands en het daarop staande gebouw gelegen in den Tafelvalley' (a certain piece of garden ground with the building standing thereon, lying in Table Valley) to 'den Collonel en Hoofd van Comps(anie) militie . . . de Manhafte Heer Robbert (sic) Jacob Gordon' (Colonel and Chief of the military company . . . the officer Robbert Jacob Gordon). Shortly after this de Bonnaire died, the transaction not completed, so the property was transferred to Gordon from the estate on 16 May 1788.*

The size of the ground was '446 quadraat roeden (square roods), 43 quadraat voete (square feet)' and the price paid for the whole was 12 000 guilders. Of this 9 000 were for the property and 3 000 for the furniture.[3]

The man who had bought the estate was the famous Colonel Robert Gordon, a Dutchman of Scots descent, who was Commander of the Dutch garrison from 1790 to 1795. He was a man of outstanding accomplishments and great charm. Among his many interests was a knowledge of botany which went far beyond that of the ordinary keen gardener.[4] When he owned *Schoonder Zigt* the gardens were reported to be 'the most beautiful at the Cape'. As one writer put it, Gordon showed not only the taste and ingenuity of the gardener, but also the skill and erudition of the botanist. The gardens of his home became stocked with rare botanical specimens, many of them collected during his travels into the interior of the Cape.

In 1786, two Austrian botanists, Franz Boos and Georg Scholl, had arrived to collect new specimens of plants for the famous Schoenbrunn-Tuine in Vienna. Although Boos had returned to Europe before Gordon bought his house in the Gardens, Scholl stayed on for a total of thirteen years at the Cape and there is proof that Gordon invited him to use the *Schoonder Zigt* gardens as a testing ground and repository for samples of his rare botanical collection,[5] among them certain species of euphorbia and a rare cycad or two. Some of these plants, having been established and nurtured in the grounds of Gordon's home, were then taken over to the famous public gardens in Vienna and some introduced to Kew Gardens. Even the Australian settlement benefitted from the experiments conducted by Gordon in this botanical haven, as a result of a visit which the founder of that settlement paid to the Cape on his way to Australia.[6] It was from this same garden that Rex too was to send some rare plants to important collections in Europe.

After Gordon, tragically disturbed at what he regarded as the ignominy of the handing of the Cape over to Britain on instructions from the Prince of Orange, died by his own hand at *Schoonder Zigt* on October 5 1795, his widow, Susetta Nicolett Gordon, and children stayed on there until the property was sold on 8 March 1797, to Philemon Pownall,[7] from whom Johanna van der Stap (the Widow Freislich) bought it in March of the following year.[8] Pownall

*Appendix D

paid Gordon's widow 13 500 guilders for the estate, with no furnishings mentioned this time, so the fixed property had appreciated by roughly fifty percent in value.

This then was the house and the rare botanical collection which Rex came to possess five years after Gordon's death and it is clear that the keen interest in botany which he later showed when living at Knysna was stimulated during his ownership of these unique gardens.

So on 18 November 1800, Rex bought from the Widow Freislich 'her house, garden and premises called *Schoonder Zigt* together with their appurtenances lying in Table Valley'.[9] Even in the present century, when the house had met the fate of so many spacious old homes and been converted into an apartment house, it was possible to detect the sound proportions and clean lines under the hideous twentieth-century additions and 'improvements'. Today Erf 44, Orangezicht indicates the site of a garage and houses at 17 Prince Street, near the top end of Schoonder Street.

The architecture was distinctive and the material excellent. The doors were wide and the ceilings lofty; the walls were exceptionally thick and the floors either flagged or of broad wooden boards. All the woodwork was of either teak or stinkwood, the teak, of course, imported but the stinkwood local, because the tree from which it takes its name grew fairly profusely on the slopes of the mountains surrounding Cape Town at one time. Now the dwelling has gone in the path of progress and dozens of buildings jostle each other unceremoniously where *Schoonder Zigt* once stood alone in its elegance.

Our capacity for imaginative reconstruction is limited by time but it is not difficult now, with this knowledge of the fine house, to imagine the suppressed excitement with which the new owner in 1800 would have taken over the keys, would have strolled from one spacious room to another planning the use of each, and with what zest he would have set about supervising the cleaning and furnishing of his new home – the first home, so far as we know, that he had ever possessed.

Another emotion, even stronger than pride of ownership, had prompted this important move – love. For the purchase of *Schoonder Zigt* coincided with his taking into partnership a 'wife', Johanna Rosina van de Caab (of the Cape), also familiarly known as Roosje.[10] 'Van der Caab' was the suffix or surname indicating a slave born at the Cape. For her and for his own children-to-be, he had acquired this lovely house. His mind was made up; he would settle in the fairest Cape, create a home and rear a family. He had not only taken transfer of the house: he had signed a contract with life itself.

George Rex, for reasons best known to himself, did not marry this woman (he states as much catetorically in his will[11]), but one fact about his life is secure – this was not a casual, sordid encounter. There is, in fact, every evidence that he loved Johanna Rosina and was proud to have her bear his children. He was an Englishman, with none of the intense colour prejudice which nowadays seems to amount almost to an obsession with certain sections of the population in South Africa, regardless of their descent.

On this question of slave descent, no one thought any less highly of Aesop, Plato or Epictetus because of their having been enslaved. Pushkin boasted *ad nauseam* about his descent from a Negro slave and Alexandra Dumas père was certainly physically more negroid than European.[12] On the local scene we have only to think of the young Simon van der Stel who, when he was sent to school in Holland, had it explained in his papers that his capital had to remain in the custody of the Orphan Chamber in Batavia 'in view of the fact that he is a person of mixed blood'. His grandmother, Monica da Costa, is thought to have been Goanese or Singalese.[13]

The results of such investigations should surprise nobody with a sense of history. The Netherlands, for example, has for centuries been the home of tolerance and in Europe in general there was little prejudice against inter-racial marriage in the seventeenth or early eighteenth century. Readers of Scottish or Irish descent will be amused to learn that one distinguished geneticist is prepared to go so far as to say that, whatever their status, black people in Britain in that period were rather more cherished than were the Irish or the Scots.[14]

A distinct hardening in racial attitudes in South Africa can be fixed firmly as having started in the last year or so of the eighteenth century, being attributed with near-certainty to the influence of the Anglo-Indians – Britishers who called at the Cape on their way 'home' after having spent several years in India. The strict caste system in India, based at least partly on pale skin colour, had given the light-skinned European *Caucasoid* an initial advantage. After the Battle of Plassey, it was to the advantage of the British victors to impose a system which the Indians would accept as placing them (the British) even above the light-skinned, superior Brahmins in caste. And this is what happened. Pale skin colour, a criterion already acknowledged by the Indians as representing a higher caste, became inextricably linked with rank.

By 1800 racial discrimination was more pronounced in most

British territories than in those of other powers and it seems reasonable, therefore, to ascribe opposition to interracial breeding to the effect of the new British caste-consciousness and to see it as a contradiction of the more tolerant traditions of the forebears of the Afrikaner.[15]

So Rex took Johanna Rosina as what some chroniclers euphemistically termed a 'wife in common-law'. But the term 'common-law wife' was even then not legally recognised and had not been for many years, but he did take her as a partner and helpmeet. There was, incidentally, no clergyman of the English Church in the Cape at that time except the military chaplain.

It is not normally the business of a biographer to speculate, but it does seem appropriate here, if we are to gain some understanding of the man and his motives, to hazard a guess as to the reasons for his having declared himself in his will as 'not having submitted myself to the matrimonial laws of the Colony'. He may well have been married before he left England. This is admittedly surmise, but it is not such wild surmise as that freely proffered regarding many other aspects of Rex's origins and early life and is a possibility which has suggested itself to more than one investigator when they have come to the question of Rex's bachelor status in South Africa.

Rex was at least thirty-two when he left England (thirty-seven, if one accepts Sanni Metelerkamp's suggestion of 1760 as his birth-date) and he had been practising for eleven years as a qualified lawyer, in receipt of a good salary. It would have been the most normal thing for him to have married in, say, his late twenties. If such a marriage had not worked out well, there would hardly have been a question of divorce, for the simple reason that in those days this was a prohibitively expensive luxury reserved for the very rich. On the other hand, he may well have set out for the Cape in 1797, as other British officials and civil servants did, accepting that this would be a temporary occupation of the Cape and that he would be returning within a year or two to a loving young wife. She may have tired of waiting for him and become involved with another man in his absence, or it may have been merely a case of circumstance and inclination conspiring to keep him in South Africa, in which case he acted correctly – according to his lights – in not entering into a marriage contract with another woman, although he intended treating her in every other respect as a wife.

Judge Holland, Rex's superior, would obviously have known of his marshal's marital status. Any historian attempting to conjure George Rex out of the past and present him with his strengths and his weaknesses, his virtues and his failings, his courage, doubts, idiosyncracies and intimacies, should in fairness take this possibility into account. He was now far from home and he started his new life as best he could. He could not – and would not – marry Johanna Rosina without committing a criminal offence of which at least a few other persons at the Cape would have been aware. This theory could account for his remaining officially a bachelor all the rest of his life and for his extreme reticence on the subject with his own family in the years to come.

The woman he had taken to bed and put in charge of his new home (their first child, Edward, was born nine months later)[16] was then still legally a slave. She was aged about twenty-seven or twenty-eight and had already borne four children of her own by another union.[17] The Reverend Arthur J. Rex Beddy, who has dealt objectively (and, in the South African context, courageously) with the origins of Rex's two 'wives' in his *Genealogy of the Rex Family*, has virtually established that Johanna Rosina was born at the Cape, although where the genes that fashioned her had come from a hundred years previously is unknown. There may well have been Eastern blood in her veins, since *all* the slaves at the Cape had been imported since the time of Van Riebeeck. Also it was not unknown for the stock of slaves to be changed in character and 'improved' on occasion through white sires exercising their *droit de seigneur*.

A very old man in Knysna who remembered the first Mrs. Rex. is said to have commented to a Rex descendant in the last century that she was dark in colour but 'not of our land'.[18] Beddy quotes Dr. I. D. du Plessis, author of *The Cape Malay*, as affirming that her own names, Johanna Rosina, and those of her own four children, Emmerentia, Hendrik, Carolina Margaretha and Christje (Christina Maria) were Dutch names, not of Eastern origin, but names, of course, are not conclusive proof of origins one way or the other.

Beddy's reconstruction of a possible background for Johanna Rosina is a credible one and, in view of certain facts to be discussed presently, could well be the correct one. Here it is: a certain Johanna Rosina Greyling, who was born at the Cape in July 1747, married when she was sixteen years of age, a Jan Theunissen, formerly of Amsterdam, Holland, and at one time captain of the hooker, *Neptunis*. After the birth of their first child, Theunissen died. On 6 April 1769, the twenty-two-year-old widow married Jan van Coeverden, a Hollander from Dordrecht, who had settled in Stellenbosch. The van Coeverdens had nine children. It is suggested that when Johanna Rosina (Roosje) was a child, both her mother and she were in the service of the van Coeverden family and that her mother gave her Mrs. van Coeverden's baptismal names out of

An artist's impression of SCHOONDER ZIGT, Cape Town, the home which George Rex bought in 1800. (By A.A. Telford from photographs by Miss Mary Gunn and Dr. Mary Cook)

'A View of the Cape of Good Hope with a Dutch Squadron at Anchor and an English squadron coming to Anchor in the Bay'. A water colour by John T. Serres in 1804. (By permission of the Africana Museum, Johannesburg)

Sketch of the old Knysna Drift by an unknown artist (thought to be Frederick Knyvett) who visited Knysna and called on George Rex in 1832. (From the Mendelssohn Collection, by permission of the Library of Parliament)

admiration for a kind mistress. This was a common custom among slaves and even, in much later days, among devoted servants of long standing in a happy household. Also of interest is the fact that Beddy suggests that 'Govert', the second name of the fourth child which Johanna Rosina was later to bear to Rex, may have been a contraction or corruption of 'Coeverden'. But this is related to a domestic drama which was to take place some years later. This background story, put forward by Beddy, could easily account for a minor legend which flourished for a while, that Johanna Rosina was the widow of a Dutch sea captain.

The surname of three of Johanna Rosina's own four children was throughout their lives given as 'Ungerer'. The Death Notice which was filled in when Carolina Margaretha (the second daughter) died in 1866 describes her as Carola. Marga. Ungerer, daughter of Johanna Rosina Ungerer and Hendrik Ungerer.'[19] This suggests that these three children ('Van Wyngaarden is given as a surname for the first girl, Emmerentia[20]) were fathered by an Ungerer. A Johan(n) Hendrik Ungerer landed with his brother at the Cape in 1788 and both seem to have been in the Würtemberg Regiment of the Dutch East India Company. The former, however, is believed to have abandoned his military calling, moved to Swellendam and married Elizabeth Magdalena Fourie in 1798.[21]

The Cape Directory of 1800 (compiled from a series of tax returns known as *Opgafrolle*,[22] lists the residents of Cape Town and its environs at that time, with their places of residence, and reveals some interesting information about two other persons with the name of Ungerer and about other families which seem to have featured significantly in George Rex's life.*

From the fact that Mrs. Johanna Rosina van Coeverden, the woman who is presumed to have formerly employed Johanna Rosina (Roosje); that two men whose surname, Ungerer, was bestowed on three of Johanna Rosina's pre-Rex children; and that the Freislich family, from one of whom Rex bought *Schoonder Zigt*, are listed here as living fairly close to one another, it may reasonably be assumed that this little circle provided the *milieu* in which George Rex moved for at least part of the time in Cape Town before he bought his lovely new home.

Several of the men of this circle were obviously of German extraction. Of the various nationalities composing the population of the Colony by the turn of the nineteenth century, Germans accounted for more than forty per cent, so there were bound to be

*Appendix F

several such interesting groups in Cape Town at that time. George Rex may well have found these decent and worthy people more friendly and less rigidly class-conscious than the ranking officers of the garrison who then made up the major part of the cultured English community. Three outstanding men of German extraction who are shown by the Cape Directory of 1800 to have been living in the centre of town, were Anton Anreith, the sculptor from Freiburg, Herman Schutte, a draughtsman, from Bremen, and Heinrich Joseph Klein, teacher and artist.

It is unlikely that Johanna Rosina was still in the service of Mrs. Johanna Rosina ~~Greyling~~ *van Coetzerden* when Rex met and fell in love with her, because on 24 January 1800, it was Hester Catharina Horak, widow Blankenstein, who was the signatory to an agreement whereby she agreed to transfer to George Rex her slave, Roosje van der Caab, and the latter's three children, Emmerentia, Hendrik and Christje.[23] The widow Blankenstein had presumably been Johanna Rosina's owner for some time.

Rex's reputable intentions towards this slave woman are underlined by the fact that fourteen months later, on 11 April 1801, when she was roughly five months pregnant with their first child, he petitioned for her emancipation from slavery. At the same time he petitioned for the emancipation of Emmerentia, Hendrik and Christje too.[24] The actual purchase and transfer, whereby Johanna Rosina and her three children became free persons, took place on 29 May 1801, George Rex and Egedius Benedictus Ziervogel being signatories of the document of purchase.[25]

Johanna Rosina was obviously an attractive and competent woman and there is something very touching in the humility Rex displayed in deciding to share his life with her and not to indulge in a casual, temporary affair, as he might so easily have done. Unions between men of European stock and slave women were not uncommon in those days, resulting largely, of course, from the acute shortage of European women in the Colony. Van Riebeeck had urged the Council of Seventeen as early as 1659 to send out to the Cape a large number of healthy daughters of 'lusty farmers' to help solve the problem, because he considered 'working with unmarried men is very unstable'.[26]

That the problem was still unsolved towards the end of the eighteenth century is shown by the fact that the marriage registers and the records of the *Requesten* reveal repeated intermarriage between European men and women of colour. At this distance in time, it is possible to see the problem not in terms of either vice or virtue, but in terms of humanity.

Three months after George Rex had applied for the emancipation from slavery of Johanna Rosina, on 6 July 1801, J. H. Ungerer, who must have been still the owner of the second daughter, petitioned for the emancipation of 'Carolina van de Caab'.[27] This was the girl later known as Carolina Margaretha, who was to become Rex's second 'wife'. She may have been held back because she was particularly useful or particularly attractive when Ungerer married in 1797, but may have been so unhappy without the comfort and company of her mother and brother and sisters that her owners realised that the situation was untenable.

She was manumitted in response to Ungerer's petition and presumably joined the rest of the family in Rex's household at *Schoonder Zigt*. The *vrybrief* took some months to come through, but was finally granted on 23 December 1801. This document was signed by J. H. Ungerer, G. Rex and E. B. Ziervogel,[28] emphasising once again the close ties which existed between Rex and Ziervogel.

When, at the end of March 1801, George Rex requested (as has been mentioned) to be released from his duties as Advocate for the Crown, it is not unlikely that he was also beginning to be preoccupied with the greatly increased weight of his domestic responsibilities. Johanna Rosina was carrying his first child and although she would undoubtedly have fulfilled her household tasks efficiently and created a pleasant atmosphere of home in the spacious rooms, Rex would have multiple duties too, of course, in dealing with the family finances, the upkeep of the house and outbuildings and, in particular, the overseeing of the garden and the orchards.

Just about this time, among other things, he was most concerned with the supply of water to his estate, a problem he had inherited from the previous owner. The particularly hot, dry summer had – as so often happens at the Cape – played havoc with his garden and, to add insult to injury, his water supply had been cut off. In a petition to the President and Members of the Burgher Senate on 12 January 1801, he stated that 'in consequence of the cutting off of a small leaden pipe that supplied him with water from the Great Public Water Course, he had 'lost all his vegetables, which are entirely burnt up, but with deepest concern sees his fruit trees, with which the garden is stocked, also decaying fast and several hundred of the young fruit from his best Lemon and Orange trees daily withering and falling off'.

The Burgher Senate was sympathetic and sent a letter almost immediately to the Governor, Sir George Yonge, urging for 'a small ray of water to be run into Mr. Rex's garden'. They tactfully reminded His Excellency that, in response to an earlier appeal from the previous owner of this property, they had written to him on similar lines five months previously. 'We could wish' they wrote, 'to give some answer to Mr. Rex, but are unable to do so, more important occupations having not yet allowed Your Excellency to answer our letter of the 4 August last respecting the Public Water-pipes and the arrangement which we proposed to effect between Mr. Hurling and the Widow Freislich.'[29] (Fredrik Hurlingh and his wife, Maria Jacoba, incidentally, as well as a Coenraad Nelson and his wife, Maria Elizabeth (born Hurter), lived next door to *Schoonder Zigt* in 1800 at *Tuyn Buytenzorg*.[30])

The Governor was probably occupied with nothing more important than planning his dances, concerts, races and theatricals. It is not known how long he took to accede to the Burgher Senate's request on Rex's behalf, but it was certainly before September 1801 because in that month George Rex wrote a letter simply acknowledging the receipt of the diagram of Hurling's garden, adjoining his, and making no further mention of any shortage of water.[31]

Like every other householder in the town at that time, he owned a number of slaves to work in the house and to keep the lands in good order. His roster included the names of at least four imported slaves, because he had applied on 29 November 1799 (a year before he bought *Schoonder Zigt*) for an order to the Customs House 'to admit four slaves of the *Sceptre* to an entry.' His Majesty's ship, *Sceptre,* was one of the six ships driven ashore by a strong north-westerly gale on 5 November that year and the Captain, his son, some of the officers and the greater part of the ship's company perished in the wreck. It was an appalling tragedy which was talked about in Cape Town for many a month afterwards. On 3 December, only four days after Rex filed his application, it was approved by the Deputy Secretary.[32]

The British authorities at the Cape, knowing the disapproving attitude of the home Government to slavery, but at the same time being subject to constant pressure from the merchants and burghers of the Cape to step up the importation of these unfortunate human beings, were on the horns of a dilemma where slavery was concerned.

Man's inhumanity to man always becomes more evident in times of war. The jackals and the black marketeers are never far away when it comes to taking advantage of a situation of stress. There is, in the official records of the Cape Colony for this period, a sordid repetition of names of certain Cape Town merchants suspected of shady dealing in slaves and even of outright graft. This was especially the case during the weak Yonge administration, when fraud and favouritism flourished so openly that Judge Holland of the Vice-Admiralty Court swore on oath that a certain official close to the Governor 'openly avowed that he himself was concerned with Hogan in the profits arising from the sale of prohibited slaves in the Colony'.

Just about this time, this Mr. Michael Hogan, a local merchant, fitted up a private brig of war which the commander of the vessel used for the transport of slaves whom he bought illegally and then fobbed off as having been taken from captured prize ships. Three times this ship, *The Collector*, returned to Cape Town bearing cargoes of slaves and always there was a story of the prize ships, from which the crews had allegedly been taken, being found abandoned by their masters and, in one case, destroyed by fire. Suspicions were aroused, and finally the Port Captain, Captain D. Campbell, became so incensed that he wrote directly to the authorities in London: '. . . . . How the Court of Admiralty could have been so imposed upon . . . so glaring and pernicious a Traffic should not pass unnoticed . . . I never thought it could escape the knowledge of the Court (Vice-Admiralty)'.[33]

The Courts of Justice had confiscated all the slaves while Hogan blandly denied all knowledge of the illicit trading. Sir George Yonge had tried every tactic to prevent the Courts of Justice from dealing with the charges of smuggling of slaves, but finally reluctantly had to agree. By the time the Court assembled, all nine persons, who had undergone interrogation in the Vice-Admiralty Court earlier, in connection with *The Collector*, had left the Colony.[34]

Life in this court was obviously not easy and seldom dull. The picture emerging from the official documents is one of tension and acrimony from a gubernatorial level down to that of minor officials, such as poor Mr. Ponterdant, Examiner of the Vice-Admiralty Court, who, through a piece of indiscreet comment, fell foul of both the Governor and Judge Holland and was summarily fired.

The navy were dissatisfied about the handling of prize ships and their cargo, the Judge was equally unhappy about it for different reasons, and Sir George Yonge did nothing to improve matters by over-ruling senior officers. No doubt the Marshal of the Vice-Admiralty Court could hardly have failed to be affected by the atmosphere of tension.

A scandal which involved the firm of Walker and Robertson, (who did a profitable trade in slaves on the side and were well in with the Governor) was the apprehension early in 1801 of *The Chesterfield* on the Rio de la Plata. This ship, which belonged to Messrs Walker and Robertson, had been seized while 'carrying on an illicit and nefarious Trade with the Enemy' and was brought to CapeTown, where the Vice-Admiralty Court took charge of it. A Court of Piracy was assembled, at which George Rex, the Marshal, was in attendance. Two men were sentenced to death, but the Governor arbitrarily ordered – without informing the captain who had apprehended the ship or any of the persons most concerned – that the men should be allowed to return to London to await the decision of the Crown lawyers.[35] The Vice-Admiralty Court had again been over-ruled. Within four days of this fracas, Yonge was summarily dismissed from office and recalled to England.

On the home front, Johanna Rosina's busy life of housekeeping and catering for her growing family (Edward was born in July 1801)[36] must have been affected by a widespread crisis of a different type – a critical shortage of grain in the Colony.

Now her ingenuity must have been taxed, as was that of every other housewife in the Colony, to find ways and means of keeping her family healthy and satisfied when all grain products were unobtainable. A grain Commission had been set up, early in 1801 to investigate ways and means of alleviating the shortage and, if possible, to prevent 'the impending Calamity of a Famine'.

At the height of this crisis, Mr. Hogan's name appears again, this time in a dispute with the Grain Commission, involving indirectly the Marshal of the Vice-Admiralty Court. Hogan, as agent for a captured Spanish prize ship, *La Balena*, seems to have prevailed on Rex to agree to what the Commission described as 'very exorbitant charges' for a quantity of flour and biscuit which they had commandeered from *La Balena*. The Commission informed Mr. Hogan sharply that they had 'marked on the Certificate of Mr. G. Rex, Marshal of the Admiralty Court, wherein it was asserted that the said Biscuit and Flour were delivered in order to be paid for by Government according to the appraised value thereof that no such condition was ever mentioned or thought of' and that the price fixed by the Commissioners was final.[37]

But it is impossible to recreate in words the tensions of a bygone age. The crisis of history can never have for us the same urgency and impact as the actual happenings did for those concerned.

George Rex in his official position – quite apart from his commitments as head of *Schoonder Zigt* and father of an increasing family – must have been subjected to niggling strains among the grasping and warring factions on every hand. Also, any semblance of order and permanence in his private life must have been dissipated by the rumours of the preliminary peace negotiations which began to filter through to the Cape towards the end of 1801. These inevitably fore-shadowed the end of the Vice-Admiralty Court. On 15 December, General Dundas announced the King's proclamation of 1 October, that all hostilities with France should cease immediately 'putting an End to the Calamities of War, as soon as and as far as may be possible.'

Protracted peace negotiations had actually been going on for some time and, three months earlier, on 28 September, the acting Governor had already issued a proclamation directing that no British subject or foreigner would be permitted to remain in the Colony without having obtained a special licence from the Commander-in-Chief or been furnished with a passport from the Secretary of State's office.[38] Unless his position exempted him from complying with this injunction, George Rex must have presented himself before Mr. Andrew Barnard or the other members of the Commission, as instructed, and stated his reasons for wishing to remain in the Colony. His mind was obviously made up. He had bought a large house, had assumed family responsibilities and had decided to make South Africa his home. His interview with the Commission, had it been recorded, would have told us a great deal.

For the ordinary citizens of Cape Town it looked as if the troubled year were about to end on a brighter note. Their nerves were rudely shattered, however, when on 8 December, looming Table Mountain contributed its own quota of excitement to life in the town below. About ten o'clock in the morning, a huge landslide of terrifying proportions took place in the Platteklip ravine, high above *Schoonder Zigt*. One can picture vividly the startled mistress of the house clutching her four-month-old baby in her arms, her own children crowding round her skirts in terror, rushing out of the house at the first ominous rumble which heralded the slide.

'It presented a sublime and awful spectacle . . . A small cloud was seen resting above the gorge when suddenly it became violently agitated and . . . moved down the mountain with the noise of rushing waters which continued for half a minute.' When the dust settled, it was clear that a huge mass of rock had become detached from the mountainside and shattered everything in its path as it skidded down the slope.[39]

In February 1802 (two months after the proclamation of peace,) Judge Holland was writing to Lord Hobart, who had been appointed one of His Majesty's principal Secretaries of State, about the arrangements which he was making for terminating the causes pending in the Vice-Admiralty Court 'that will not in all probability be finally determined upon previous to the surrender of the Cape'.[40]

It was to be a drawn-out business, but he was beginning to tackle it systematically.

Again it is necessary to underline the snail's pace of communication in those days and the cumbersome nature of the machinery of war which took months, if not years, to grind to a halt. It is, for us, like looking back at a slow-moving film. Our imaginations are circumscribed by the times in which we live and it is difficult for us to digest the fact that the preliminary peace negotiations were not broadcast simultaneously on the radio from the main cities of the world on the night of the announcement.

George Rex, closely involved in the procedures to bring about the closure of the Vice-Admiralty Court, must also have been energetically planning an alternative career for himself on South African soil, because at this time Johanna Rosina was pregnant with their second child. (John was born on 26 October 1802). Rex's life was now completely metamorphosed. While all official activity was geared to getting out as swiftly as possible, he was concentrating on ways and means of implementing his earlier decision to stay on at the Cape permanently. It is not surprising that there are no letters or records of a personal nature covering these years of change: he had effectively loosed any remaining ties with England and was now putting the past behind him for once and for all.

Apart from his planning to remain in South Africa, his second vital decision, to pull up the roots he had put down in Cape Town and travel hundreds of difficult and even hazardous kilometres to establish himself in an isolated beauty spot, cannot have been made overnight. The issues involved were far too complicated. In order to understand something of the man's motives in making this major move, which had such far-reaching personal and social repercussions, it is necessary to turn back the clock a little and learn something of the varied career of one of the more picturesque characters who probably had a significant influence on Rex's future plans.

This was James Callander,* a well-born master shipwright and one-time ship owner, who had had an adventurous career in the service of the British East India Company and in the British navy from 1772 onwards. He had seen service in many parts of the world for a quarter of a century, had come to South Africa in 1797 (the same year as George Rex), following the disastrous loss of two of the three ships he owned,[41] and for roughly a year skippered a brig belonging to John Murray, who owned a trading store in Mossel

*Appendix G

Bay.[42] Murray, a successful businessman, conducted a lively trade between this port and Cape Town, thanks partly to his sturdy fellow countryman who during 1797 and most of 1798, several times brought the brig up the coast laden with goods needed by the scattered Boers in the remote eastern districts and returned with it heavily laden with valuable timber from the forests of Outeniqualand. John Murray, with Rex, incidentally, was one of the signatories affirming loyalty to the establishment in the tense days before Macartney left the Cape.

At the end of 1798, Callander was commissioned by Macartney and Dundas to follow up Barrow's and Rice's findings and examine the forests, bays and rivers of the Knysna and Plettenberg Bay area and, if the report was favourable, to supervise the cutting and shipping of timber from there.[43] He travelled overland to Knysna and obtained some sort of squatter's right to build himself a small wooden cabin near the Knysna Heads.[44] Here he lived in isolation, putting all his time and skill into charting the Knysna lagoon and making other necessary observations. His knowledge of the currents, shallows, winds and storms which might endanger shipping was first-class and from the beginning he minimised the difficulties – then thought to be insuperable – of bringing vessels in over the dangerous rocky bar between the Heads. This unusual son of the sea apparently also had some sort of dwelling at Plettenberg Bay.

In July 1799, when the Kaffirs and Hottentots had been raiding the Lange Kloof and had murdered eleven white men and four white women, it was Callander who reported on these disturbances to the authorities in Cape Town and pointed out that the farmers of the district urgently needed powder with which to defend themselves and their homes. The situation was indeed critical. The country people had abandoned their houses and properties, the Hottentot servants had to a man deserted their masters and the country was completely overrun by Kaffirs and those Hottentots who had joined 'the Renegadoes'. Callander, however, seems to have received no issue of powder to meet the need he had described, but a letter urging him 'as an Englishman' to set an example and calm the fears of the surrounding luckless inhabitants.[45]

Sanni Metelerkamp put forward the theory that soon after Rex's arrival at the Cape, his interest in the Knysna area was stimulated by James Callander and that 'it is certain he must have accompanied Callander on one or more of his trips to Plettenberg Bay and travelled overland with him to Knysna'.[46] This is quite possible, although they probably became better acquainted after

105

Callander had completed his survey of the Knysna area and returned to Cape Town.

It is certain anyway that some time before the end of 1803, Rex heard from the Scottish seaman of the idyllic lagoon with its – in Callander's opinion – illimitable potential as a harbour, and about the magnificent indigenous forests on the surrounding slopes which grew down almost to the water-line. He must have heard too about the ill-starred succession of owners of the fine property, *Melkhout Kraal,* soon to be going for a song very probably, following its being plundered and virtually destroyed by the Kaffirs during the uprisings of 1799, 1800 and 1802.

Here was a goal for Rex to work towards; there he would gain his *ultima Thule.* He would be his own authority, beholden to no man.

But first the restoration of the Cape to the Batavian Republic was to take place. On 19 December 1802, the Dutch squadron arrived in Table Bay and four days later the warship, *Bato,* brought the Commissary-General, Jacob Abraham de Mist and the Governor and Commander in Chief, General Janssens. The ceremony of the restoration of the Colony to the Dutch was to take place on New Year's Day. About noon on the day of 31 December, however, the *Imogen* dropped anchor in Table Bay and there was delivered to Dundas with great despatch a communication from Lord Hobart marked *Most Secret.* This contained nothing less than instructions to delay the restitution of the Colony to the Dutch, but at the same time to avoid at all costs 'creating an apprehension of its (the action's) arising from a hostile motive'.[47] A task to tax the wisdom of Solomon.

It was an explosive situation and one would have said an untenable one, except that tact, forbearance and courtesy on both sides did, in fact, preserve the *status quo* for longer than anyone thought possible. On 19 February a despatch arrived from Lord Hobart bringing this extraordinary situation to an end. Arrangements were made for the postponed restoration of the Colony to take place two days later and this went off splendidly. Dundas warmly praised 'the good policy, moderation and humanity of the Commissary de Mist . . .' during the time of waiting.[48]

Less than three months later Britain was again at war with France and Holland.

*　*　*

There is no evidence as to how George Rex was occupied during this time. As a result of all this vacillation he must have said goodbye several times to the men with whom he had worked in the

Vice-Admiralty Court and to friends he had made among the officers and men of the British forces. One would give a great deal to know what went through his mind as, from the stoep of *Schoonder Zigt*, he watched the ships carrying his compatriots set sail, to grow smaller and fainter, until they finally disappeared over the blue horizon.

Because his job had come to an end and because he had a family to support and a home to maintain, he must have earned some income in the two years following the closing of the Vice-Admiralty Court in 1802, possibly by doing some private legal work, possibly by marketing the produce of the *Schoonder Zigt* estate, but most likely by trading and other dealings. Most of the British subjects – between seventy and eighty in number – who chose to remain behind, were merchants who had vested interests in Cape Town. Incidentally, all but ten or so of these Britishers signed the oath of allegiance to the Batavian Republic.[49]

Rex seems to have had a keen sense of business and by this time had many useful contacts among the better-heeled citizens of the town. One thing we do know for certain is that his position was rudely affected, as was that of all remaining British subjects, by an untoward incident which occurred shortly after the restitution of the Colony to the Batavian Republic.

An English whaling vessel, *Mary*, which had been captured by a Dutch sloop, was brought into Table Bay and her officers and crew, twenty-six in all, were held as prisoners by the Dutch Government. A cartel ship (carrying prisoners to be exchanged for others), *Matilda*, carrying French prisoners of war who had surrendered to the English at Pondicherry, also put into Table Bay and the Governor proposed to Captain W. Shaw of the *Matilda*, that the men from the *Mary* be put aboard his ship preparatory to being conveyed back to England. The transfer of the prisoners accordingly took place, but the Englishmen, far from being grateful for the promise of being transported to their homeland, escaped from the *Matilda* in the dead of night on 4 February 1804, boarded their own ship, *Mary*, and 'cut her out of the harbour'.[50]

Janssens reacted swiftly. He ordered all British-born and naturalised British subjects to leave the country within two months. Citizens of Dutch or other nationalities were forbidden on pain of banishment, corporal punishment, and other severe penalties, to associate in any way with the British.[51] The consternation among the British subjects was intense. The sailing times of ships were irregular and widely spaced and when they did sail, accommodation on them was limited.

Even if a man did succeed in getting a passage for himself and his family, there was usually no question of their possessions, trunks, furniture, their *lares et penates* being accommodated. A number of families panicked and fled at the first opportunity, having sold all their possessions for next to nothing. A few seem to have abandoned their homes almost as they stood. Notices of forced sales were common at this time in the *Kaapsche Courant,* the official and only newspaper during the Dutch regime at the Cape. It is possible, in view of his commitment to stay and of his increasing family (John, his second son, had been born in October 1802)[52] that George Rex, during this period of upheaval and uncertainty, acquired some of the fine furniture and interesting *objets d'art* with which he is reputed to have furnished *Melkhout Kraal.*

In the event the notice to quit was not enforced, but those British subjects who had stood firmly by their decision to remain, or had simply been unable to obtain a passage on a ship, seem to have spent the following eight months in a state of uneasy indecision. Not Rex, however. His plans were by now well formulated and he knew what his next move was going to be. In more ways than one, he knew exactly where he was going.

Five days after the unfortunate incident of the escape of the prisoners from the *Matilda,* the sale of *Schoonder Zigt* was advertised on Rex's behalf by E. B. Ziervogel in the *Kaapsche Courant,* and three months later, on 12 May, the same newspaper carried the following announcement (in Dutch):

PUBLIC SALE
on Thursday next, 17th May,
at a Public Auction
To be sold in the garden of Mr. Rex
Some household effects and furniture, consisting of mirrors, chairs
sofas, tables, a writing desk etc. besides carts, a wagon and a
Chaise with metal (studded) bridals for two thoroughbred horses
and whatever else there may be.'

On the twenty-third of February 1804 the sale by auction took place, the buyer being none other than the advertiser, the same Egedius Benedictus Ziervogel who, with Rex, had signed the document of purchase of Johanna Rosina and her children some three years earlier. Ziervogel took transfer of *Schoonder Zigt* on 27 September 1804.[53]

It is clear that there were close personal ties between Marshal Rex and Translator Ziervogel of the Vice-Admiralty Court. At one stage they jointly owned a boat, *The Young Phoenix,* and in 1809, when Rex had been several years at Knysna, he gave his power of attorney to Ziervogel.

The day before the sale of the house, Johanna Rosina presented George with his first daughter, Elisabetta Carolina.[54] For a man who loved children as warmly as he later proved he did, this must have been a joyful day but it is doubtful whether he could, during this traumatic period of upheaval and change, have been able to anticipate fully the even tenor of the rural days to come when he would enjoy the company of his children most.

Two months after the sale of his big house in the Gardens, Rex bought the *opstal* (buildings and improvements) of *Melkhout Kraal* out of the estate of one Richard Holiday.[55] John Murray, who had been in partnership with Holiday and had owned a property on the Brenton side of the Knysna lagoon jointly with him, was now executor of his will and it was with Murray that Rex had to deal in this transaction.

This was the same, seemingly ubiquitous John Murray, who had employed Callander to skipper his brig up and down the coast and who had, in 1798, bought a large whaling business when the affairs of the previous owners, Messrs. Fehrsen and Company, were wound up. Under Murray's astute management, the company flourished and was enlarged but in 1802, with the return of the Batavian Republic, he was forced to stop his activities and sell his plant to the agents of a chartered fishing company which had obtained in Holland exclusive rights to kill whales in the bays of the Cape Colony. When, at the end of three short years of Dutch rule, the Cape again reverted to Britain, the fishery was seized and the whaling again thrown open to all comers. Murray, the only colonial shareholder in the company, triumphed and continued to add his whaling ventures to his other profitable enterprises.[56]

For the eight months following his purchase of *Melkhout Kraal*, Rex must have been fully occupied with his preparations for the move to Knysna. There were probably a certain number of slaves employed on the estate when Holiday died in 1803[57] and these would have been taken over by the new master, but other labourers would have to be signed up, strong wagons procured (capable of standing up to weeks of buffeting over rough tracks), decisions taken about which domestic items could be transported in the wagons and which should be sold, certain legal and financial arrangements made, and many items, which would be quite unprocurable in the remote eastern part of the Colony, purchased. This was a time of intensive planning, hard work and strenuous organisation.

On 8 October, Governor Janssens indicated that, although he had not enforced his earlier banning order, he still had suspicions about the trustworthiness of the British subjects and issued a proclamation ordering all British-born and naturalised British subjects to be 'interned' at Stellenbosch.[58] It was a very gentlemanly form of internment, however. The aliens had to reside in Stellenbosch and could only leave with the permission of the Governor for a stated time and purpose, but those who had married into families of colonists or who had farming interests to attend to, were given special permission to continue living in their own places of residence. Rex probably spent a little over a month at Stellenbosch, because in November he applied to the authorities for a longer absence from Cape Town than the usual eight days, 'in order to return to his farm at the Knysna, where he has already thirty-three slaves at work under their overseers'.[59] From the fact that he applied for 'a longer absence from Cape Town . . .' one might assume that he was one of those allowed to stay in his own home, but Sanni Metelerkamp states that he was actually interned.

James Callander his job of charting the Knysna estuary and reporting on the surrounding forests complete, had returned to the Western Cape and was also one of those detained at Stellenbosch.[60] How these two men, both intensely interested in 'this fine navigable river and noble harbour' (Callander's own words) would have talked in those frustrating weeks in the sleepy little town! Rex would have absorbed and, in his trained, legal way, have noted down every useful detail that the down-to-earth Scot could tell him.

At Knysna, some nineteen months or so earlier, Callander had met Governor Janssens, who was visiting the Eastern Cape with the intention of getting to know its inhabitants and their problems first hand. He was accompanied by Captain Paravicini di Capelli, a surgeon, as his aide-de-camp, and the two respectable burghers, Dirk Gysbert van Reenen and his son, Daniel, to assist him with their knowledge of the people and their language.[61] Van Reenen, Senior, (whose journal of the expedition is one of the most valuable sources of information on the country at that time) wrote of James Callander, whom they found in his timber cabin at The Heads, that 'he lived there some time as an anchorite'. He goes on to say that Callander 'presented the Governor with a map of the Bay showing its lie and depth, as well as of the river, certifying that the latter was quite navigable, even in its upper reaches. If this could be verified by investigation, ships could find a safe harbour there in all seasons, and also everything needed for repairs would be within easy reach, seeing that the forest encloses the river on both sides.'

110

The Governor also discussed with Callander the possibility of establishing a saw-mill at Knysna and developing the surrounding forests.

The Governor's party then lunched pleasantly under the orange trees in the grounds of the burned-out and deserted *Melkhout Kraal,* then in the estate of the late Richard Holiday, who had acquired this loan farm from Johann von Lindenbaum.

Dirk van Reenen himself was sceptical about Callander's enthusiastic report. He was convinced, in fact, that any ship would be dashed against the rocks outside The Heads in stormy weather, but admitted that 'inland the sea forms a lake of about three hours' on foot, where the water is always calm and abounds with fish . . .'[62]

After this promising encounter with those in high places, Callander would have been justified in feeling he was getting somewhere in his persistent attempts to have 'this fine navigable river' opened as a harbour and if the iron entered his soul when the years passed and no attention was paid to his painstakingly drawn charts and detailed report, he had some reason for bitterness. His interest in Knysna, however, never waned and as will be seen later, he applied, many years later, to return there as 'Resident'.

The Attorney General, Mr. Beelaerts van Blokland (whom Rex, with his legal background, would certainly have met) supported Rex's request to the Governor and wrote warmly that 'as the British subject George Rex has received due permission for residence and has furnished security for his good conduct, and as his agricultural pursuits deserve every encouragement, and as he is certainly one of the best and least dangerous of the English subjects in this Colony, I venture to advise you to permit him to return to his farm under the conditions mentioned in Art. II of the Proclamation of the Governor and Commander in Chief of the 27 September last.'[63]

Rex had obviously given the Batavian authorities every confidence in his integrity and motives, and they were anxious – as the British had been before them – to encourage in every way possible the right type of colonist to settle anywhere between Swellendam and the ever-troublesome eastern frontier. Rex's petition was granted expeditiously. On 29 November 1804, the Governor agreed to 'grant permission to George Rex to return to his farm at the Knysna' provided he report to the Field Cornet once a week.'[64]

The actual date of the family's departure from Cape Town is not known, but probably some time in December Rex set out with his wife and children, several ox-wagons, some slaves and a complement of artisans, some of the latter accompanying the little caravan on horseback. If a coach or carriage were included in the train of vehicles, this would have of necessity been drawn by at least six horses, not because of 'a desire for pageantry or magnificence, but of necessity',[65] on those appalling country tracks.

Johanna Rosina had to show remarkable faith in her man to undertake this long, bone-shaking journey into the unknown, over rough and often precipitous paths, with not only the four children from her previous alliance, now aged between fifteen and five, but three-and-a-half year old Edward, John, just over two, and the baby, Elisabetta, to care for, feed and keep happy through the long, tedious and uncomfortable days of the journey. The changing of clothes and washing of napkins alone must have presented difficulties almost unimaginable to the modern mother. Johanna was pregnant again and December is one of the hottest months of the Cape summer. The mind of any woman today who has undertaken a much shorter but similar journey, with all modern facilities, shrinks from the thought of such an ordeal.

Much of the magic of the ever-increasing beauty of the countryside as they passed Mossel Bay and wound their way slowly and painfully along the chain of lovely lakes that leads the traveller into the heart of Outeniqualand, must have been lost on the poor woman, but at last the weary cavalcade topped the rise at Keyter's Nek and saw Rex's future empire, the pearl of the lagoon in its priceless dark setting of forest, waiting below them.

An artist's sketch of George Rex's brig, **Knysna,** *putting to sea through The Heads, Knysna. This brig was built mainly of stinkwood. (By A.A. Telford)*

A reproduction of a water-colour of MELKHOUT KRAAL, Knysna, painted by Major A.C. Gregory on 29 October, 1834. (From the private collection of Mr. Harry Oppenheimer, by permission of the owner)

A scene in the Knysna forests, the timber from which largely provided George Rex with his income. (Photo: Geoff Causton)

6 En Passant

Apart from the Knysna lake 'of most surpassing loveliness' what was the nature of the countryside surrounding George Rex's new home?

There is no shortage of descriptive material on it, for traveller after traveller – scientist, botanist, naturalist, explorer, government official, trader and even what we today would call tourist – was beginning in the late eighteenth and early nineteenth centuries to take an interest in the *hinterland* and the eastern seaboard, including the green belt of country lying between the Outeniqua and Tzitzikama ranges of mountains and the sea. Most of the travellers left an account, or at least some sketchy notes, of their experiences in traversing the country and every one of them commented on the almost impassable nature of the terrain, particularly the hazards involved in crossing the precipitous mountains which are so effortlessly breached by spectacular highways today.

Each in turn commented on the deep kloofs running from the mountains to the sea in Outeniqualand and intersecting the coastal peneplain, with rough paths which were little more than Hottentot cattle tracks. The tangled paths through almost impenetrable forests, rivers with dangerously steep banks, swollen with floods in winter and presenting dry, stony beds in summer, treacherous marshes, 'stupendous rocks', surf-washed estuaries, pleasing to the eye but concealing pocketed traps for the unwary rider – all these added up to a picture of rare beauty, tinged with difficulty and danger.

Although by no means the earliest, one of the more colourful accounts of the type of travel which was routine for pioneers in this part of the Cape came from the lay pen of an emancipated young woman, Julie Phillippe Augusta Uitenhage de Mist, nineteen-year-old daughter of the Commissary General during the rule of the Batavian Republic, who accompanied her father and his official party on an expedition to the eastern frontiers of the Colony towards the end of 1803, just a year before George Rex and his family arrived at Knysna. These, then, are much the same conditions the Rex party would have encountered on their journey.

In her diary, Julie de Mist writes:

'Farther on we found forests of several days travel in diameter, where the intertwined branches and broad-leafed shrub which eventually filled the intervening places, intercept all the rays of the sun and prevent them from penetrating; while the thickly interlaced lianes entwined round the tree trunks impeded our passage. The road which we followed was only the work of elephants whose tracks we frequently discovered, and despite the extent to which the colonists had broadened it, progress between the rocks was hampered by tree-stumps, particularly since we either had to climb or descend all the time. Thus we struggled on for many days against all kind of difficulty in the road, while we were exposed to the burning rays of the sun and to downpours that resembled cloudbursts; the nights we spent mostly under one or other tree or some overhanging rock without removing our clothes and using our saddles as pillows . . .'[1]

The roads themselves were described by C.I. Latrobe, the missionary who was travelling this way and visiting George Rex's home in 1815, in these words: 'We soon entered upon roads, not easily described, so as to give an Englishman an adequate idea of them. How those African wagons can bear such a thumping, bouncing, twisting and screwing between rocks, and large masses of broken stones, regularly piled upon each other, is almost beyond belief.'[2]

These are glimpses of the conditions still prevailing about forty to fifty years after the first scattered European settlement of the eastern Cape began. Thanks to the comprehensive work of Vernon S. Forbes, *Pioneer Travellers of South Africa,*[3] we have an excellent account of the movements and motives of the venturesome men who undertook what were in the main shoe-string journeys to the eastern interior before the dawn of the nineteenth century.

Their youth and daring has often been overlooked. Carl Peter Thunberg, Francis Masson, Anders Sparrman, Francois Le Vaillant, William Paterson were all in their twenties or early thirties. The wealthy Hendrik Swellengrebel, at forty-two, was comparatively old. These are the counterparts of the intelligent young men, prompted by ambition, drive and the spirit of enquiry, who would today head research teams, perform brilliant operations, hold senior executive positions before the age of thirty, or even, when there is so little of the earth's surface left unexplored, set out for the moon.

Comparatively few of these intrepid pioneers were able to travel deeply into the densely forested region then known as Outeniqualand, but tended instead to cross the Outeniqua Mountains north-

114

wards, sometimes by the Attaqua's Pass (five or six kilometres west of the Robinson Pass), sometimes by the Duivelskop route (about twenty kilometres east of today's Outeniquà Pass) and then to continue eastward along the Lange Kloof, that fertile, elongated valley bounded in the south by the Outeniquas and on the north by the Kamannassie hills. The scattered settlers in the Lange Kloof, because of the good, 'sweet' soil, were comparatively prosperous[4] and most were prepared to offer hospitality to the weary travellers.

So what was almost a recognised waggon-road slowly took shape along the trunk route to the east, the 'road' being little more than a series of tracks connecting one important farm house with another. The owners of these overnight stopping-places could usually be relied upon to produce a meal (even if it was sometimes only bread and sour milk) and a bed, and very often horses for the following phase of the journey. It was these isolated farmhouses which made progress to the eastern districts possible and bearable.

By 1772 some of these homesteads had become really important. Masson, the Scot who came out to collect plants for the Royal Gardens at Kew, gave a glowing account of a farm much further east than Rex's, the home of Jacob Kok, a Hessian, who 'used us with great civility'. He had built a handsome house, made gardens and vineyards, possessed numerous herds of cattle and had upward of a hundred Hottentots in his service 'whom he employed in taking care of them'.[5] This is very similar to the descriptions which were to be given of Rex's estate and hospitality forty years or so later.

The fact that comfortable homesteads such as these were singled out for special mention is a clear indication of the isolation and comparative humbleness of the dwellings *en route*. The warmth of welcome, however, at these humble farms, the civility and inborn courtesy of the Boers, is commented on appreciatively by several of the pioneers. A few were critical of the lack of civilised amenities, a lack which could not in fairness be blamed on these isolated families, struggling against odds, pests and natural disasters to make ends meet.

Our picture of *Melkhout Kraal,* Rex's home-to-be, as one in the chain of hospitable farms dotted along the route to the east, is likely to be painted in truer colours if the background is filled in from the often disjointed, but always valuable observations of those 'through' travellers who did breach the formidable mountain range southward from the Lange Kloof to visit Outeniqualand, or make a side trip from the Mossel Bay area to come directly eastward to Knysna, 'the land where it is always afternoon'. Many of them were bound for Plettenberg Bay, the possibilities of which as a harbour were already being explored. Whether they were concerned with scientific enquiry, the need for defence of the coast, the execution of government orders or – not least – the exploitation of the vast and valuable timber resources of the Knysna and Plettenberg Bay districts, each of the wanderers had his own good reason for coming this way.

Dr. Thunberg, 'the father of Cape botany', visited Knysna and Plettenberg Bay on his first journey east in 1772 and, incidentally, gave us an account of the first recorded crossing of the massive mountain range from south to north, from Plettenberg Bay to the Lange Kloof, by a route not dissimilar from that which was to be followed nearly a century later by Thomas Bain's splendid Prince Alfred's Pass road.[6]

Thunberg mentioned the farm *Melkhout Kraal* and 'the colonist Peter Plant' as being in possession of it at that time.[7] There is no other mention of a Peter Plant in the records of the travellers and it seems possible that Thunberg might have misheard or interpreted phonetically the name of Piet Terblans (farmer in the Goukama Valley) and confused it with that of his brother, Stephanus Terblans, already the owner of *Melkhout Kraal*. Alternatively, Plant may have been occupying the land casually as so many stock farmers did in those days when it was virtually impossible for the authorities at the Cape to enforce payments on the so-called 'loan farms' and so regularise the position in the remote interior districts.

The whole question of land tenure in the Cape was a vexed one for all concerned two centuries ago.[8] The following résumé will given the reader some idea of how George Rex came to acquire his large tracts of land around the Knysna lagoon. Resentment of any authority, the inability of the local market to absorb agricultural production in normal years, an inclination on the part of the sons of the Dutch, German and Huguenot settlers to take up the untrammelled, comparatively easy-going life of the stock farmer, a determination – in spite of repeated bannings – to trade with the Hottentots; all these factors had resulted in a swift, leap-frogging movement of the colonists and a dangerously rapid pushing out of the Colony's frontiers. The borders were inexorably extended, especially along the valleys folded into the ranges of the Cape mountains towards the heavier rainfall areas of the east.

There were the freehold farms, mainly wine and grain farms clustered comfortably close to Cape Town, but the tendency of the stock-keeping Boers to wander off in search of new grazing grounds necessitated some quick thinking on the part of the authorities and this resulted in the introduction of the 'loan farms'. In the first years of expansion, nothing more than a grazing licence had been granted to the stock farmers inland. If the grazing became worked out after a year or two, they simply moved on and settled elsewhere. The supply of land was apparently inexhaustible.

The accepted method of choosing one of these loan farms sounds haphazard to modern ears. The would-be farmer would decide on a central point – the *ordonnantie* – which was usually the essential spring or *fontein* near which his house was to be built. He would then ride out on horseback, *at a walk*, for half an hour in the direction of each point of the compass. This accepted habit of measuring distance by time often caused amusement among visitors from overseas.

There was no likelihood of calculating the estimated boundaries of a farm so measured too exactly, but this method of staking a claim to land usually resulted in an area of something between 1 200 and 4 100 hectares being allotted; 2 400 hectares being an average. The farmer then put down his name for this area and waited to see whether any objection would be raised. It was said that these loan-farmers felt crowded if they were able to see the smoke from a neighbour's chimney, so this was a complaint which might be made if the new tenant proposed putting his house too near an established boundary. If no objections were raised, he was then granted the farm on payment of a rent – a tithe – fixed by the Government on the understanding that his lease would be renewable annually.

This gave the loan farmer little security of tenure, of course, and towards the middle of the eighteenth century a new form of land holding was introduced, the 'quitrent', or *erfpacht*, system. The main difference between the two systems was that quitrent land was granted for fifteen years, the rent still being payable annually.

The few freehold and many loan-farm agreements, plus some quit-rent leases, were the terms on which all land was held up to 1813. Under all three systems a sale could take place, but only the buildings and improvements – the *opstal* – could be charged for, although it was not unknown for the value of the land to be discreetly included in the purchase price. Loan farms were originally granted on an annual rent of twenty-four rix dollars a year (calculated at that time to be worth £1-16s a year)[9], so it can be seen that it was possible to be a landowner on a grand scale for a rental of little more than £5 a year.

The man to whom *Melkhout Kraal* was first granted in 1770 was Stephanus Jesias Terblans.[10]. On Frederici's and Jones' map of 1790[11], this Terblans is also shown as being the occupier of *Sandk-*

raal, another large estate of 2 500 hectares, upstream from *Melkhout Kraal,* which was also later to be bought by George Rex. The original grant of *Sandkraal* was made on 16 December 1780.

It was Stephanus Terblans who was the proud owner of *Melkhout Kraal* when Governor van Plettenberg, on his historic expedition to the interior and the eastern frontier in 1778, made this farmhouse a stopping place at 1 p.m. on 5 October on the party's homeward journey, in the course of which he side-stepped from the usual route to visit Plettenberg Bay.[12]

The Governor was returning from Algoa Bay, the party having followed the established trunk route down the Lange Kloof and then crossed the mountains near Duivelskop and turned eastward towards Knysna.

Having passed Pieter Terblans' farm, *Buffelsvermaak,* 'they reached the farm of Stephanus Terblans called *Melkhoute Kraal'.* Although Olof de Wet, the Governor's secretary, does not say so specifically in his diary of the journey, it is probable that they enjoyed lunch in this lovely setting. They then proceeded to the bay 'which had recently been inspected by the officers of the *Catwyk aan Rhyn'* and spent two nights at the farm of Cornelis Botha. This man is shown as a landowner in the Piesang Valley, Plettenberg Bay, on the map of 1790, so this was presumably the same man. The club-house of a fine eighteen-hole golf course now occupies the site of Botha's residence.

The next morning the Governor and some of his party rode round the beautiful bay, over the name of which confusion had grown more confounded as the years rolled by. Known to the early Portuguese explorers from the fifteenth century onwards, it had first been dubbed, most aptly, the Bahia Formosa (the Beautiful Bay), but had also been known as the Angra d'Alaguoa or the Bahia das Algoas, both these names referring to the lagoons which spread out so noticeably at the foot of the Piesang River, behind today's Beacon Island, and at the confluence of the Keurbooms and Bitou Rivers, where the water is banked up behind the long stretch of sand-dunes of the Look-out Beach. The bay had also been known to the succeeeding straggling colonists, as the Bay of Content (or Contant), Piesang River Bay, Keurbooms River Bay and Bitou River Bay. The Governor now settled the issue once and for all by naming it 'Plettenberg's Bay'.

Here, on his orders, was erected a beacon in the form of a slab of dark blue slate, a little more than two metres high and carved with the coat of arms of the United Provinces, the monogram of the Dutch East India Company and the Governor's own coat of arms.

This was what has been called 'a possessional cross', indicating the company's ownership of this area. The following morning early, the Governor's party left Cornelis Botha's home, stopped only to change over the oxen in the wagon-teams at Stephanus Terblans' farm, and crossed the Knysna River about eleven o'clock.[13]

The Governor had, on this brief visit, judged Plettenberg Bay to be a suitable port from which the riches of the forest might be shipped to Cape Town. Nine years later a woodcutting post was established there with every confidence and the first load of timber was taken out by the Frenchman, Captain Francois Duminy in the *Meermin*, in August 1788. Captain Duminy, domiciled at the Cape, was in the employ of the Dutch East India Company.[14] But this all belongs to another and fascinating story.

George Rex, until the Knysna River was opened for shipping about thirteen years after his arrival, shipped out from Plettenberg Bay in the meantime the timber in which he was by then industriously trading. But this bay, so alluring when tranquil, can prove treacherous beyond all imagining when lashed by the south-east gales and, after several tragic occurrences, the scale of exporting timber from here declined rapidly.

Stephanus Terblans, after enjoying the loan rights of *Melkhout Kraal* for twenty years, died, but his widow, Hester, continued to run the farm with the help of her now grown-up children. In 1798 she married again, this time Johann von Lindenbaum, a German from Alsace, to whom she had sold *Melkhout Kraal* three weeks previously.[15]

It was to this home, carrying letters of introduction from von Lindenbaum, (who was away in Cape Town), that young Robert Semple (author of *Walks and Sketches at the Cape of Good Hope*) and a friend came riding one evening in 1801. They were on their way to Plettenberg Bay on business connected with the friend's coastal vessel, which had been driven ashore there during a violent gale.

As the sun was setting, the men rode along the sandy shore of the lagoon, noting the 'noble trees' on their left and the 'wild fowl of all descriptions' on the tranquil lake on their right, until they saw *Melkhout Kraal* on gently rising ground ahead of them.

'We spurred on our horse, which, tired as they were, seemed to scent the stables, and brought us to the door of J. Lindenboom. Our letters of introduction were found hardly necessary to this hospitable family. The mother did every honour to her husband's letters, and her children, all the fruits of a former marriage, vied with each other in procuring us every little refreshment that we needed. In an hour we were no longer strangers, and on retiring to rest, it seemed as if we were in the bosom of a family, with which we had been formerly intimately acquainted, and now met after a long separation![16]

Few warmer tributes to the open-hearted inhabitants of the remote eastern districts are met with anywhere in the writings of the day.

In May, 1801, von Lindenbaum sold the *opstal* of *Melkhout Kraal* to one of John Murray's business partners, Richard Holiday, who lived to enjoy it for only about a year. When he died in 1802, John Murray, as executor of his estate, was left to dispose not only of *Melkhout Kraal,* but of another large undeveloped property on the west side of the estuary, which he and Holiday had owned jointly.[17] This was *Uitzigt,* which comprised the whole area known today as Brenton and Belvidere.

It was in 1801, the year that *Melkhout Kraal* changed hands for the second time that the second Kaffir uprising of serious proportions (referred to in the previous chapter) broke out. Black brigands swept through the Lange Kloof and, in lesser numbers, through the Tzitzikama, Plettenberg Bay and Knysna areas, burning, looting, plundering and murdering.

The once substantial homestead of *Melkhout Kraal* was razed to the ground and this was how Governor Janssens and his party found it in April 1803, when they picnicked there after conferring with James Callander.[18]

This too was how Commissary General de Mist and his party found it later in the same year. Martin Heinrich Karl Lichtenstein, the German professor who had arrived in December of the previous year to act as tutor to Governor Janssens' son and who was now a member of the de Mist party, had a sufficiently perceptive eye to appreciate that this farm, although devastated, 'had once been an arcadian retreat'. He refers in his journal to the owner of *Melkhout Kraal* as 'an Englishman by the name of Holiday', apparently not realising that Holiday had died the previous year. He also inferred that the property had been ravaged in the uprisings of 1799, whereas most of the destruction he saw had obviously taken place only the year previously. Apart from these minor errors, his account is invaluable as the only indication we have of the spaciousness of the buildings which had once graced the estate and the extent to which the grounds had already been developed with taste and care.

Having described the fury with which the Kaffirs had burned all the household goods of the inhabitants of the homestead and then destroyed the buildings, Lichtenstein continues: 'We scarcely found a place among the ruined walls where we could make a fire,

120

but the vast heaps of rubbish, and the extent of the ground over which the ruins were spread, showed at the first glance the dimensions of the buildings . . . The vegetables grew wild in the beds, and the paths were overgrown with grass and weeds. In the vineyard I found a red-deer feasting upon the ripe grapes: I followed his example and found the flavour of them even in this degenerate state such as shewed the excellent stock from which they were descended.'

Lichtenstein lyrically describes the hedges of roses and jasmine in full blow, the orange trees bent under the weight of their fruit, the peaches, apricots, almonds and bananas having ripened on the trees. 'Not the hand of art alone, and the industry of man, but nature seems, imitating them, to have formed this singular abode in one of her most fantastic humours. I could not help indulging myself in the vision that it was inhabited by some benevolent super-human being, such as is created by the fancies of poets or romance writers.

'The free unconstrained forms and luxuriant growth of the plants and trees destined for the nourishment of man, the wild overgrown walks between the rose-hedges, which seemed to be trodden by no human foot, filled me with a sort of secret awe, as I stretched out my hand to gather some of the neglected fruit. I conceived that I had just the feeling which anyone might be supposed to have, wandering in the pleasure garden of some enchanted prince.'[19]

Stephanus Terblans, Johann von Lindenbaum and Richard Holiday had obviously created a paradise in this isolated spot. Lichtenstein also mentions that the estate was first made in the middle of the eighteenth century 'by a very active, clever and industrious man' and that, by reason of its fertility, it soon became one of the most famous properties in the Colony.

Even Theal, the historian, who was not normally given to superlatives, reported that it had acquired before the close of the eighteenth century 'the reputation of being more like a fairyland than an ordinary South African cattle run'.[20]

Now it was the far-sighted and ambitious Rex who had become the owner of this fairyland.

7 Man of Property

To this Garden of Eden, then, came George Rex and his family just a year later. *Melkhout Kraal* had been in his possession for eight months and it is reasonable to assume that his slaves (whom he mentioned in his petition for leave to return to his farm at the Knysna) must have tidied up by now the worst of the devastation so tellingly described by Lichtenstein. It is extremely unlikely, however, that without his supervision the labourers would have managed to repair the gutted buildings to any extent. The probability is, therefore, that instead of bedding her children down in comfortable, welcoming beds the night they arrived, desperately tired after their long journey, Johanna Rosina had to continue to improvise under more-or-less camping conditions for some time.

Rex had the foundations of a comfortable home to build on, the means of livelihood at hand in the forests, a once-enchanting garden to restore and a superb setting for the scene of his endeavours. He could now visualise the fulfilment of all his dreams, but it was to take years of skilful planning, organisation, supervision and back-breaking work before the dream became a paying reality. It must have been with mixed feelings, therefore, that he and Johanna Rosina approached the ruined house and overgrown garden clinging to the gently rising hill above the eastern shore of the lagoon.

He must have called on all his undoubted resourcefulness and tenacity of purpose to restore this property to what it had once been, let alone to build it up into the gracious estate which it would eventually become. He had, up to that point, little first-hand knowledge of agriculture, except what he had absorbed in the established gardens of *Schoonder Zigt,* and he had no experienced hands to help him because, unlike the sons of distinguished English families who came to this fair corner of the land of promise some thirty to forty years later, he did not bring out from England any artisans, gardeners or servants. Nor were his sons, with the possible exception of his young stepson, Hendrik Ungerer, old enough to be of assistance to him yet. It will be seen shortly that in later years there was to be a place for each of his older boys in the thriving agricultural-cum-

122

business concern which he created out of his tranquil domain.

But this land of promise had disappointments in store for him as it was to have for would-be agriculturists ever since. The affluent families in this area today, apart from the small handful who have drawn their wealth from the bountiful forests, are those who have accumulated their capital elsewhere and then retired there to savour the peace and beauty of their surroundings. There are few large-scale farmers and those who have succeeded to any degree have done so by dint of, not only their hard labour, but by the utilisation of modern methods of improving the quality of the soil and replacing those elements which are so quickly drained out of it.

For the *bosgrond*, the newly-cleared ground, is very productive at first and this leads the settler's hopes to rise in anticipation of an indefinite continuation of the same rich crops. The sandy loam, however, deteriorates rapidly and after a few years of intensive use becomes seriously low in plant foods which in earlier times could not be replaced by means of scientifically-balanced fertilisers, as is done today.

The frequency and distribution of the rainfall can only be described as erratic. The rain is distributed over the year, although unevenly, which largely account for the perennial greenness of the tough indigenous growth.[1] It was largely this greenness which so beguiled Rex and other early colonists.

The whole agricultural situation was recently summed up thus: 'Farming is generally unimportant in the local economy of the area. Farm sizes increase west of George, although they remain small by South African standards .... inaccessibility to markets inhibited growth and development'.[2] How much more did this inaccessibility inhibit growth and development in Rex's day.

So, in spite of its obvious attractions, the verdant slopes which enchanted traveller after traveller, the warm, temperate climate, the lack of frosts, the abundance of water and the hourly and daily miracle of beauty abounding, this is not – strictly speaking – agricultural country.

The graphic records left by the Honourable Henry Barrington, who was to buy a portion of what had been Rex's land and to struggle doggedly against odds with an astonishing range of agricultural enterprises, nearly forty years later, give a fair picture of the same type of problems as those with which Rex was beset from the beginning.[3] By the end of the last century there was at *Melkhout Kraal,* little vestige to be seen of the agricultural activities which Rex pursued.

But fortunately this disillusionment lay locked in the future and there were – until man's reckless depredations began to threaten them – the mighty forests. George Rex's slaves were the nucleus of the labour force he was going to need and to these he added at various times, when a particular undertaking warranted it, numbers of the unfortunate Hottentots, who, dispossessed of what land they had previously used for grazing their cattle, were more and more being employed as labourers by the colonists. This labour force served to get his house, barns, workshops and stables built, to get the already laid-out grounds re-planted and to get his business enterprises under way.

He seems to have adapted well to the master-servant relationship with an assortment of peoples who were differentiated from him by language, customs and heredity, and to have treated them well. Interdependence created a loyalty and some of his employees appear to have stayed with him fifteen years and more.

We get a good idea of the layout of *Melkhout Kraal* (although several of the buildings mentioned in the following extract were added years after his arrival) from a letter which Rex addressed in December 1830, to Messrs. Nisbit and Dickson, Cape Town, 'requesting to have Insurance effected in the Alliance Office against loss from fire on the several buildings on my Quit Rent place, *Melkhout Kraal,* situate on the left Bank of the river Knysna in the District of George . . .'[4]

The main house, described as a 'Private dwelling house with thatched roof', was built of brick, in two wings, and measured 21,9 metres across the front by 15,2 metres deep. It stood away from the other buildings and had a fireplace in the sitting-room as well as in the kitchen.

Then follows a list comprising 'a brick building housing a store-room and other offices (with no fire-place); a stone building containing bedrooms and a loft (with no fire-place); a brick building containing a servants' kitchen, with a fire-place at one end, a carpenter's workshop and servants' bedroom at the other end; a brick building used as a wine-cellar at one end, a slaughter-house and iron-store at the other, and finally a waggon-house and two adjoining storerooms, with a loft which was used as a granary.' All the buildings were thatched and all, except the stone building and probably the guest-cottage, were described as having brick walls 'partially of timber within the walls.'

The total value of these six buildings was estimated for insurance purposes to be £562-10s. No wonder the impression grew among the woodcutters and the simple country folk around that a very important personage had arrived to settle at Knysna.

Naturally not all the buildings of *Melkhout Kraal* were constructed immediately on arrival, but were added at various times as George Rex's family and his agricultural activities increased. A tremendous undertaking in all, when one tries to visualise the work involved in the making of bricks alone, the gathering of reeds for thatching, the mixing of mortar with sand laboriously brought up from the river, the casting of foundations and the actual construction of the houses. No doubt the wood-work would all have been of stinkwood, ironwood and yellowwood from the adjoining forests. As there is no mention anywhere of an architect's services, we may infer that Rex was practical and versatile enough to turn surveyor, draughtsman and clerk of the works in turn, to design each structure and then supervise its erection.

A description which restores *Melkhout Kraal* in our imaginations to the handsome homestead it eventually became, came from the pen of Captain John Fisher Sewell, who married the youngest of Rex's five daughters, Maria, and after half a lifetime at sea settled down to farming at Holt Hill, not far from Plettenberg Bay. His description of the Rex home, although written long after Rex's death, is vivid and fills in the blank spaces in the plans of the fire insurance document.

'It was a splendid place,' Sewell wrote. 'The road up to the house was through an avenue of oak trees and the drive terminated in front of the dwelling, which stood a little back, and in front of it was a row of giant oaks, which sheltered it from the midday sun.' Having described the 'large oblong hall', the drawing-room, parlour and other smaller rooms, the writer continued: 'From the front door, westwards, extended an avenue of pear trees which led down to a garden and plantation of oaks, with orange and naartje trees on the one side and a vineyard on the other. The view commanded the lake and Belvidere on the opposite side of the river, and was magnificent. A princely heritage for, with its barns, waggon houses, water-mill, outbuildings and servants' quarters, it was a much larger establishment than the village of Knysna.'[5]

The proprietor had obviously extended his gardening activities considerably after the year 1815, in which C.I. Latrobe visited *Melkhout Kraal* and wrote later: 'After dinner he (Rex) showed us his gardens, which are at some distance from the dwelling, towards the valley. They are well stocked with a great variety of produce, but no attention has been paid to ornament.'[6]

Roughly six months after he took possession of *Melkhout Kraal* his fourth child, Jacob Govert, was born[7] and he, who loved children, must often have had quiet satisfaction in watching the toddlers

125

tumbling on the grass and his baby lying in his basket under a tree, fascinated as all babies are, by the interplay of light and shade in the shimmering leaves. There would have been this quiet content, undoubtedly, but the impression which has come down to us of these years – through sundry jottings, journals and letters – is necessarily a more humdrum one, showing him concerned with a score of more practical issues.

In the first place he purchased, in addition to *Melkhout Kraal* and *Sandkraal* (already mentioned) *Welbedacht* (1 238 hectares), which he re-named *Eastford*.[8] A condition of purchase of all these loan farms adjacent to the sea or any tidal water was that the government retained the right to resume possession of 17,1 hectares on each, should this be required later for public use. A morgen (0,86 hectare) of land on the eastern Head was reserved for a pilot's house out of the 2 525 hectares of *Melkhout Kraal*,[9] and a little circle on the top of the eastern Head for a flagstaff.

Later he also purchased *Jackals Kraal*, a lovely 514 hectares at the head of the Piesang River,[10] near Plettenberg Bay. To the north-west of Knysna, he bought in 1817 from Solomon Terblans, roughly 889 hectares out of the vast Leeuwenbosch area, which was to become *Portland*[11] and – many years later – the home of the indefatigible Henry Barrington. Rex's last large purchase of land was that of *Uitzigt*, which comprised the whole of the rugged Western headland, later to be divided into Brenton and Belvidere.[12]

There are two confirmatory references to the approximate date of his purchase of *Uitzigt*. Andrew Steedman, who spent two days in 1833 at 'the hospitable mansion of Mr. Rex,' wrote in his '*Wanderings and Adventures in the Interior of Southern Africa*', 'Mr. Rex having recently purchased the land on the opposite side of the river, now possessed nearly the whole extent of the Knysna, comprising upwards of twenty four thousand acres.'[13] And George Rex, writing to his sister, Sarah, in October 1830, wrote '. . . to which I have lately added by purchase of an extensive farm of contiguous land, the possession of which only was wanting to make it complete, so that we now have in perpuity both sides of the River and Harbour from its entrance all the way up nine or ten miles, and as far as navigable by boat.'[14]

To enable the present-day reader to visualise his property in 1830, it must be mentioned that *Melkhout Kraal* itself included the areas on the eastern shore today known as *Hunters Home* and *Woodbourne*, so that his purchases of *Eastford*, *Westford* and *Uitzigt* alone, gave him ownership of a vast U enclosing the Knysna basin. Special interest attaches to another of his properties, an

126

area lying east, in the direction of Plettenberg Bay, because of the claim which has persisted over the years that this was a special grant of land from the Crown (implying, of course, from King George III). This was *Springfield*, 1 604 hectares in extent.[15]

The mundane truth of this matter is that Richard Holiday, when he bought *Melkhout Kraal* from von Lindenbaum, acquired the right to this adjoining area 'by preference without payment' once von Lindenbaum had no further use for it. A condition of Rex's purchase of *Melkhout Kraal* when Holiday died, was that this adjoining farm would be transferred to him too 'by preference without payment'.[16] In May 1804, a few weeks after he had bought *Melkhout Kraal*, Rex applied formally to the Council of Policy of the Batavian Republic for the use of this farm, but it was not until 9 December, 1807, that he received this notification from C. Bird (Colonial Secretary): '*Nongna* It has pleased His Excellency to grant the memorialist the land in question on loan.' Rex made his first payment of 26 rix-dollars on this farm (which he re-named *Springfield*) in the same year.[17] It was as simple as that.

In 1830 his farms totalled nearly 10 000 hectares.

A change in the system of land tenure was inevitable. Sir John Cradock, when he succeeded the youthful Lord Caledon as Governor of the Cape in September 1811, was concerned about – among other things – the faults of the existing system of loan places. On 6 August, 1813, a proclamation was issued which allowed – in fact, persuaded – occupants of loan farms to have their tenure converted into that of 'perpetual quitrent'.

Rex's farms were registered under the new conditions in 1816 and the total quitrent payable on them was 182 rix-dollars, or roughly a little more than £13.10s. sterling at that time. The rents seems to have been raised slightly as time went by, because a receipt dated 13 July 1818, for 'Quit Rent on *Melkhout Kraal*' is for the amount of 81 rix-dollars,[18] instead of the 70 rix-dollars originally agreed upon.

Meanwhile, in the years immediately following his arrival, there was plenty to engage Rex's attention and he must have, in spite of his slaves and Hottentot labourers, worked extremely hard himself.

Not only was the reconstruction of the main house a matter of urgency, but he would have been clearing bush, fixing the watercourse to the house, planting trees and shrubs, fencing off pastures and trying out his first crops. By dint of hard work and admirable husbandry, he restored the vineyard and orchards, the flower garden and the vegetable garden; he planted fig, quince, apple and mulberry trees and an avenue of almond trees leading from the homestead down to the lagoon. Grain, barley, spelt (a German wheat) were grown over many years and trial crops of flax, hemp and tobacco were planted at various times.

He was nothing if not industrious. Cider was made from the apples, brandy from the grapes and one year it was even recorded that the Rex daughters had spun several pounds of raw silk from silkworms fed on the mulberry trees. Cattle, horses, sheep and chickens were all kept and 'at one time the yield of milk was so great that it was the duty of a special slave . . . to do nothing but churn'.[19] The surplus butter was exported to Cape Town, Algoa Bay, St. Helena and Mauritius in kegs and barrels.

But in spite of these varied activities on the home front and the animated scene conjured up by the record of them, George Rex's main source of revenue was obviously the export of timber from the surrounding forests. As the transport of this timber overland to Plettenberg Bay, from whence it was shipped out, was an operation which wasted time, labour and money, Rex never slackened in these years his efforts to have the Knysna River opened to shipping. His hopes in this connection, eventually to be realised, were temporarily dashed in 1808, by the failure of the very first attempt to prove that the Knysna bar could – winds, tides, currents and all other things being set fair – be safely crossed.

In this year the gun brig, *The Staunch,* was sent 'with some carpenters to endeavour to cut timber in the Knysna, 'a small harbour near Plettenberg Bay'. *The Staunch,* however, found such a heavy sea running when she arrived at the bar between the Heads, that Lieutenant Street, in charge of her, wisely proceeded to Plettenberg Bay, where he took in some timber to justify the voyage.[20] For nine years following the voyage of *The Staunch,* timber needed for the naval yard at Simonstown continued to be obtained from Plettenberg Bay and there is no doubt that, of this, George Rex supplied the major proportion, as he was by far the most astute man for many miles around dealing in timber.

In spite of the experience of *The Staunch,* Sir Jahleel Brenton, Naval Commissioner at Simonstown from 1815 onwards, made a point of collecting all the information he could on the Knysna river and formed the opinion that it could be 'admirably adapted as a shipping place for the timber required for the use of the dock-yard, as well as for cargoes to send to England'.[21] He therefore decided to travel, in un-nautical fashion, overland to Knysna in 1817 to judge for himself its potential as a harbour.

He stayed for several days with George Rex, who had arranged, at the Naval Commissioner's request, for woodcutters to prepare a quantity of wood to be a cargo for the brig, *Emu,* which had been despatched from Simonstown with instructions to enter the Heads and collect the timber at the riverside. In attempting to enter the mouth, however, the *Emu,* met a strong head wind in the narrows between the Heads and was driven on to a sunken rock. She was so badly damaged that her captain beached her a short way within the Heads at Steenbok Island (today's Leisure Island). Rex's hopes were once more dashed on the rocks.

The sloop-of-war, *Podargus,* was then sent to fetch the crew and stores of the unfortunate *Emu.* Finding on arrival off the Heads that the wind was fair and the water calm, *Podargus* sailed in and anchored 'with the utmost ease'. Captain Wallis, in command, made a survey and sent in a most favourable report on the possibilities of the lagoon as a harbour.[22]

Sir Jahleel Brenton, who was an artist of outstanding ability, painted a few pictures while at Knysna. He never had the opportunity of returning to this lovely spot, but he continued to be vitally interested in its development as a harbour.

Following the triumphal entry through the Heads of the *Podargus,* loads of timber destined for the naval arsenal at Simonstown or for the dockyards in England, were regularly shipped out from between the Heads, and coastal trading between this port, Mossel Bay and Cape Town developed most satisfactorily. From 1817 until the time of George Rex's death in 1839, a total of one hundred and sixty-two ships visited Knysna and only four of them were wrecked in that period.[23]

Sir Jahleel Brenton, satisfied that the Knysna river was fulfilling its promise as a haven for shipping, next decided to conduct an experiment with shipbuilding here.

It is clear from the protracted correspondence which passed between the Commissioners of Enquiry and the Navy Board, between Brenton and Sir Rufane Donkin (then in charge of the Colony during Lord Charles Somerset's absence on leave), between the Government and the Admiralty that this transaction caused strong crosscurrents and undercurrents.

In a letter written on 14 February, 1820, to Donkin,[24] Brenton records, 'Sir, as soon as the Knysna was ascertained to be a safe port, and well calculated for an outlet for the timber from the forests in its vicinity, I submitted to the Navy Board the expediency of a Naval Establishment being formed on its banks, and requested His Excellency Lord Charles Henry Somerset to allot a piece of ground in that neighbourhood for the purpose ... to which His Lordship was pleased to consent. I soon after visited the Knysna to ascertain what spots might be best calculated for the proposed settlement, but found the whole of the left bank of the river as far as the forests to be in possession of Mr. Rex. This gentleman, however, consented to give up a piece of his land on condition of receiving an equivalent from the Colonial Government'.

The writer goes on to record the various obstacles encountered; the unsuitability of the site selected on Westford, the unsatisfactory reports received on stinkwood as a timber suitable for shipbuilding, disasters which had overtaken quantities of hemp seed which was intended for the foundation of a hemp farm near Knysna, the fact that 'all land of any value between the Knysna and George, or between that river and Plettenberg Bay, had been disposed of, and that he (Mr. Rex) informed me that it was no longer his wish to dispose of any part of his property'.

In spite of all discouragement, Brenton then put forward his proposal as to how his scheme might still be implemented. 'As Government holds liens of twenty morgen each upon each of his (Rex's) five estates on the Knysna . . . I suggested to Mr. Rex that he should give up forty morgen on the eastern bank of the Knysna, between *Melkhout Kraal* and the *East Ford,* extending four morgens along the bank of the river and ten in length from the beach inland . . . In these proposals Mr. Rex has consented. As this ground which I have selected would be of the greatest value in the event of a village or town being built on the Knysna and contains the only good shipping place and spring in the harbour . . . and Mr. Rex has already given up a portion of *Melkhout Kraal* for the Pilot's establishment, I feel no hesitation in requesting Your Excellency to take the subject into consideration . . .'

With great dispatch, the Acting Governor sent word to Brenton later in February that he 'had caused measures to be taken for giving effects to your suggested arrangement with Mr. Rex as to the appropriation of a certain portion of land in his possession for public purposes'. Donkin also made it quite clear that, although he strongly wished to encourage the development and opening up of the Colony, he had strong reservations about the choice of land decided upon for Brenton's purpose.[25]

The deal was, however, done. Rex, who had been planning to divide up and sell portion of his property for small farms, rather reluctantly agreed to cede to the Admiralty a block of forty morgen (34,3 hectares) on the east shore of the lagoon, the government in return ceding its claim to twenty morgen (17,1 hectares) on each of his other four farms. The area at *Eastford* eventually appropriated was named Melville in 1825, in honour of the first Viscount Melville, formerly our old friend, Henry Dundas.

It was very much later, after Rex's death, that a further area, called Newhaven, was added to the east of Melville and the two areas together formed eventually the village of Knysna.

Meanwhile the Navy had acquired its site for a dockyard near the present Yacht Clubhouse and in July, 1820, three shipwrights and ten labourers were sent from Simonstown to build a brig there. The whole venture was ill-fated. Neither the timber nor the labour was as cheap as had been anticipated, the difficulties of bringing the timber out of the dense forests were formidable and, on top of everything, an accidental fire caused heavy damage to the embryonic shipyard. In January 1822, a ship was sent to Knysna to pick up all the workmen, the frame of the hull of the brig, and other materials salvaged from the fire.

So, even though the harbour was now officially commissioned, all was not plain sailing. The efficacy of the pilot station which had been established in 1819 had for some time been in question and in 1826 it was abolished altogether.[26] This created new problems for Mr. Rex, now heavily involved in the timber export business. Insurance on cargoes bound for Knysna were almost doubled, few ships were prepared to risk the sudden shifts of wind and tide which could make the Heads a death-trap and freights rose in proportion to the obvious risks. With the courage and decisiveness which were characteristic of him, George Rex decided to build his own ship. He engaged a master shipwright, Captain James Smith, former commander of the brig, *Usk,* two assistant shipwrights, two caulkers, a joiner, a blacksmith and four labourers, all on contract for eight months.

In 1826 the keel of the brig, which was to be of one hundred and forty tons, was laid on the right bank of the river at Westford. The Historical Monuments Commission has marked the site of the slipway one kilometre upstream from the old Phantom Pass road-bridge, with a granite monolith on which is a suitably inscribed bronze plaque. The old stinkwood slipway was only re-discovered in 1946 by Mr. Robert Veldtman and the beams which were laid at George Rex's command today grace, appropriately enough, the Chamber of the Divisional Council of Knysna in the form of a magnificent board-room table and set of chairs.[27]

James Holman, the blind traveller, who visited Knysna while the brig was being built, reported that 'about two hundred yards below the ford, there was a vessel moored, which had been lately launched from the opposite side of the river. She was the first vessel ever built on its banks, and was from that circumstance, named *The Knysna*, by her owners, Messrs. Rex and Robinson. She was built by Mr. Smith, of native oak, commonly known by the name of the stinkwood tree...' The vessel in question was about 140 tons burthen, and was intended to be loaded for Cape Town, and from thence with wheat for England.[28]

George Rex had thought of calling his brig the *Britannia,* but Cowper Rose, who visited *Melkhout Kraal* in 1828 and went up the river with his host to look at the vessel in the course of construction, wrote: 'It's name was to be the *Britannia,* but I begged hard to have it called the *Knysna,* as the first that had been built from its forests, or launched upon its waters.'[29]

There were vicissitudes in plenty in the five years that it took to complete the *Knysna* but she finally sailed from the Knysna harbour with her first cargo on 16 July 1831. She was the first seagoing ship to enter the mouth of the Buffalo River, East London, and for many years plied with cargo between Cape Town and Durban, calling at intermediate ports as well. Her long life (she was known to be still afloat in this century) was as much proof of the durability of the wood from which she was built as a tribute to the men who built her.[30]

From now on Rex's business enterprises proliferated, but above all the world of wood was his oyster. In spite of the extraordinarily variegated nature of the cargoes which the *Knysna* sometimes carried – and they ranged from fowls and geese to pickled pork and sausages, from bacon and biltong to walnuts and almonds – there is no doubt that she was in the main loaded with timber for Cape Town.

Andrew Steedman, already mentioned in this chapter, reported: 'The inhabitants of this district principally support themselves by felling timber in the government forests, which they bring to the Knysna for sale, where Mr. Rex and a few others engaged in the wood trade reside, and from thence it is transported by small vessels to Cape Town.[31]

Obviously Knysna would have been no place for the ascetic essayist and philosopher, Henry Thoreau, who wondered why the village did not toll the knell every time a tree was felled.

The depredations and uncontrolled felling by unlicensed woodcutters in this section of the Crown forests of the Cape had, even by 1812, caused concern. Captain A.F. Jones, of the Royal Navy, reported in this year that the forests were not nearly as extensive as had been thought, that considerable damage had already been done by reckless, greedy men, that the difficulties of bringing the timber out of the forests were almost insuperable and that the only type of wood suitable for shipbuilding was stinkwood, which grew sparsely in comparison with other types of trees. Official attitudes to the problem vacillated inexplicably and little attention seems to have been paid to preservation, let alone re-afforestation, in those early days.

In 1811 the forest in the Plettenberg Bay area had been reserved exclusively for the use of the naval yards at Simonstown and the following year a large section was closed altogether, because of the increasing scarcity of good timber reported by Captain Jones. By the time George Rex was in a position to contract for substantial amounts of timber from the forests surrounding his home, some semblance of control had been introduced, even if it was limited, and the abuses were fewer.[32]

Theal records that when Rex's lands were registered under the new perpetual quitrent system in 1816 and the Knysna harbour was eventually opened to shipping in 1817, he 'then introduced labourers and carried out his plans until the artificial beauties at *Melkhout Kraal* were nearly as great as the natural ones.'[33]

Certainly the various *opgawe* (official returns for tax assessment purposes) between the date of his arrival and 1816 show no great number of slaves or other employees on the strength. The *Opgaaf* of 1816, one of his best years to that date, shows him to have two female slaves, ten male slaves, ten child slaves, twenty-five horses, a hundred and fourteen oxen, two hundred and sixty breeding stock and sixty-two sheep and goats.[34]

The fact that Theal was right and the situation then began to improve is reflected in Rex's Day-book of 1818 to 1822,[35] the only record to survive from the mass of business correspondence and other such documents which he must have written during this period.

On 26 August 1818, for instance, we find John Wing, the Chinese carpenter, taken on at a wage of fifty rix-dollars a month (the rix-dollar was then fixed at 1/6d.) It was Wing who was to be responsible for many of the fine pieces of furniture which in time graced *Melkhout Kraal* and which so impressed many of the visitors. Jonathan Redford, a gardener, and Robert Colville, an overseer, were both taken on to the staff at twenty-six rix-dollars a month each, while the following year Robert Scott started work in January at sixty rix-dollars a month and James Blake, in March, at thirty-six rix-dollars a month. Adam Henter, a seine-maker, John Black, a woodcutter, and Esau, the shoemaker, all started work for Rex in 1818. Esau was to be paid twelve rix-dollars a month.

This day-book tells us a great deal, not only about Rex's forest-workers, gardeners, apprentices, Hottentots and slaves, the other landowners in the area (with all of whom he traded), but also about the ships that called to load timber or buy provisions, and about his *modus operandi* generally. The owner of every name in the book is debited with 'goods from the store' in varying quantities.

Other pages headed *Forest Work* or *Permits for Timber for Exportation* indicate the extent of his involvement in the timber business and the comfortable income which he derived from it.

Among callers during this period to whom he supplied timber or other goods – often provisions for a ship's crew – were John Weakner, Master of the *Adolphus;* John Hope of the brig, *Good Hope;* Captain Wm. Dean, of the ship, *Juno;* Captain Thos. Jeffrey, master of the brig, *Ocean;* Marthinus Hoets and William Robertson, of Cape Town; A.G. van Kervel, Esq., (first Landdrost of George); Agidius Petersen, the land surveyor from George; Major F. Rogers, Military Secretary, Cape Town; and Richard Peek, a shipwright, of Melville. The Burgher Senate too was responsible for an order for 542 beams in 1818, for which it paid the satisfactory sum of 3 473,6 rix-dollars. John Gough (the pilot) bought 'I muid potatoes' and John Smith and others of the pilot's crew stationed at the eastern Head bought stores in September, 1818.

Among the thinly scattered colonists whose names are listed as debtors in the day-book, are Matthys Zondagh of the Lange Kloof (an hospitable farmer whom James Edward Alexander, a traveller, described in 1835 as 'a burly old fellow, with a voice and back like a miller . . .'); Solomon Ter Blans of Leeuwenbosch, north-west of the Knysna lagoon; Nicholas van Huysteen of Wittedrift (the van Huysteens were among the earliest settlers from Holland in this area); Cornelis van Rooyen, Jan van Rooyen and Michael Kap of the Piesang Valley; Renier van Rooyen of Ganse Vallei; Martha Weyers of Swarte Rivier ('Tea 2 lbs. and 1 Doek' seems to be the extent of her purchase); Cornelis, Batter and Jacobus van der Wat of Stoff-pad (at the head of the Bitou River near Plettenberg Bay); Martinus Jarling of Keurbooms River; Tyse Jarling of Buffels River; Jacobus Meeding of Ruygte Vallei and Carl Rosenberg, the blacksmith, of Goukamma. Kobus and John Barnard, sad to relate, are noted as still owing amounts from 1814 and 1813 respectively. The contents of 'Store at the Bay' are listed here too, so presumably Rex also owned a store at Plettenberg Bay.

Apart from the nine slaves – Primo, Hector, Damon, Africa, Sousa, July, Caesar, James and Colombo – nine apprentices and nine Hottentots are listed in this book, each with a long list against his name of items such as tea, sugar, rice, sout (salt), pepper, botter (butter), candles, meal, rum, brandy, sheep, tabak (tobacco), a hamel (wether) or a pig debited to him. Sometimes these employees, but more often the surrounding farmers, bought more durable goods, such as 14 ells linen (an el is a little over a metre), 4 ells fustain, 5 ells flannel, 4 ells green baize, 1 shawl, 3 doeken (head scarves), Pak spelde (pins), 1 fine Hat, 1 pair schoenen (shoes), 4 velle (hides), or a gun stock.

The mixture of English and colloquial Dutch makes quaint reading, but shows that Rex had made a laudable and determined attempt to learn the language of his 'people' – as he always called them.

An interesting group of workers who are shown both as purchasing goods from the store and being paid for timber supplied to George Rex, comprised Hendrik Ungerer (about 26 now), whose address is given as *Melkhout Kraal*, Alexander Kock, Gert and Hendrik Stroebel, all of *Springfield*. The extent to which their lives were linked with those of the family at *Melkhout Kraal* will become apparent in the following chapter. The practice of encouraging the woodcutters to bring down timber in payment for goods which they wanted from the store is reflected in an entry for Monday, 19 August 1833, in George Rex's personal diary for the period 7 July 1833-14 November 1834:[36] 'J. Barnard, Voslo and several others here for goods they say John promised and for which their timber is ready.'

Under the heading *Permits for Timber for Exportation* are listed the number of loads shipped out in each of the five years covered by the day-book and only in 1820 did the number drop below a hundred. In this year 97 loads of timber are accounted for. The names of ships in which loads of timber were shipped out are given and the orders are broken down into 'waggon-wood, planks, beams, spars, spokes and bowsprits'. Permits are noted as having been 'sent this day to Squire for 50, or 80, or 100 loads'. John Squier was at this time Resident at Plettenberg Bay, and it was his duty 'to superintend the Government Woods and Forests in the vicinity of Plettenberg Bay and to render assistance to Ships driven into the Bay in distress'. Under the heading of *Timber Purchased* in the day-book, the biggest item of expense is that of 'provisions for 19 workmen' amounting to more than 1 000 rix-dollars per year. Rex's profits from timber sales in the period covered by the day-book fluctuated from just over 3 000 to 8 000 rix-dollars per year.

The diary, covering a period of sixteen months (some thirteen years or so after the day-book) clearly shows the spread of Rex's business interests in the thirties and the basis on which his whole commercial and agricultural enterprise operated. Activities at *Melkhout Kraal* were now at a peak. The Knysna harbour had been in use for some years, Rex's own brig was in commission, his labour force was steady, and he had his three eldest sons – Edward (32), John (31) and Jacob (28) all living at home and working hard for him. He himself was now sixty-eight years of age, still holding the reins and taking the major decisions, but content to sit back a little and leave the execution of his plans to his sons. Probably this was the first time since his arrival in Knysna that he had found time to keep detailed notes of the activities affecting his life. Personal emotion has no place in this factual record of events and opinions are minimal.

And a detailed record it is, showing not only a remarkable grasp of the many facets of his own business arrangements – tenders for timber; the number of beams, planks, spokes, felloes, axle-trees and draft-booms shipped out in a load; the number of sheaves of barley gathered at *Belvidere;* the names of the slaves, Hottentots and apprentices who had gone to help Edward construct a road; the offers to charter his brig; damage to his lime kiln; the possibility of a sale for timber at Mauritius; a trespasser cutting wood illegally in his forests; the purchase of some sheep, and so on – but a keen and kindly interest in the activities of everyone with whom he came in contact one way or another.

'Squire makes wagon sides now and charges rds 80 in wood, 15 feet – Squire was paid rds 325 for the St. Helena's mast, 64 ft. long – called on Jan Polsen who very much doubts Coomans getting his timber delivered – Ungerer's wagon has just delivered a load of beams at the landing place – When Edward was at the Drift on Wednesday, Bell the Mate was making a raft for Squire with some stinkwood planks which had been promised to Coomans – Long sold his young wolf for rds 40 – the *St. Helena* at the Cove – Garcia accepts for rds 2 500 at 4 months dated 30th September – Cornelis van Rooyen has purchased the quarter place Piesang River at public sale for rds 1 510. Garcia was to bid to rds 1 400 for it for H. Ungerer – Munting passing to Plettenberg Bay – Came upon a receipt for Wickham's taxes, 18/- – about noon Col. Wade proceeds to Plett. Bay intending to stay the night at Klaas van Huyssteen and to go a long stage tomorrow to Meedings – They have got no whale yet at Plettenberg Bay and have seen only one – Williams from the Bay there who says the whale fishery will not be continued.'

The last two remarks applied to the whaling industry then in its infancy at Plettenberg Bay, but to be revived enthusiastically towards the end of the century.

On Sunday, 10 August 1834, Rex reflects on disconcerting trends in the coastal trade with which he was so vitally concerned. 'The ships coming from England to Algoa Bay direct and vice versa, and those vessels bringing in cargoes – partly for Table Bay and partly to Algoa – take in at the Cape for the latter port at very low freights; being obliged to go there. A great deal of underhand work going on at the Cape by those who sell on Commission. Manufacturers and others in England, to get rid of their goods, consign them to these Commission Houses who advance on the goods about 33 percent. And they are sold at public sale without regard to anything else than their commission money. Findlay caught this morning at the ship, a shark 10 feet long – 2 young ones within, 4 feet long.'

Another unusually interesting comment is that made on Tuesday 2 September 1834: 'Captn. Brown, of the *Test* much displeased with the place of Knysna and tells John he will undeceive other vessels – that none shall come there in future. He says it is all the merchants' fault now . . . The *Test* not half loaded, and Sinclair says the woodcutters bring down only stinkwood since its amount in value sooner pays their debts.' The unfortunate Captain Brown had obviously been waiting an abnormally long time to load his ship, owing to this tendency on the part of the woodcutters to scour the forests for the comparatively rare stinkwood. The price of stinkwood, incidentally, in the early years of the nineteenth century, was 3/10d per cubic foot;[37] today it is about £10 for the same amount.

A fairly typical entry in the diary is that of Friday 16 August 1833: 'Received from J. R. Captn. Smith's extended Account Sales of A/C, also letter he wrote to Col. Thompson renewing my tender for timber. Also Memo of Mr. Skirrow for 36 frs. Knee timber – see dimensions S.P. Also Memo of Watermeyer of an error in discount paid to Zeederberg. Also copy of his letter to Duthie. He returns me the Title Deeds of Jackals Kraal – power of attorney from me being wanted to transfer. Papers of particulars for the sale of place, Krombeks River.'

This was a man with his finger on the pulse of the whole community in which he lived and prospered and of the wider world beyond. Comments on people and events in Cape Town are common and entries such as, 'At Plett. Bay this season taken 2 fish – 26 leaguers oil, but little bone – price of the oil in London £20 per ton last season from September to March. 46 seals – all males – price of each skin if in good merchantable condition, well prepared – hair on and fast – no hole in the skin, 20s at market (Sunday 25 August, 1833)' and about meetings of the slave proprietors to discuss arrangements for compensation connected with the impending emancipation of slaves, show that his horizons were by no means bounded by the hills encircling the Knysna lagoon.

He himself visited Cape Town on business from time to time on his own, it seems, when he took the opportunity to enjoy some urban social life with his friends, the Judges Menzies and Kekewich, and Baron von Ludwig among others.

Postal arrangements occupy quite a lot of his attention and the arrival and despatch of every letter is meticulously recorded. As early as 1809, George Rex, as a result of an offer which he made to the government authorities to take charge of postal matters, had been put in charge of the mails for Knysna and Plettenberg Bay, and the entries in the diary nearly a quarter of a century later make it clear that he was still fulfilling this function conscientiously.

But it brought him as many headaches as some of his major operations. The Hottentot postriders were sometimes drunk, frequently late and produced a variety of cock-and-bull stories to account for their tardiness. The postal service was a perennial source of irritation, the more so as letters held an infinitely more vital place in the scheme of things than they do in these days of telephones and telecommunications generally.

If George Rex was the owner, chairman and managing director of the business, controlling operations from his study at *Melkhout Kraal*, John, his second son, was the general manager. Edward, his first-born, seems to have been a quiet man, not as forceful as John, but he was primarily responsible for getting the precious timber out of the forests and delivering it to the landing-place – a most important task. Most entries relating to him are simply 'Edward to the Bosch (forest)', but he was also responsible for keeping things running smoothly at *Melkhout Kraal*. He was the farm manager, who looked after the wood-cutters, repaired the watercourse to the house, repaired the wagon, arranged an elephant shoot, made a *veldbrand* (veldfire) two days running in February 1834, trapped the 'wolf, shored up the gable-end of the school and sometimes went fishing or shooting.

Jacob was concerned primarily with looking after the stock. He drives fifty-two head of cattle to *Springfield*, takes a span of oxen to the landing-place, helps Edward kill the 'wolf', searches for missing oxen and obviously is a born veterinarian.

But John was here, there and everywhere – in Cape Town, George, Mossel Bay, Algoa Bay, Plettenberg Bay and the Lange Kloof. He was on the *Knysna* brig when it made its historic entry up the estuary of the Buffalo River at East London, to land stores for the troops on the eastern frontier. His activities were multifarious.

138

He put in tenders, interviewed captains of various ships (and on occasion 'set them right'), entered into contracts, attended sales, arranged discounts for certain merchants, supervised the loading of the ships and general acted as his father's righthand man. It was he who applied for and received in 1838 a licence to sell or barter gunpowder 'at any private magazine duly approved of by the Governor of the Colony, on his premises situate at *Melkhout Kraal,* and not elsewhere.'[38] He was often up before dawn, returned home after dark and on occasion rode through the night. A very fine man of business was John.

Here, in the yellowing pages of the day-book and the diary lies the answer to the question which has puzzled those who have queried the existence of the alleged royal grant of £1 000 a year – where did George Rex's money come from? It came largely from the virgin forests. For the rest Rex had a virtual monopoly of trade within a radius of 40 or so kilometres. The neatly organised economy of his estate provided his family with meat, vegetables, fruit, meal and grain; fish abounded in the lagoon and hardly a week went by without a buck or two being shot on the hillsides.

He had put down his roots in a spot where nature, impartial in her bounty, was at her most generous to the enterprising.

8 Father, Family and Friends

No one, besides the two persons most intimately concerned, can know the whole truth about the dissolution of a marriage or any other emotional tie. Even when the couple and their domestic circumstances are well known to a friend and when the details of a break-up are related in sorrow or in anger by one or other of the parties concerned, it would be a rash observer indeed who would presume to apportion the blame fairly in such a situation.

How unwise and uncharitable then to attempt to pronounce judgement on a man and woman whose union broke up one hundred and seventy years ago. For the bald fact is that George Rex and Johanna Rosina (Mrs. Rex I) parted, almost certainly, sometime before September 1808. Confirmation of this break lies in the fact that in June 1809, Carolina Margaretha Ungerer, Johanna's second daughter, bore the first of her many children to George Rex.[1] She had obviously supplanted her mother in Rex's affections at least nine months earlier; a situation unusual enough – although she was no blood relation of his – for it to have caused slanderous gossip and unsavoury speculation ever since. It was she, already six months with child and described as the daughter of Hendrik C. Ungerer and Johanna Rosina, who was a sponsor at the baptism of four-year-old Jacob Govert Rex, her step-brother, which took place in the Dutch Reformed Church at Swellendam in March of that same year.[2] Carolina Margaretha, born on 9 April 1793 (according to a note in Thomas Henry Duthie's diary[19]), was only fifteen years old when she conceived her first child. This was not an unusual age for a pregnancy in those days. What was less usual, of course, was the twenty-seven year gap between her age and that of her lord and master. Rex was now forty-three, was in his prime, and presumably he saw in this young girl the fulfilment of his dreams of himself as a patriarchal figure, keeping open-house for all comers, with numerous happy children clustered round his board and an imposing home as background for the idyllic scene. The same quality which had caused Carolina Margaretha to be singled out by Johann Hendrik Ungerer (presumably a blood relation) for retention when

her mother, brothers and sisters had gone to George Rex's household originally, was possibly the quality that appealed to the latter
now. That she was attractive was patent; that she was dark-skinned
we know from the recorded comments of Carl Drège, the German
apothecary who visited Knysna in 1831[3], an unknown artist
(thought to be Frederick Knyvett), who visited *Melkhout Kraal* in
1832 or '33)[4] and by Johan Fredrik Victorin, the talented young
Swedish naturalist, who spent several months in Knysna in 1854,[5]
fifteen years after Rex's death, but while Carolina Margaretha was
still very much alive.

This young woman, was to bear Rex nine children over the next
quarter of a century and to earn the devotion, not only of these nine
offspring of her own, but also of the four children of the previous
alliance, Edward, John, Elisabetta and Jacob. These four young-
sters, her half-brothers and sisters, now became, of course, her
stepchildren as well.

There may have been any of a number of reasons for Johanna
Rosina's departure from *Melkhout Kraal*, or a combination of
reasons. In 1808, she would have been (according to Arthur Beddy's
estimate) about thirty-six years of age, no longer young, and had
already borne eight babies. There is the possibility that she could
not, or was unwilling to, bear any more children and that Rex had –
as was later proved – set his heart on a large family. There is also the
real possibility that cultural differences, which had seemed negligi-
ble when set against their strong initial attraction for each other, had
now assumed the proportions of a high wall between them.

Johanna Rosina, who had grown up in the slave quarters of her
previous owners, could hardly have taken more than an elementary
interest in Rex's business concerns, let alone shared his intellectual
pursuits, his love of books and of music, his knowledge of world
affairs and his penchant for attracting stimulating company. Comely
though she undoubtedly was, she could not have found it easy to
take her place as hostess to the increasingly important personages
who were beginning to visit *Melkhout Kraal* for one reason or the
other. Her's was a poignant situation. Her fine qualities, which came
out so strongly in the four children which she bore Rex, were
apparently not enough to compensate for her lack of background or
to enable her to hold her own in the new world which had opened
up for her on the impressive Knysna estates.

Another factor which would contribute its own quota of awkwardness to what was probably by now a strained situation, was the
presence in the establishment of Johanna Rosina's own three children, Emmerentia, Hendrik and Christje (Christina).

Even where no marked difference exists between the social or racial backgrounds of two generations involved in a step-relationship, the very presence in a household of children who have been fathered by a man other than the current head of the family, creates difficulties hard to envisage by members of an ordinarily united family. In George Rex's case, however good his original intentions were in this respect, he would by 1809 have realised that any idea he might have had of bringing up all these children as his own was impracticable.

It would be futile to pretend that the disruption of this eight-year-old alliance between Rex and Johanna Rosina was not a traumatic experience. Whether it began with a slow attrition of their feelings or whether the break was accompanied by swift, violent scenes, one can only guess. Unfortunately inventive minds and malicious tongues have tried to fill the gaps left by history with highly-coloured speculation and, to this day, lurid, apocryphal versions of the end of Johanna Rosina's regime are animatedly recounted to newcomers to the Knysna district. The true story, though unusual, seems to have been comparatively prosaic. Johanna Rosina Ungerer, described as the mother of Hendrik Christiaan Ungerer, reappears rather surprisingly in the *opgaaf* (official return of residents) of 1 June 1812,[6] four years or so after she had been supplanted by her daughter.

It is patently impossible to discern the realities of the situation out of the mists of the past century and it is more than likely that Rex's impulses and motives were obscure even to himself. Undoubtedly, in addition to the strong patriarchal urge, there was an almost Pygmalion-like element in the man's make-up.

Here was a girl, Carolina Margaretha, who for half of her short life had been brought up in his *ambiance;* he would train her, mould her, and breathe his own kind of life into her as Aphrodite had breathed life into Pygmalion's statue. It was not too late for her inherent traits to be circumfused with the training and education he could give her. On a purely practical level, in fact, it is extremely likely that he himself gave her most of the formal education she received.

There were few schools in the Cape at the beginning of the last century and none at all in the country and there is no record of the older Rex children having been sent away to school or having a tutor at home in the very early days at *Melkhout Kraal*. It is not certain when Mr. Thomas Carter, the Rex tutor, formerly a midshipman in the Royal Navy, joined the household. It is reasonable to assume that the young step-mother, only a few years older than Edward,

142

John, Elisabetta (Betsy) and Jacob, had received at least some of her schooling with her half-brothers and sister, probably at the hands of the master of the household. Rex was well-educated, ambitious for his children, and anxious that his new 'wife' should create a milieu which would be a credit to him. In addition to any book-learning which she acquired (and she wrote a good letter in later life) she would inevitably have absorbed the nuances of culture in the Rex home as naturally as she breathed the clear air of Knysna.

From the moment her first baby, Anne, was born on 8 June 1809, however, Carolina Margaretha had little time for the next quarter of a century to worry her young head about anything but the running of a large household, the arrival of her next baby and the care of those already born. For she bore Rex a further eight children, in this sequence: Frederick (30 August 1811); Carolina (7 August 1813), Christina Wilhelmina (17 September 1815), Louisa Georgina (4 May 1818), George junior (4 December 1822), Sarah (29 April 1824), Maria (1 January 1827) and Thomas Henry (24 July 1834). All the children, of course, were given the surname Rex.[7]

In regard to the question of Rex's antecedents, the godparents cited on Maria's baptismal certificate – a John and Maria Liptrap, of Essex – have special significance, as will be seen later. The ceremony took place at home ('op de plaats van De Heer George Rex') on 20 January 1827,[8] and the babe was clearly named after this Mrs. Liptrap.

The record of Rex's remarkable family of thirteen children (which includes the four born to Johanna Rosina) speaks well for the stock of the parents and the healthy atmosphere in which they were born and thrived. Not one child of the thirteen died in childhood or predeceased their father, and several of them lived to a ripe and fruitful old age. Anne, the pretty second daughter, (Carolina Margaretha's first-born) was the first to go when, at the age of twenty-nine, she died from complications following an attack of measles some eight months after her father's death. Her unmarked grave is next to his at *Melkhout Kraal*.

In the meantime the large, exceptionally united family grew in stature as well as numbers, at first engaged in the timeless pursuits of all country children anywhere and later taking their places in the smooth running of the farm or the busy household.

It is not difficult for us now, having the details of the comfortable homestead, the grass and trees sweeping gently down to the calm lake, the multifarious activities of the farm – the workshops, the dairy, the storage lofts and the big kitchens – the genial character of the man presiding over this domain and the untiring concern of the young mother for the needs of her family, to imagine what a jolly, bustling household this was and what a full and satisfying life its members enjoyed in what may have seemed to outsiders like a quiet backwater.

The most complete picture of the comings and goings of the family and friends in the heyday of *Melkhout Kraal* is, of course, drawn from Rex's diary of 1833-34[9] and a batch of family letters written also mainly in the eighteen thirties. What one gleans from these dusty documents enables the reader to reconstruct, in part at least, the prevailing atmosphere in the busy home, the characteristics of the widely-differing personalities involved in its communal activities, and an impression of the way of life which had evolved in the quiet procession of days, weeks and months of the preceding thirty years.

From the time of the family's arrival in Knysna until after 1834, when the thirteenth child had been born, this was a household in which there was always a baby or two to be fussed over. When the older boys were being set to their lessons, playing their games or, on a Saturday, perhaps being taught to handle a gun, set a trap or catch a fish, were little girls 'helping' mother in the kitchen or sewing their first sampler under Carolina Margaretha's gentle eye, small boys getting up to mischief or being sent off to school in Cape Town, and a baby girl or boy being spoiled by all age groups.

Later the older boys began to take the weight of responsibility off their father's shoulders, the little girls had become young women who painted and sketched, wrote long and loving letters, made their own dresses from materials which Father imported for them, and became skilled in the many household tasks necessarily ever recurring in a family which entertained as frequently as this one did.

Nearly every one of the children learned to play some musical instrument – violin, harp, spinet, accordion or fluitjie (mouth-organ) – and the provision of music for impromptu dances never presented a problem. They all sang, old-time ballads, sea-shanties or the latest 'hit' when new sheet-music arrived from London.

Harmony was the key-note of this exceptionally happy family, the key being set, of course, by the paterfamilias. Any parent today, no matter how superior the educational, social or material advantages enjoyed by their children over those obtaining at *Melkhout Kraal* in the early years of the last century, would be proud to have such telling evidence of powerful family bonds as that which illuminates the letters of George Rex's family. Whether it is Rex himself, writing to his wife or children, children to their parents, sister to sister, brother to half-brother, or older girl to smallest son – through

144

every one of the letters runs the shining thread of genuine affection and a deep love of their home. 'With duty to Papa and love to all brothers and sister' was a common ending for the children to use when writing to their mother, while Rex's to his sons and daughters was frequently 'Your ever affectionate father, G. Rex'.

Perhaps one of the most revealing letters of those extant is the one which the sixty-one year old Rex wrote in August 1826, to his 'wife' then aged thirty-two. He was in Cape Town on business and several phrases in the letter indicate the depth of understanding existing between the couple, as well as his genuine nostalgia for his home and family. In these letters and in his diary he usually referred to Carolina Margaretha (Mrs. Rex II) by the pet name of 'Bess'.

'I have been very anxious for a letter from you and it is with the greatest pleasure that I have received yours of the 30th July, and see that the child is recovered and yourself so much better, and all the rest well. George and Sallie, I have no doubt, are *stout* (mischievous) enough by this time. [George was then four and Sallie two.] When I shall have the happiness of seeing home again I do not know. I am not able yet to fix a day, as the time of my leaving Town is uncertain.'

Having commented on a fire at the drostdy at George, accidents to Primo and Antony (slaves) and the probability of the Government wood being ready for delivery, he goes on: 'You mention the boat of the Government at Plettenberg Bay having to be sold. John has seen it – I have not – but I think we had better purchase it on the recommendation of Captain Harding ... The Life Boat at the Knysna I saw just before I left home. It is all gone to pieces and good for nothing.'

Then follows news of a dinner engagement and a little kindly gossip about Mr. Blair, the new Commissioner, someone apparently known to Carolina Margaretha. 'The latter is to be married to a daughter of Mr. Nourse, the Merchant . . . . . Mr. Blair is of a very good family. I have just now heard he has settled five hundred pounds a year on her, which is a very good thing for Mr. Nourse.'

His mind swiftly returns to his home and children. 'I am glad you have sent a list of things for the Children as well as for the people [the workers on the estate], as we should not otherwise have known what to buy. I shall not forget the Basilie powder for Maria, poor little thing, though I am so glad to find she is well again. As I shall hardly have time to write to Edward by this post, pray tell him that John has ordered his clothes, but that they are not come from the Taylor's – and Jacob's also . . . . .'

'Give my love to all. I have written to Mr. Carter, who has given me a very good account of the school children, particularly of Caroline (aged thirteen) which has pleased me a good deal. Kiss the little ones for me . . .'[10]

Apart from the love of home and family apparent in almost every line, two pointers as to the quality of his relationship with Carolina Margaretha emerge from this letter – his genuine delight at receiving a letter from her and the very natural way in which he takes her into his confidence over business matters, such as the possible purchase of the boat at Plettenberg Bay.

Confirmation of the boat's having been bought by the Rex family exists in the copy of a Vendue Roll of a quantity of stinkwood and one boat, both belonging to the government, sold at Plettenberg Bay on 26 August 1826, by public auction. The record of the sale is signed by H. van Huysteen, Field Cornet.[11]

This good father took the keenest interest in his children's progress with their studies and encouraged them in every way, partly by providing them with a sound selection of books from which to study. A box of carefully selected books used to arrive from England periodically – works by Shakespeare, Bunyan, Jane Austen, Sheridan, Walter Scott, Byron, Southey and Coleridge – as well as essential text-books, and it was probably due to his constant habit of reading aloud to them that all his children showed in later life an excellent feeling for the English language and wrote extremely good letters.

Rex made a note in his diary when Maria, aged seven and a half, 'commenced writing' and of the fact that young George, when he entered Mr. Collins' school in Cape Town, was not so far behind his classfellows as he had expected to be. In the letter quoted above he mentioned his pleasure at receiving a good report on Caroline's progress with her studies and in his diary recorded the fact that Louisa, who was then at Mrs. Sinclair's boarding-school in Uitenhage, had written requesting that 'A History of Rome, a History of Greece, Magnall's Questions, a drawing-box and cardboard, a slate and pencil', be sent to her. Both the boys and girls seem to have inherited his own love of natural history and made collections of shells, pressed flowers, seaweed, butterflies, moths, beetles, and sometimes stuffed birds and fish.

In addition to their formal studies, the children learned the social graces of singing and dancing, painting and sketching, riding and chess-playing. All in all they made up an accomplished family and their good manners, social graces and intelligence were remarked on by more than one visitor to *Melkhout Kraal*.

Collectively they charmed all comers; individually they developed as diverse temperaments as is possible among the members of any other families which are controlled by an exceptionally dominant parent. The characters and interests of the older offspring, the young men in particular, are captured and crystalised for us most clearly in the slice of life portrayed for us in their father's diary. He was then rising sixty-nine.

John, as already noted, was the ears, eyes and capable hands of his father, but he was much more than merely an astute young business man. It was he who was deputed to ride out to greet important guests as they approached Knysna, or to see others safely on their way when they left *Melkhout Kraal*. He went to Cape Town and other centres more frequently than any other member of the family and, as has been mentioned, acted for his father in numerous business transactions. The fact that he had apparently inherited, more than most other members of the family, his mother's colouring, did not in any way affect his being on cordial terms with his father's friends and business acquaintances. (John's swarthy complexion caused some astonishment among the servants at Protea – later Bishop's Court – when he called on Bishop Gray and his wife there.)[12] Nor did his appearance, although it did occasionally give rise to casual comment, lessen the respect and affection which he inspired in others.

When John Findlay, captain of the Rex brig, the *Knysna*, possibly having prematurely celebrated Hogmanay, behaved 'in a very rude and disrespectful manner towards Edward' on New Year's Eve, 1833, 'John went down himself . . . and found it a proper opportunity set him right.' John, so 'circumstanced', did not invite Findlay to dine the following day, as had been intended; he was too forthright and forceful a character to do this immediately after having exchanged angry words with the man. Mr. Rex, however, healed the breach by sending a note to be delivered to Captain Findlay on board and the latter presumably joined the Rex family for dinner on New Year's Day.

The fourth son in the family, Frederick, a high-spirited and venturesome youth, was the only one who chose to cut the ties binding him to his home and to make a career for himself outside of Knysna. Having had some training in Cape Town as a land surveyor, he decided at the age of twenty-three to volunteer for service on the eastern frontier when the major Kaffir War broke out towards the end of 1834. His career bespeaks an astonishing versatility. Having been made a quartermaster and finding that he thoroughly disliked the work, he soon managed to be appointed an ensign in the 1st Battalion. His lively letters to all at home, but

147

particularly to 'My Dear Papa', give a vivid account of the vicissitudes of war in that rough terrain against a primitive and unpredictable opponent. His father's letters at that time were full of concern for his son's safety and a quiet pride in the young ensign's daring, a trait more than once commented upon by his superior officers.

After the end of the war Frederick obtained various commissions to survey and lay out, in turn, Fort Beaufort, Winburg and Smithfield. He was the only son to get married in his father's lifetime. Having been engaged briefly, while on active service, to the daughter of a staff surgeon, he thought better of it and later married instead Johanna Elizabeth Bain, daughter of the famous Andrew Geddes Bain, geologist and pioneer road engineer – a match which delighted his family. This was in September 1838, so George Rex had the satisfaction of seeing the most spirited of his sons happily settled down just seven months before he died.

A fine portrait of Frederick, in the possession of the family, is by an unknown artist, thought to be F.T.I' Ons. It is characteristic of the work of this artist who had settled in Grahamstown in 1834 and it is very possible that he and Frederick would have met.

Young George, who was said to be the image of his father and who had a warm, outgoing personality, was only seventeen when his father died, but was already undertaking a number of useful tasks around the farm. He was an excellent shot, having dropped his first buck at the age of ten. In July 1834, when he was twelve, his father recorded proudly, 'George shot owl in vineyard.'

Another terse entry in Rex's diary, 'Child born 4 p.m.' against the date 24 July 1834, recorded the arrival of the youngest child, Thomas Henry Rex. It is apparent from various entries and references in letters that this baby engaged the family's affections in a special way. Anne, in a letter to Louisa a few months later writes, 'Dear Little Tom is just three months today and you can't think how forward he is for his age. He knows every one of us perfectly and put out his little hands when he sees Papa, who is become his horse and rides him to Rondebosch. Cry he seldom does . . .'

George Rex mentions Tom in a letter to Anne too: 'He is, I can assure you, perfectly well, and as saucy and engaging as ever.' And in a letter to his only sister, Sarah Rex, who lived in Bath, he wrote, '. . . little Tom grows a fine boy, active and intelligent.'

This child of his old age gave Rex great joy. He was rising sixty-nine when Tom was born, a fact which must have been a special source of pride to him. To become a father when nearly seventy is a remarkable achievement enough, but if the date – 1760

– put forward by Rex family tradition as having been Rex's birth-date is correct,[13] he would then have become a father at seventy-four, an event which would surely have hit the headlines, even in those days.

Betsy, the eldest daughter, was a stay-at-home, who never married. She took on many duties around the farm, in particular the care of the poultry yard, but was also an intelligent and well-educated woman. She was singled out for special attention by several of the important guests who called at *Melkhout Kraal* in the course of their travels eastward. She was presented with an exquisitely carved set of chessman by Lord Charles Somerset, with a calf-bound album by Baron C.F.H. von Ludwig, a particular friend of George Rex, and with a butterfly net by Louis Verreaux, the French naturalist who visited the Cape in the eighteen-thirties.[14] She had helped the last-named with his collections of moths and butterflies during his prolonged visit to Knysna, during which he stayed with the Veld-man family at *Springfield*.

Anne, when she was nearly twenty-eight years old in 1837, was left for six months in Cape Town to stay with various family friends, among them Judge and Mrs. Menzies, who reciprocated the hospi-tality the judge enjoyed at *Melkhout Kraal* whenever he was on circuit. (Readers will remember that William Menzies, who had served as a Register's Clerk in the Vice-Admiralty Court, was an uncle of this judge).

Her father too was in Cape Town for part of the time, because an affectionate letter, dated 17 March and addressed to 'Myn Lewe Bess' (Carolina Margaretha), throws an interesting sidelight on Anne's stay in town and was most likely, therefore, written in 1837. Rex warns 'Bess' of a pretty large party of people connected with the circuit court who are about to visit *Melkhout Kraal* and hopes she will not be too greatly inconvenienced. He gives her news of the three children in Cape Town at that time, George at school but spending every week-end with his father for as long as the latter is in town; Sally whom he hopes to get into a good school, Miss Mathews', at Rondebosch, and Anne, who had been staying with the Ludwigs, but is now with Mrs. Menzies.

There appears to have been an unfortunate *contretemps* while Anne was with Mrs. Ludwig, because Rex goes into some detail about Mrs. Ludwig's rude behaviour to Anne and the fact that the older woman now wanted back the ill-advised letter which she had written to the girl. Rex, tactful as always, writes: 'I appear to know little about the matter and go and dine there or she sends me some Dinner here from her Table as usual'. From this it sounds very much as if he, too, was staying with the Ludwigs. Ludwig, of whom more later, was a business associate and fairly close friend of George Rex.

Always solicitous for his children's welfare, Rex reports that he has spoken to Major Michell (Major Charles Cornwallis Michell, then surveyor-general and superintendent of works in the Cape Colony) about Frederick and has no doubt that the Major will do what he could for the young surveyor, says that John will write to Jacob about some sheep of Piet van Rooyen's, and asks his 'wife' to thank Edward for his kind letter and information on the *opgaaf* paper (census) that has been sent to everyone in the district. The writer sends his love *to all on both sides of the river* (a reference, of course, to the Duthie household at Belvidere), and concludes, 'Kiss the Children all for me, Your ever affectionate, G. Rex.'[15]

Anne's letters home at this time are lively proof of two things – that she was poised and attractive enough to hold her own in the round of parties, dances, balls and luncheons which largely made up the way of life of Cape society at the time, and that once the initial excitement had died down, she was longing for the security of her own home at Knysna and the companionship of her brothers and sisters. Perhaps she had some vague premonition that she was soon to die. It was 'Brother John' who set out with the wagon for Cape Town and brought the homesick Anne back with him.

Christina and Louisa, aged eighteen and fifteen respectively at the time when Rex began his daily record of events and comments, were caught up in the cheerful round of domestic activities, when not at their studies; accompanying their mother on little visits to friends in the vicinity; helping to prepare for the numerous house guests; joining in picnics and riding parties, and even being allowed to stay up late, no doubt, when games or dancing were on the schedule for the evenings.

Christina was not only helpful to her mother; her father in his late sixties was delegating more and more of his duties to his children and to Christina fell the task of dealing with postal matters. Letters exchanged between Rex and his fourth daughter make it clear that she was conscientious and sharp-witted in dealing with her responsibilities.

The youngest daughters, Maria (six) and Sallie (nine) merited no more mention at this stage than an occasional 'Maria hurt her arm in lathe' or 'Maria and Sallie come home from Veldmans', but were no doubt underfoot at every turn, thoroughly enjoying the comings and goings in this busy household.

But it is on Caroline, the lovely twenty-year-old Caroline, that most attention was focussed in the early thirties, in spite of some odd lacunae in her father's diary. She, the only daughter to marry in her father's lifetime, had been wooed for nearly three years, in the leisurely manner of the day, by the handsome Lieutenant Thomas Henry Duthie of the 72nd Highlanders (Duke of Albany's own Regiment) who was stationed for several years at the Castle, Cape Town. Duthie, who had studied at St. Andrews' University and the Military Academy, Edinburgh, before coming to South Africa,[16] who was personable, well-educated, exceptionally charming and *persona grata* with all the leading personalities in Cape society, met Mr. Rex in Cape Town on several occasions, once preparing for a ball at the Castle; one evening over dinner at Judge Kekewich's home; at Government House; at Colonel Munro's and at a New Year's Eve party at Mr. Oliphant's at Camp Bay.

(George Kekewich, who was an old legal friend of Rex, had served in the Vice-Admiralty Court for seventeen years during the second British occupation, before becoming a puisne judge of the newly-established Supreme Court with the learned William Menzies in 1828.[17] It has been said of the latter that no one matched him in the mastery of legal principles at this time.[18])

When Thomas Duthie mentioned that he was anxious to arrange a shooting trip to the eastern Cape, naturally Mr. Rex warmly invited him to stay at *Melkhout Kraal* when passing. Thanks to Duthie's facile pen, we have an exceptionally vivid account of the impression made on him by the happy family at Knysna, the hunting and fishing parties (shark fishing too), the picnics, dances, games of chess in the evenings or delightful days spent idling away the time down at the swing in the garden. A pastoral idyll emerges from the word picture he drew.[19] George Rex had lately purchased *Belvidere* on the bank of the lagoon opposite his own home and Duthie was even then struck with the possibilities of this quiet haven. 'Much pleased with all the family, particularly Miss Caroline', was the first of many enthusiastic entries in his journal, as he fell increasingly in love with dark-eyed Caroline, the beauty of the family.

There were further visits, more picnics and dances, more shooting trips, and eventually the joy of becoming engaged, in December 1832, to his 'beloved Caroline.' One of the qualities about her which most attracted this young man of the world, was her unspoilt, unsophisticated outlook on life, she who had never travelled further than about thirty kilometres from her home.

They were married in the Military Chapel in the Barracks, Cape Town, on 12 February 1833. Mr. Rex, John, Anne and young

George travelled to Cape Town for the occasion and Caroline, who stayed with Judge and Mrs. Menzies at their home, *Sans Souci*, before the wedding, was given away by the judge. After a brief honeymoon at Wynberg, in a cottage which had been lent them by one of Duthie's brother officers, they sailed for England where for well over a year they visited relatives, among them Thomas Henry's brother, the Reverend Archibald Hamilton Duthie, at Minster, in Kent, and his sisters and aunts in Edinburgh.[20]

Although the Duthie clan were delighted with the modest girl from far-off South Africa and she most grateful to them, she was aching for the long-planned visit to her own aunt, Miss Sarah Rex, of Bath, 'thinking I will feel her more my own'. Sarah was, of course, George Rex's only sister, a spinster. Aunt and niece were charmed with each other and Miss Rex gave Caroline a pair of dainty ear-rings which George Rex had given his sister forty-two years previously.

Miss Sarah Rex got on famously too, with Caroline's debonair young Scottish husband and in years following included many affectionate messages for him in her letters to Knysna. Typical was a letter of September 1837, in which she writes to Caroline, 'Pray let me hear from you soon. Tell me of my dear Brother, a constant source of pleasure. The anecdotes of your little nursery amuse me – indeed I shall be interested in all you say and I hope I may congratulate Mr. Duthie on his rising prospects. Remember me most kindly to him . . . . .'[21]

While the Duthies were still in Britain, their first child, a daughter, was born, in November 1833. She was named Caroline after her mother and grandmother. Ten months later, on 13 September 1834, the little family of three landed back in Table Bay, full of hopes and plans for the home which they had decided to build at *Belvidere,* recently purchased by Thomas Henry from his kindly father-in-law.

Excitement was mounting at *Melkhout Kraal* for weeks before their return. Caroline Duthie was the only one of the family so far to have ventured further than Cape Town and would have wondrous tales to tell her Rex brothers and sisters. Besides, the Baby Caroline was Rex's and Carolina Margaretha's first grandchild. Their own three-month-old baby, Thomas Henry Rex, was, quaintly enough, eight months younger than the grandchild, the new baby's niece, and one can imagine the fussing, exclaiming and comparing of nursery notes that went on between mother and daughter when the two babies were bedded down together at *Melkhout Kraal.*

Brother John, stalwart as always, took the eldest daughter,

Betsy with him in the bullock wagon to fetch Duthie, Caroline and the baby back from Cape Town. George Rex wrote to the Duthies to reach them at Cape Town, on their arrival in the *Lord Hungerford,* and again to catch them at Swellendam, where they would be bound to stop on their way home. The despatch of these letters was recorded, along with the usual minutiae of the daily round, the loading of timber, postal troubles, movements of ships and so on, but strangely enough as the actual date of the Duthies' arrival drew near, Rex seems to have been pre-occupied with other matters, in particular the arrival on 26 October of Major A. C. Gregory and his friends, Mr. Wallace and Mr. Halliburton.[22]

On Tuesday, 28 October, two wagon-loads of Duthie's and Rex's goods – including ten rabbits – were brought up to *Melkhout Kraal* and the following day the postboy reported having seen John's wagon at Swartvlei that morning. John and little George rode out to meet the homecoming party and at halfpast nine that evening, the travellers returned. Apart from listing the cost of the sheep which Duthie had purchased on the way home, there is no reference in Rex's diary for that or any following day to the fact that his daughter, who had been absent from home for a year and nine months, his first grandchild and his well-liked son-in-law had returned. He was obviously not a man given to committing his deep feelings to his diary. (In corroboration, his only entry for Christmas Day, 1833, is 'To the fishwater'.)

For the week following the Duthies' return, Major Gregory and his friends provided subject for comment every day, usually a note of the number of bushbuck or snipe they had shot. One day a fishing party with Duthie is mentioned. Although Major Gregory, whose well-known sketch of *Melkhout Kraal* is reproduced on Plate 7, was the recognised artist of the party (Mr. Harry Oppenheimer possesses an album of his sketches), it is Mr. Wallace only, strangely enough, who is three times mentioned by Rex as having been occupied with sketching. Possibly he was practising under Major Gregory's expert eye.

Thomas and Caroline Duthie built their spacious home at *Belvidere* – 'this enchanting spot' – and thanks to Rex's help in the matter of procuring materials and marshalling a labour force before their return, it was ready for them to occupy by April 1835. Here they lived, prospered and brought up a large family. There was regular communication between *Belvidere House* and *Melkhout Kraal* and when visits were not convenient, notes were ferried back and forth across the Knysna lagoon.

By the mid-thirties the backwater of Knysna was no longer so quiet. There was an almost constant stream of visitors and from both their own accounts and Rex's jottings, we get a clearer picture of life on the hospitable farm than at any other time. The visitors fell into several categories – Government officials with business to see to in the area; missionaries; military men, often on their way to and from duty on the troubled eastern frontier; members of the circuit court; Anglo-Indians on furlough taking the opportunity of seeing something of this country before returning to India; Rex's friends and business associates, and last, but most numerous, the families living round about Knysna, at Springfield, Goukamma, Portland, De Poort and Plettenberg Bay.

A bare list of names of these numerous visitors, some well-known and of distinguished rank, is of limited interest except to a zealous historian, but excerpts from their accounts do help to clarify traits in the character of the genial host of *Melkhout Kraal* and the life there better than his own detached comments do. For instance, C. I. Latrobe, a missionary appointed by the United Brethren to visit the mission settlements at Genadendal and Groenekloof, arrived in Knysna in 1815 with a small party and accompanied by Mr. Melville, the land surveyor.[23] Mr. van Kervel, the landdrost at George, had kindly sent word of their approach ahead to Rex.

The missionaries and Mr. Melville received a warm welcome not only from the head of the house, but from 'Mr. Rex's lady' who insisted that her servants should assist the ladies in the party with certain household tasks. 'Mr. Rex found in Mr. Melville's company and conversation much pleasure and information respecting the measurement of land . . .' and was anxious that they should stay for more than one night. It was with difficulty that they persuaded him that they must press on to *Jackals Kraal,* near Plettenberg Bay, which Latrobe was to inspect with a view to starting a mission establishment there. Although Rex had recently applied to the government for ownership of *Jackals Kraal* with a view to putting up a small hunting lodge there, he was generously prepared to forego his claim if Latrobe and his brethren should decide it was suitable for their purpose, 'and rejoiced in the hopes of seeing the land cultivated and a settlement of Christian Hottentots formed in the neighbourhood.'

The host rode part of the way to Plettenberg Bay with them (he was then fifty) telling them as they went the horrifying story of the murders which had taken place at a particular point on the road, De Poort, during the Kaffir uprising of 1802.

Jackals Kraal as a site for a mission, however, was later rejected as being too small by Dr. J. T. van der Kemp, who as chief representative of the London Missionary Society in the Colony had the final

154

say. It was also rejected by the Hottentots accompanying Latrobe on account of its being 'sour veld'. Leaving *Jackals Kraal* to cross the mountains, Latrobe's party called at Veld Cornet van Huysteen's house at Wittedrift, where they were again most hospitably entertained and presented by Mrs. van Huysteen on their departure 'with two cocks, a large square bottle of honey and some other useful articles'.

Another caller who visited Knysna a number of times from 1818 onwards was James Bowie, a botanist from Kew Gardens. He became very friendly with the Rex family, who helped him with his collections of rare seeds and plants. Sometimes he stayed with them for several months at a time and there are many tributes in his diary to their hospitality and helpfulness: 'I once more quitted the friendly home of Mr. Rex, who, with his family, treated me with the greatest respect, and with whom I always considered myself at home' was one of the last entries he made before leaving South Africa in 1823.[24]

George Thompson, the merchant (whose book, *Travels and Adventures in South Africa*, published in 1827, was considered by Theal as 'one of the best that has ever been written upon South Africa') gave the following description of a visit to Knysna in 1823: 'At nine o'clock I reached the home of Mr. Rex, from whom I met with a very cordial reception and was prevailed upon by his hospitable intreaties to defer the prosecution of my journey till the next morning. Mr. Rex is a gentleman of excellent education and elegant manners, who has been in the Colony upwards of twenty-six years. On his first arrival he occupied a high situation under the Colonial Government, but having soon afterwards received an extensive grant of land at this place he retired hither, and has since augmented his estate by considerable purchase.'[25]

Cowper Rose, of the Royal Engineers (whose role in the naming of the brig, *The Knysna*, has already been mentioned) was lyrically enthusiastic about the setting in which Mr. Rex lived and his whole way of life: 'It will be long ere I can forget the beauty of the scenery among which Mr. Rex lives, or the kind welcome that he gave to a stranger; and to meet the information and manners of the polished life, without its hackneyed and wearying forms, in a situation so wildly remote, has an effect not easily described, and one from which I found it most difficult to escape. Through the whole establishment there was an air of active industry, and it seemed to possess every thing within itself – carpenters, masons, saddlers, etc. – while the house and gardens were in the nicest order.'[26] This was in 1828.

James Holman, the blind but intrepid traveller, was another

caller about this time who commented that he 'met with a most gratifying reception from Mr. Rex and all his family, having been previously acquainted with that gentleman, and his two eldest sons, at Cape Town.'[27]

When Andrew Steedman was a guest at *Melkhout Kraal* in 1833, Rex's brig had broken away from her moorings during a gale and was high and dry upon the shore for four days. His description of the efforts of the Rex sons, the neighbours and numerous workmen to refloat her, complements the following notes made by George Rex about this dramatic episode: 'Weather cloudy, After breakfast came on to blow very hard from NW. At 12 very heavy – at I the Brig on shore on the Island . . . The gale increases and is very heavy at 2 o'clock – about high water.'

The following day, he noted that it 'Blew very hard all last night in squalls with rain. The Brig high and dry on the Island. The weather moderates this morning but still blows from NW.' On Wednesday 'all our people from the Bosch with wagons and oxen' took the cargo out of the brig, but it was not till the following day, Thursday, that Rex was able to report 'All hands at work getting out the timber etc. The Brig floated to her anchorage at 3 o'clock, just before high water.'

Andrew Steedman regretfully left 'the hospitable mansion of Mr. Rex, from whom I had received that kindness and attention which is so unversally experienced by all who visit him.'[28]

In 1834 the Ludwigs, of Cape Town, spent more than three weeks at *Melkhout Kraal*. Of all George Rex's friends, more is known about Carel Ferdinand Heinrich Ludwig than about most of the others, thanks to his own account of the Ludwigs' visit and to the impressive research of Frank Bradlow, author of the delightful biography, *Baron von Ludwig and the Ludwig's-Burg Gardens*.[29] There are certain analogies in the careers of these two contemporaries, which possibly explain not only their friendship and shared interests, but also reveal parallels in their personalities and histories.

Ludwig was an exceptionally able son of a poor church clerk in the little town of Sulz, Württenberg, who came to the Cape in 1805 (a year after Rex had settled at Knysna) in answer to a newspaper advertisement to fill a vacancy in a pharmacist's business in Cape Town. He had qualified as an apothecary in Württenberg. Within a short time he married in the Lutheran Church, Alida Maria van de Kaap, the widow of one Carel Freidrich Heinrich Altenstaedt. (She was Ludwig's first wife, the second being Eliza Griffith, whom he married in 1847). From her first husband Alida inherited a thriving tobacco business which she continued to run and, thanks to this source of steady income, Ludwig was able to devote himself largely to his special interests, which were scientific and botanical. He established a unique collection of rare plants, established the famous Ludwig's-Burg Gardens, and his services to science were so remarkable that, in recognition of them and the credit he had brought to his country of origin, the King of Württenberg acceded to his petition to be created a Baron of Württenberg. He was thus entitled to prefix his name with the distinguished 'von'.

Rex's notes on the Ludwig visit indicate that a close friendship existed between the two families and it is of interest that this was almost the only occasion on which Mrs. Ludwig is reported as having been involved in any of her husband's social activities. There are mentions of John going with Mr. Ludwig and Verreaux to see the Strelitzias (the *Strelitzia angusta*, the indigenous wild banana, which can grow to a height of seven metres and more); of the Ludwigs' party going in the wagon to *Eastford;* of the Rex daughters preparing garlands with which to deck the door of Mrs. Ludwig's room on the morning of her fiftieth birthday; of 'Bess' (Mrs. Rex II) and Mrs. Ludwig going in the family wagon to see the 'Hout Bosch' (forest); and of the invitation from the Ludwigs to take one of the girls back with them to Cape Town to stay the winter with them. It was agreed to allow Betsy Rex, then over thirty years old, to go with them.

Their itinerary included a visit to the Cango Caves and then a return to George, Worcester, Paarl and Swartland on their way back to Cape Town. John, on horse-back, accompanied their wagon as far as George to see them safely over the precipitous Cradock's Pass above it.

As often happens when men of humble origin are outstandingly successful in their careers, grandiloquent stories are spread about their backgrounds. Extravagant rumours about Ludwig's origins began to circulate and, with variations, were repeated by certain of his descendants after his death. It was given out that he was a German nobleman; a son of the Chief Justice of Württenberg and a bosom friend of King Wilhelm; that he had come to the Cape in 1800 as a result of a duel which he had fought at home and that his children had grown up and been educated with those of the King of Württenberg!

He was reported as having driven every day in a superbly mounted equipage, drawn by six white stallions, to release his wife from her labours at the shop and take her back to the lovely house in Kloof Street, whereas, in fact, he at no time possessed a house in Kloof Street and his carriage was a neat little phaeton, drawn by four cream-coloured ponies. Another claim stated that 'What is today known as *Loretto* was his residence where he lorded it in feudal state.' *Loretto* was never his residence; he lived in St. George's Street, comfortably but not in feudal state. And so it went on, each generation probably contributing another highly-embroidered tale to follow on top of the others, until through sheer repetition, some descendants came to believe them to be true.

Ludwig's achievements were indeed remarkable and varied enough, in all conscience, to earn him a place in history without any such tarradiddle being added to his story. Through him Rex was at this period kept in touch with new thinking in the world of science, as his friend was closely associated with many of the leading scientists of Europe at the time.

In November 1838, only five months before Rex died, George Washington Walker, of Newcastle-upon-Tyne, accompanied by his friend, James Backhouse, both Quaker missionaries, came to *Melkhout Kraal*. The latter was a shrewd observer and lively recorder of their experiences. From his pen we have the usual appreciation of the warm hospitality for which *Melkhout Kraal* was famous and also a few succint observations on persons who played some part in Rex's life.[30] Having described a prayer meeting at *Melkhout Kraal*, held to set forth the blessings of the gospel to the family, servants and a few friends, Backhouse continues: 'The family had received a good education, and their schoolmaster, a feeble diminutive old man, more than eighty years old, was kindly provided for among them.' This was, of course, Mr. Carter, the 'little white dwarf', as another traveller described him earlier, who had been living with the family for many years. He lies buried in an unmarked grave in the family encosure at *Melkhout Kraal*, together with the remains of George Rex, Anne, and Mr. and Mrs. George Rex junior.

Backhouse then went on to describe the lack of medical facilities at Knysna and how he had perforce to act as locum tenens for the unlicensed apothecary, Wickham: 'No medical man resided nearer this place than George, forty miles distant, but an intelligent mason usually supplied the defect; he was ill at this time, and I was therefore applied to on behalf of the Captain of the cutter now lying here. I found him in a critical state from the use of strong drink.' The cutter, the *Friends Goodwill*, with the *St. Helena* and *The Knysna* (Rex's brig), was lying in the harbour.

The 'intelligent mason' was Robert Henry Wickham of Plettenberg Bay, who was unfortunately ill at this time, but who followed an unusual combination of callings in that he supplemented his income from stone-cutting by practising as a much-needed apothecary for the local population. He eked out his career as a stone-mason as best he could but also ranged far and wide visiting the sick. His services were undoubtedly much in demand and he was either skilled or lucky – or both – because no dissatisfaction with his treatments is recorded. He attended 'Bess' (Mrs. Rex II) both before and after the birth of her last infant, Thomas Henry.

One may smile at Rex's cryptic entry, 'Wickham on his way home from Boshof's wife', indicating – one hopes – yet another successful confinement. This stone-mason-cum-apothecary-cum-farmer was somewhat dilatory in settling a certain debt to the Rex family and the sorry business dragged on for many months. On one occasion George Rex wryly commented on the versatile Wickham staying on uninvited, when he had called officially as a part-time census enumerator, seating himself at the dinner-table and 'is one of the company in the sitting-room afterwards for the whole evening'. But on the whole good relations existed between the apothecary and the family at *Melkhout Kraal* and it was Wickham who attended the *grand seigneur* himself in his last illness.

The last visitor of note to *Melkhout Kraal* before Rex died was the scientist, Dr. Ferdinand Krauss, later to become Director of the famous Botanical Museum at Stuttgart. He mentions in his diary of January 1839, the 'European-style' environment which Rex had created, the attractive surroundings in which he lived and the wealth of interesting flora and fauna of the district.[31]

* * *

Not least important of the many facets of life reflected in the faded jottings of the worn diary, is the light thrown on the course of the lives of Johanna Rosina's own three children – Carolina Margaretha's siblings – after the dramatic rift with her protector several years before.

Johanna Rosina herself, as the *opgaaf* of 1812 reflected, was still alive in that year, living quietly at Springfield with her family, Emerentia (also referred to as Emmerentia Helena van Wyngaarden), Hendrik Christiaan Ungerer and Christina Maria – Christje (sometimes with the surname Nieuwel or Newell).

But Johanna Rosina was soon to die. Her death probably took place on 9 November 1814.[32] It does not seem likely that another Johanna Rosina van de Caap, who died in 1820 at the age of sixty-six years and six months, could – in view of her age – have been Mrs. Rex I.[33]

Beddy, who has gone to immense pains to locate the exact site of her grave, after many years has satisfied himself that she is buried near the eastern boundary of *Springfield* on the road to Plettenberg

Bay, just beyond Brackenhill. The exact site, unmarked, may lie in a clump of cottonwood poplars near the *four* seventeenth kilometre stone on the national road, or the road itself may have swept right over it. Her family had seen to it that her body received a seemly burial.

Rex, in his diary, frequently refers to 'Emmerens – Emerentia – Emmarens – Amerentia – Emmerentia or Esmerens' (his spelling of names is nothing if not erratic) visiting *Melkhout Kraal* and sometimes staying over for a few days, her name being linked with that of her husband, Gerhardus (or Gert) Stroebel, whom she had married in 1817.

A sisterly note was struck when a little more than a fortnight *before* the birth of George Rex's and Carolina Margaretha's last baby in July 1834, 'Ammerentia came' and on 4 August, ten days *after* the birth, she left, indicating that she had remained at *Melkhout Kraal* for this period to help her sister over the period of her confinement. Sadly, she died in July 1838, leaving three sons aged eighteen to twenty-one years.[34]

Hendrik Ungerer was quite an important cog in the agricultural and commercial complex of *Melkhout Kraal*, as evidenced by the fact that his wagon was often hired for special purposes; that he brought timber down from the forests for loading at the landing-stage; that he asked John to bring him back a saddle from Cape Town; that he asked John to bid for him for some land in the Piesang Valley being sold by auction; that he owned oxen and, later, his own property, at Concordia.[35] Altogether he seems to have been a hard-working and independent man, whose activities were closely related to those of the family at 'the Big House'. In 1816, Hendrik had married Anna Christina Kap,[36] who during their subsequent half-century of married life, produced a large family. At the baptism of their son, Hendrik, in 1822, John Rex's name headed the list of witnesses.[37]

There was a little family tension on one occasion when Gert Stroebel, an expert woodman, had encountered and shot an elephant and was to be paid a hundred and eighty rix-dollars for it by Verreaux. Hendrik Ungerer had transported the carcase from the forest for him and a disagreement ensued over Hendrik's demand for his share of the money which Gert had been paid by Verreaux. After some days of strained relations, came the entry in the diary: 'Emmerens and Gert –to keep good friends it seems – agreed to pay Ungerer the amount he demanded.' On New Year's Eve 1833, Edward, John, Jacob, Frederick and George Rex (junior) went to Gert Stroebel's home – presumably to celebrate.

References to 'Chris – Chris Veldman – Christje – Chris V – or C. Veldman, her child and nurse' do not occur as frequently as those

160

IN
MEMORY
OF
GEORGE REX ESQUIRE
PROPRIETOR
AND FOUNDER OF KNYSNA,
DIED 3ʳᵈ APRIL 1839

George Rex's tombstone in the ground of Old Place (MELKHOUT KRAAL) a few metres off the National Road east of Knysna. The omission of a birthdate in the inscription on the stone has intensified speculation about Rex's origins. (Photo: Geoff Causton)

At this Court It was found by the homage that present Hopkins widow of & &
Thomas Hopkins dyed seized and so and that Theodore Hopkins her daughter & &
afterwards marryed Mr Thomas Rex a Distiller and that they are both dead and that &
they left Issue out only Son named John Rex now of Goodmans fields Distiller and that he &
the said John Rex is heires as Grandson of the said Thomas Hopkins and present his &
wife and also as only Son and heir of the said Thomas Rex and present his wife to All those
three acres and three Roods of Land be the same more or lesse lying in Bromley in &
the parish of West Ham in the said County of Essex formerly in the Tennure of Ralph & &
Thomson and afterwards of Joseph Robibout and now of John Warren with their & &
Rights Members and appurtenances Now at this Court Came into Court the said
John Rex and brought into Court the last Will and Testament of his late Grandfather the

John In the Name of God Amen.
Rex.
I John Rex of the parish of Saint Mary Whitchapel
in the County of Middlesex Distiller being somewhat
weak in Body but of sound and disposing Mind Memory
and understanding praised be God Do make and publish
This my last Will and Testament in manner and form
my first Debts and funeral Expences be fully paid and
satisfied In the next place I give Devise and Bequeath
unto my beloved wife Sarah Rex and her Assigns all
that my Messuages after of Land lying and being Appointment Ware in Distilton Quand in the parish of West
Ham in the County of Essex and also all those my two-
acres of Land lying and being in Plaistow Quand
aforesaid with their and every of their appurts part
of which said Lands are Freehold and other part thereof the

An extract from the application of John Rex (George's father) to inherit the lands in
Plaistow Marsh which were specified in the will of John's maternal grandfather,
Thomas Hopkins. (By permission of the Essex Record Office. Ref. D/DPé M5)

of the other two children of Johanna Rosina. This was Christina Maria, or Christje, the youngest of Johanna Rosina's own children, who was married to Frederick John Veldman. Christina bore two daughters to Veldman, but less than a month after the arrival of the second in 1834, she died at Kruysfontein *(Springfield)*, aged about thirty-five years, [38] probably from complications arising from her confinement. Of a generation of seventeen souls, related through Johanna Rosina and Carolina Margaretha, she was the first to go. In his journal, Thomas Henry Duthie commented sympathetically that 'poor Mrs. Veldman' had died during the night.

All the evidence points, therefore, to Rex (far from having cast Johanna Rosina and her family into the wilderness) having humanely helped them to lead their independent but somewhat interlinked lives on his ground at *Springfield*. Here they went about their humble occasions, without fuss or compulsion. Sometimes the little community descended on *Melkhout Kraal en masse* and the diary lists the names of the Ungerers, Stroebels, Veldmans and their in-laws, the Kaps, 'etc. etc. etc.', this indicating, in Rex's drily humorous way, their numerous progeny and possibly nursemaids.

*   *   *

The only extant correspondence with any member of his family in England with whom George Rex had maintained links was that with his sister, Sarah. There is no known record of his having written to his brother, John, and unfortunately even among the letters to Sarah the earliest available is dated 1830. Any letters written during the preceding thirty-three years, since Rex had left England, have been lost or destroyed. The tone of the letters to Sarah is unstrained and affectionate, giving no indication of any sort of a rift having existed between them, so it is very probable that many earlier letters were written but have gone the way of most family letters. It is curious that even among those which have survived, there are parts missing and even signs of excisions here and there.

In his letter of 14 October 1830, (the earliest one extant)[39] Rex gives his sister details of the progress being made by the children, of the visitors to *Melkhout Kraal* (Sir Lowry Cole, then Governor of the Cape, had called there shortly before this letter was written), of his shipbuilding and business activities and the improving land values at Knysna.

He makes only one reference to family and friends belonging to his former life in London: 'I shall be happy to hear of the welfare of Maria and John (for so I claim the privilege of calling him). They may perhaps touch at the Cape on their return from India and take *Melkhout Kraal* in their way, which I should in that case certainly promise myself.'

He was referring here to the Maria, to whom Sarah Rex refers in her letters as 'my niece'. In 1825, long after Rex had settled at the Cape, Maria had married John Liptrap, who did exceptionally well in the British army in India, was at this stage a first-lieutenant, expecting to be promoted to captain*. This is the same couple whose names appear as sponsors on Maria Rex's baptismal record in 1827, but this did not necessarily mean that they were present at the ceremony.

In the few surviving letters from Sarah to her brother over the next eight years, there are further references to Maria and John Liptrap and to other members of the Liptrap family – to 'Amelia, the only surviving daughter of our friend Liptrap', to 'Mrs. Sam Liptrap who is very stout and her husband very thin', again to 'Mrs. Samuel Liptrap, the daughter of our old Friend, who was always very much attached to me' and to the death of 'friend Samuel Liptrap' who died after a lingering illness.[40] Four members of this family were beneficiaries under Sarah Rex's will[41] and the significance of the friendship between the Liptraps and the Rexes will emerge in the next chapter.

In Sarah's first letter, a young woman named Emma, is mentioned, but there is no indication of her relationship to the Rexes. She died in October 1830, 'in a rapid consumption', to the great grief of the stricken Sarah. It is possible that the spinster, comfortably off and lonely, had adopted this 'beloved girl' at some stage. It would be fascinating to know more about the enigmatic Emma. Whose child was she? She was only eighteen months old when she first came to Sarah.

Matters of wider interest, such as the death of King George IV and the cholera epidemic in London in 1832, crop up in Sarah's letters now and again, but for the most part her news is related to her own health and holidays, her and George's old friends, and to repeated requests for news of her dear brother and all her nieces and nephews.

In July 1832, Sarah wrote to Rex, *inter alia:* 'I hear constantly from dear Maria. It is only the expectation of seeing her that lures me on to brighter prospects. John Liptrap is by this time Captain and I suppose he will soon think of taking his furlough. I have often wondered that none of your sons wished to enter the Army or Navy,

*Appendix I

162

but you are happy in having them at home.' The spinster's devotion to her 'niece' is deep and touching.

Rex's last known letter to Sarah was written in June 1837, when he had returned from his lengthy stay in Cape Town, leaving George at school and Anne staying with the Menzies. He reported that he – seventy-two years of age – had suffered a fall from his horse at Hottentots Holland on the return journey and had travelled the remaining five hundred kilometres home in great pain. He was now almost recovered. He mentions John going to Cape Town, Edward being busy in the forest, Jacob occupied with sheep farming and 'Frederick returned from the wars safe and sound.'

By Sarah's last letter of this affectionate exchange, written in July, 1838, she sends the sad news that Maria Liptrap had arrived in England from India in May and four weeks later had succumbed to 'Water on the Chest'. The old lady, then sixty-eight, was deeply distressed by the loss of this young relative, whom she had cared for as lovingly as an orphaned child. Sarah was to survive only another four years and she and her niece are buried beneath the same tombstone in Bath.

It is most unfortunate that the letter of condolence which Sarah must have written to the family in Knysna after her brother's death has not been preserved. George predeceased her by just on three years.

George Rex died as he would have wished – as we would all wish to go – quickly and painlessly. On April 1 1839, he did not feel well enough to get out of bed, but was in full possession of all his faculties and perfectly composed. The family were disturbed enough, however, the following day to summon friend Wickham, who prescribed for him, and he appeared to be much better after taking the medicine. He slept soundly that night but at six o'clock on the morning of 3 April, he suffered a massive stroke and two hours later – before the hastily-summoned Thomas and Caroline Duthie could reach *Melkhout Kraal* from Belvidere – he died.[42]

The grief of the family is not easily imagined. Rex had not only filled outstandingly the role of loving husband and father for many years, his had been the vision and inspiration which had created the domain of *Melkhout Kraal*; his the dynamism and tenacity which had resulted in various business enterprises being successfully put in train; his the intellect and personality which had attracted outstanding men from all walks of life to this remote haven, and his the firm but kindly guiding hand on the reins of the activities of the whole family. In establishing himself as a prosperous colonist in an idyllic setting, he had founded not only a little town, but had given the country of his adoption a long succession of honourable men and women who have played significant, and often important parts, in South Africa's story.

The general esteem in which he was held is best conveyed by these words from his obituary; 'Died on his estate, *Melkhout Kraal*, Knysna, on Wednesday, 3rd April, 1839, George Rex Esquire, one of the oldest English residents in this Settlement. On his arrival in the Colony, he held the appointment of Marshal to the Vice-Admiralty Court, but soon withdrawing from official life, he entered into that retirement, where after nearly thirty-five years of rural occupation and quiet enjoyment, he has ended his earthly cares. Such was the mild, amiable and unassuming character of the deceased throughout that, not to insist here on what his family, his immediate connections and his personal friends have lost by his removal, his death will long be regretted and felt by all who had the advantage of his acquaintance. If of any person, it may truly be asserted of him, that he left no enemy behind; for it was hardly possible to resist becoming his friend.[43]

His birthdate is not mentioned in the obituary or on his grave stone.

9 Land the Link

George Rex was buried in a secluded spot within the grounds of *Melkhout Kraal,* which he loved so well. Although he had been held in such high esteem by his family and friends, fifty-three years after his death his grave lay unmarked and neglected. The surrounding bush encroached on the little enclosure, animals roamed through it, weeds and brambles almost obscured the mound which marked the last resting-place of this remarkable man.

At last, in 1892, Mrs. Johanna Elizabeth Metelerkamp, a daughter of John Rex and mother of Sanni Metelerkamp, the author, had the handsome marble tombstone erected on Rex's grave, and in 1963, a hundred and twenty-four years after his death, the grave was placed in the care of St. George's Church, Knysna.[1] It will be remembered that there is no mention in the inscription of Rex's birthdate, a fact which has only served to deepen the mystery and controversy interwoven with his memory; nor are the names of his parents mentioned on the stone, although this is not so significant an omission as the first, referring as the wording does to the death of an elderly person.

We are now in a position to fill these blank spaces, both on the stone and in the story. Shortly after Rex died in April 1839, his second son, John, filled in the statutory printed form or notice, which was required to be returned within six days after the death of an unmarried person or one 'not married in community of goods'. Unfortunately this important document is not clear enough to be reproduced here, but it reads as follows:

DEATH NOTICE
No 3452

Pursuant to the Provisions contained in Section 9, Ordinance 104

1. *Name of the Deceased* George Rex
2. *Birth-place of the Deceased* London
3. *Names of the Parents of the Deceased* Not known
4. *Age of the Deceased* 73 years and 8 months
5. *Condition in Life* Agriculturist

6. *Married or unmarried, Widower or Widow* Not Married
7. *The Day of the Decease* 3rd April, 1839
8. *At What House, or where the Person died* at Melkhout Kraal, Knysna
9. *Names of Children of Deceased, and whether Minors or Majors*

Majors
Edward Rex
John Rex
Elizabeth Caroline Rex
Jacob Govert Rex
Anne Rex
Frederick Rex
Caroline Rex, married to T.H. Duthie esq.,
Christina Wilhelmina Rex
Louisa Georgina Rex

Minors
George Rex
Sarah Rex
Maria Rex
Thomas Henry Rex

10. *Whether the Deceased has left any Property, and of what kind* . . . (The rest of the printed wording concerns instructions as to the filling up and returning of this form.)[2]

Rex's age being given as seventy-three years and eight months establishes, of course, his birth as having taken place in August or late in July 1765. Confirmation of the *month* appears to be given in a letter dated 29 August, which Thomas Henry Duthie wrote from Belvidere to his father-in-law and in which he added the note 'Congratulations on the returns of your birthday.[3] This also gives us the actual day which, even without the confirmatory evidence of the baptismal registers quoted below, indicates that George Rex was born on Thursday, 29 August 1765. Two members of his own family supplied this information which, strangely enough, seems to have been overlooked or ignored by most of those who have investigated Rex's life. If Thomas Henry Duthie was a month out in his congratulations – and such mistakes are not unknown – then there may be reasons for considering an alternative birthdate of 29 July, in view of the repetition of this date in two of his professional records of Doctors' Commons.

But the *year* of his birth is not in doubt.

Had George Rex been a son of George III, it would mean that he had been born – we now realise – four years after the King had married Queen Charlotte and after three of their royal family had been born, the third prince, William (later King William IV) arriving on 21 August 1765, within a matter of days of George Rex. Although Sanni Metelerkamp has stated that 1760 was given as the year of Rex's birth, she also, in effect, implied that he was born in 1765 (as he was) when she mentioned that he was nearly seventy in October 1834.[4]

But now for the truth about George Rex's parentage.

George Rex was, in fact, the eldest of five children born to John Rex, a distiller of comfortable means, and his wife, Sarah, at their home in Goodmans Yard, Whitechapel, London.

Up to this time, Sarah, George's mother, had led rather a tragic life for a young woman, because she had already been married twice and her husbands, both distillers, had died. She lost her first husband, William Perigoe, early in 1757 and he left her with a son, Richard, then aged about six.[5] Sarah was obviously an attractive young woman, in personality if not in appearance, but probably in both, because she was very soon snapped up by Thomas Rashdall, a widower. To him she was married in St. Mary's, Newington, on 1 January 1758,[6] a tidy date on which to start a new life.

This marriage lasted roughly four years and then Rashdall died on 15 July 1762. (His will was proved on 3 November 1762.)[7] The twice-bereaved Sarah was not left to struggle on her own, with her one child, for long. Her charms must have been exceptional and her competence will become evident later in the story.

She next attracted a man who had remained a bachelor until the age of thirty-nine, a fairly unusual thing in those days of early marriages. In the *Register of Marriages Solemnised in the Parish Church of St. Mary, Whitechapel in the County of Middlesex*, there is the following entry for 17 November 1764:

No 394) John Rex *of this parish* bachelor and Sarah Rashdall of the same Widow *were married in this* Church *by* License *this* Seventeenth *Day of* November *in the Year one Thousand* seven *Hundred* and Sixty four. *By me* H. Bennet Curate *This marriage was solemnised between us*
    John Rex
    Sarah Rashdall
In the Presence of
    Iman Bulle
    H (or W) Read[8]

The second witness was almost certainly William Read, who was either already the husband of John Rex's sister, Theodora, or about to become her husband.[9] What is more natural than that he should come to see John, who had resisted the wiles of women for so many years, happily joined in matrimony to the widow Sarah.

In contrast to the paucity of children resulting from Sarah's two previous marriages, she and John lost no time in starting a family and George was born a little more than nine months after the wedding. The fairly regular arrival of the other babies every year or two – in those days before family planning – can be seen in the Baptismal Register in the Record Office, County Hall. In a volume entitled '*A Register of Christenings in the parish of St. Mary, Whitechapel, In the County of Middlesex, Beginning in the Year MDCCLVIII. Roger Mather D.D. and Public Orator of the University of Oxford, Rector,*'[10] the entries of interest to followers of the Rex fortunes are:

2 September 1765	George Rex son of John & Sarah Goodmans Yard
16 October 1767	Sarah Rex Daughter of John & Sarah Goodmans Yard Home
11 December 1768	John Rex son of John & Sarah, High Street, Home
29 June 1770	Sarah Rex dr of John & Sarah, High Street, H.
20 September 1772	Elizabeth Rex dr of John & Sarah in High Street, H.

(The 'H' after the last two entries stands for 'Home')

The earlier volume recording christenings in this parish, from 1739 to February, 1758, contains no reference to the Rex family. This is not surprising. John's father, Thomas Rex, a distiller, had died in 1736[11] and 'Rex' as a surname was very rare in the eighteenth century, although it is common enough in England today. Up till the 1790's when one other family makes an appearance, there is no other 'Rex' in the merchant directories for the London area in the later eighteenth century, nor is there a trace of the name during this period in the very thorough compilation known as Marshall's Genealogists' Guide. There seems to have been one instance in the alternative form of 'Rix'.[12]

We glean three interesting pieces of information from this composite entry in the Register of Christenings. Firstly, that the two oldest children were born while the parents lived in Goodmans Yard. And secondly, that the first daughter, Sarah, was baptised at home and not in the parish church as George had apparently been, which suggests that she was a delicate baby, too frail to be carried to church by the parents. The fact that there is no mention of her in her father's will, drawn up twenty-one years later, is significant but the proof of her having died very young lies in the fact that her name – the name of her mother – was given to a later child.

This practice of giving the name of a baby who had died to a later child of the same sex was a common one, particularly when the name was that of one or other of the parents. The Sarah who survived and who was to bear such important witness – although after her death – to the link between the Whitechapel and Knysna families, was to take the place of the baby Sarah who had died. After the tragedy of the first daughter's early death, it seems that the parents took the precaution of having the rest of their children baptised at home.

Pendered and Mallett held the view that this pointed to the fact that the family may have been Lutherans, probably descendants of Palatinate or other German refugees.[13] Professor Christie finds this theory far-fetched. He points out that Lutheran pastors could be found in London – there was a Danish church, for instance – and one of them would have acted at the baptisms rather than the Anglican rector. Certainly the records would not have been kept in the Anglican church. Whitechapel was a predominantly Jewish area in those days – in fact, even today – but there is every evidence that the Rex family were members of the Anglican Church.

John, three years younger than George, and Sarah, eighteen months younger than John, will gain substance as this chapter progresses. The last child, Elizabeth, apparently succumbed at an early stage to one of the killer diseases so rampant in the eighteenth century, because there is no mention of her in her father's will either.

It would hardly have been surprising that two out of the five children died in those days, when the infant and child mortality rate was horrifyingly high. Epidemics were commonplace. Fever, rickets, 'convulsions' and small-pox were the deadliest of the diseases, but many small children died of simple illnesses which would today be arrested in their earliest stages. Rickets was so prevalent that it was known abroad as 'the English disease' and most of the children who succumbed to it were under five. Ten or twelve children, of whom three or four survived was a quite usual family pattern.[14] For three out of five of the Rex children to have survived and grown to healthy adulthood speaks well for their strong constitutions and the loving care which their parents gave them.

In their favour was the fact that they were born in the second half of the century when a growing awareness of the excess of the numbers of deaths over births during several decades had already led to constructive measures being taken to improve sanitary conditions in the great city. A determined cleaning up of the streets and sewers of London, for instance, took place in the 1760's. Consciences were stirred too about the lack of medical facilities for the ailing of the labouring classes and the really poor – in fact, of the great mass of the population – and this had led to the re-building of two of London's oldest hospitals and the foundation of half a dozen of the biggest medical institutions in the country. One of these, the London Hospital, had first opened its doors in Prescott Street, Goodmans Fields, Whitechapel, in 1740, for 'the relief of the sick and injured poor' and, more specifically, for 'Manufacturers, seamen in the Merchant Service and their Wives and Children'.[15] This was very close to the house in which the baby George first saw the light of day.

It is clear from the baptismal register mentioned above that some years later the Rex family likewise moved from Goodmans Yard (off Goodmans Fields, a good residential area) to High Street, Whitechapel. This must have been some time between October 1767 and December 1768, according to the records. High Street was nearer the commercial centre of Whitechapel, where things would have been livelier for the distilling business. As Mrs. Rex's two former husbands had both been in this trade, it is reasonable to assume that she brought a tidy little business into her marriage with John Rex.

John Rex, father of the household, was born early in 1726 and baptized in St. Mary's, Whitechapel, in May of that year. His parents were Thomas and Theodorus Rex, who lived 'near ye Town's end'.[16] He was apprenticed at an early age to his father and, when his father died, to his mother. It was not until 15 January 1765 (the year in which his first son, George, was born) that John Rex was made a freeman of the Distillers' Company, 'took the Oath and paid as usual'. This was noted in the Minute Book of the Court of the Distillers' Company, 1756-1781,[17] and in this same volume and the one following it, it is possible to trace the positions of increasing importance which John Rex held within the Company, one of the important Livery Companies of the City of London.

In July 1765, he was elected 'on the Livery' and can later be found exercising his Liveryman's right of voting as one of the six to seven thousand parliamentary electors in the City Constituency.[18] The government of the City was vested at that time mainly in the smaller merchants and middling shop-keepers and tradesmen who, as freemen of the Livery Companies, formed the Court of Common Hall and were strongly represented in the governing

Court of Common Council. It was a unique form of democracy.

John Rex obviously took his responsibilities seriously. In 1771 he was elected a steward of the Distillers' Company, in 1772 an assistant, in 1781 a Renter Warden, in 1782 a second Warden and finally, on 19 September 1782, was elected and sworn in as Master of the Company.[19]

Another indication that John Rex was a man of substance is to be found in a document dated 7 November 1791. This concerns the re-conveyance of several freehold and leasehold tenements and premises in the parishes of St. Mary's, Whitechapel, and St. Dunstan's, Stepney, from John Rex to William Read, his brother-in-law. It seems that Rex had lent Read £900 the previous year and, as security, Read had made over to him the indenture of mortgage on these premises. William Read having paid off the £900 in full, John Rex now agreed to return to him the titles of these freehold premises mentioned.[20]

It is now possible to place John Rex, his wife and their legitimate children more securely in their *milieu* than almost any other family of their period of their unassuming background and lawful habits. They were real people, living real and busy lives, going about their work and pleasure like millions of the middling sort all over the world, not expecting to make history but content to go about their humble occasions, to work hard, to bring up their children honourably, to live in charity with their neighbours and to fear the Lord.

Their births, marriages, deaths and wills were all duly recorded and the documents filed away in their rightful places. There, in all probability, they would have remained unscanned for the rest of time, had it not been for the claims to royal connections which inevitably turned the spotlight of publicity on the origins of the Rex family in a way most families are spared. Nobody would have been more surprised that John and Sarah Rex could they have known that two hundred years after they started bringing up their little family in London, historians and archivists would be turning over the documentary evidence of their existence in an attempt to reconstruct the life pattern of one of their children.

From the fact that the baptismal register shows the address as 'High Street, Whitechapel' and that the London merchant directories show John Rex to have been in business at 87 Whitechapel[21] (probably 87 High Street, Whitechapel) we can safely assume that this is one and the same address.

It looks therefore very much as if the home in which the Rex children spent their childhood was one of those houses common in

171

London in the eighteenth century – and even in the older parts of the city today – narrow-fronted but deep, the front room on the ground level constituting the business premises, the back the kitchen area. There would have been two or three stories above this and possibly a basement and open area below, for roads were often built above ground level. 87 High Street today has been entirely re-built, though still in much the same style.

Houses in general, except for those of the very rich, were austerely furnished and there may not have been in the kitchen much more than a table, a few stools and a cupboard, the expensive chairs being kept for the parlour and bedroom upstairs. Beds were another appallingly costly item and it is quite likely that the three Rex children, with their half-brother, Richard Perigoe, would have slept on truckle beds.

Gas had not yet transformed London and street lighting – non-existent in some areas and inadequately provided by smoky oil lamps in others – was a cause of great chagrin to the whole community. It was foolhardy and downright dangerous to venture forth after dark.

This was especially true of the crowded eastern districts of the city where stage coaches were sometimes held up and citizens robbed at gun point after dark. Because of their proximity to the docklands, these were the districts of importers, coal merchants, brokers, merchants, warehousemen, victuallers, tradesmen and manufacturers. They were also the districts which absorbed most of the stream of immigrants – German, Dutch, French, Polish and Jewish – crossing the channel into working-class London, not to mention the Scots, Welsh and Irish coming to seek their fortunes in 'the greatest Emporium in the known world.'[22]

So this was a thronging, seething, rumbustious, riot-prone quarter of the city where anything could – and often did – happen. It had a vivid cosmopolitan character all of its own. There were a few wealthy merchants, a handful of clergy and a smattering of gentlefolk, but the gulf between the eastern and the western districts of London was already widening rapidly in this period and those with means and ambition were moving steadily westwards.

From the security of their little world in 87 High Street, Whitechapel, the Rex children would have heard the rumble of the iron-wheeled traffic in the streets, the bells of St. Mary's and other nearby churches pealing out their message, the comforting call of the night-watchman, 'Twelve o'clock on a clear and frosty night. All's well,' and the multitudinous cries of London from that of the vendor of roasted chestnuts to the call of the milkmaid, who skilfully balanced the open pails of milk on her head as she went from door to door. The milk came, one hopes, from the farms on the outskirts of the city because the milk from the town-bred cows was often the carrier of dread diseases. A rich variety of wholesome produce was by now reaching London from the outlying counties, not to mention the great volume of goods arriving by sea.

The colourful kaleidoscope of life in the east end of London would have provided the normal background to George's schooldays. No definite evidence as to where he was educated has yet come to light, but it is possible that he would have attended the Red Coat School in Mile End, near to Whitechapel. This originated as a free school, founded in 1712 by a body of City merchants and retired sea captains, many of whom lived in Stepney. A benefactor of the early school was Benjamin Kenton, Master of the Vintner's Company, a fact which makes it likely that children of members of this company would have been readily admitted to it. It was originally to be for twenty boys, who were to be provided with red coats. The school on the present site originated as one for girls only and the boys' school was later amalgamated with it.[23] It is possible, in fact, that not only George, but his brother, John, and his sister, Sarah, also attended this school.

Out of school hours there would have been plenty in the life of this end of London to fascinate an adventurous boy. Running out of Whitechapel Road was Middlesex Street, which on Sundays became that rowdy, cheerful babel of buying and bartering known then – as now – as Petticoat Lane. This curiosity of east London would have been a familiar scene to the Rex children.

Surely George and his friends would have peeped too, into the gloomy interior of Mears and Stainbank's bell foundry, also in Whitechapel Road, the oldest firm in Britain. It had been running continuously since 1570 and the only change in two hundred years had been made when the firm moved from one side of Whitechapel Road to the other. The bells of Barnes Parish Church were cast here in 1572 and later the bells for the new Wren churches erected after the Great Fire of London, the bells of St. Clement's, the old Bow bells, the bells of Westminster Abbey and the clock bells of St. Paul's had all taken form in this quaint old foundry. Big Ben was to be born here more than seventy years after George's schooldays.[24]

All the time, whether at work or play, George's horizons would have been expanding and possibly his political consciousness being aroused by the cosmopolitan and factious character of the community in which he was growing up.

*   *   *

The link which enables the above word picture to be drawn with certitude, the link which establishes clearly the genealogy of the Rex family through five generations, was discovered and slipped neatly into place by Professor Christie in January 1973. This link is to be found in certain copyhold lands,* the descent of which through four generations can be traced in the family tree inside the covers. A careful scrutiny of this will help to make the following rather weighty paragraphs more intelligible.

The known facts about these land holdings take us back to John Rex's maternal grandfather, Thomas Hopkins, a farmer of Stepney, who died in 1709. Thomas and his wife, Prudence, had three daughters the eldest of whom, Theodorus, married Thomas Rex, a distiller. They had one son, John, and one daughter, Theodora, who married William Read, also a distiller.[25] John Rex, their only son, as already mentioned, married in 1764 and had five children by his wife, Sarah, of whom three survived, George, John and Sarah. This brings us to George Rex, the main character in this story. John Rex was his father, Thomas Rex his grandfather, and Thomas Hopkins his great-grandfather (on his grandmother's side).

On 20 April 1765 (four months before George was born) John Rex, his father, of Goodmans Fields, Whitechapel, came to the Manor Court of West Ham Burnells and, under the will of his maternal grandfather, claimed – among other lands – the copyhold property *all those three acres and three roods of land . . . lying in Bromley Brook in the parish of Westham in the said County of Essex, formerly in the tenure of Ralph Thomson and afterwards of Joseph Boddilowe and now of John Warren . . .'* Thomas Hopkins, John's grandfather, had left this property to his eldest daughter, Theodorus, and her heirs or, failing her, to his younger daughters, Avis and Sarah Nash.[26]

At a court held on 5 December 1710, a year after Thomas Hopkins had died, his widow, Prudence, was admitted to 'one moiety of the copyhold' and Theodorus, then a child of about ten, to the other moiety. Upon the death of her mother, Theodorus, inherited the lands outright and when she in turn died, her only son, John Rex (George's father) was then entitled to claim his inheritance. Upon payment of the customary fine, which was merely a technical term for 'payment on entry', John became the owner of these lands.

He enjoyed the modest rents – which Professor Christie estimates would have been rather less than £30 a year – until he died on

*Appendix H

174

29 March, 1792.[27] He had made and signed his will on 12 May 1788, four years before his death, and it was proved by his widow on 27 February 1793.[28]

It is a touching document, showing as it does not only a rightful concern for his 'beloved wife, Sarah Rex,' but a more-than-average concern for the legitimate issue of his own body.

John Rex obviously had complete faith in his wife's integrity and business ability, since he appointed her sole executrix and, towards the end of the wordy will, emphasises her right to execute any legal transactions upon his death. He goes further and declares that it shall be lawful for her 'to act as she may deem fit' whether she 'shall then be covert (re-married) or sole and notwithstanding her coverture.' She must have been a remarkable woman and John a devoted husband.

Having directed that all his just debts and funeral expenses be paid and satisfied, John Rex states, 'I give devise and bequeath unto my beloved wife Sarah Rex and her assigns all those my twelve acres of land lying being opposite Pullery Wall in Plaistow Marsh in the parish of West Ham in the County of Essex and also those my two acres of land lying and being in Plaistow Marsh aforesaid . . . I give and devise the said freehold and copyhold lands with their appurtenances unto Richard Perigoe of Whitechapel aforesaid distiller and his heirs for and during the natural life of my wife, Sarah Rex, upon trust . . . . . but nevertheless to permit and suffer the said Sarah Rex and her assigns during her natural life to receive and take the Rents, Issues and Profits thereof to and for her and their own proper use and benefit.'

Briefly, this meant that Sarah benefitted from the rents and Perigoe acted as trustee.

Richard Perigoe was, of course, Sarah's son by her first husband[29] and was, from February 1765, apprenticed to John Rex for seven years. From 1778 he is shown in the London merchant directories as having been taken into partnership with his stepfather.[30]

Rex's will, in condensed form, continues: 'In regard I have already advanced my eldest son George Rex considerably more than I have my other son and daughter therefore from and immediately after the decease of my said wife I give and devise the said freehold and copyhold lands . . . unto my daughter Sarah Rex and to the heirs of her body lawfully issuing . . . in default of such issue to my second son John Rex and to the heirs of his body lawfully issuing . . . or in default unto my said son George Rex and to the heirs of his body lawfully issuing . . .' In the event of all three of these lines of descent failing, the property was to be left in the first instance to his sister, Theodora (wife of William Read) or ultimately 'unto the rightful heirs of Thomas Hopkins late of Stepney . . . farmer.' By this time George Rex had been practising as a proctor of Doctors' Commons for nearly four years.

These rightful, but remote, heirs would have been presumably Thomas Hopkin's younger daughters, Avis and Sarah Nash Hopkins, that is John's aunts, or their children, as reference to the family tree will show.

In the further mass of verbiage in which the lawyers of the time were prone to wrap up the clear purpose of the author of the will, there is expressed further concern for 'all and every my other Daughters begotten and to be begotten . . .' but this is all merely lawyer's flummery. It does not indicate that there were any other surviving children of the marriage and, indeed, there is no record of any further baptism of children of this family in the parish registers for the years after 1772.

One explanation put forward by some romanticists who are well aware of the more-than-coincidental interlinking of the Whitechapel and Knysna families, is that George, John and Sarah were actually the children of Hannah Lightfoot by George III and that they were boarded out, to avoid embarrassment in court circles, 'with a friendly and unsuspecting family . . . and that not by accident was one chosen of the name of Rex.' In Sanni Metelerkamp's view, at least, this 'would divert suspicion from the true quarter.'[31] *Pace* Miss Metelerkamp, but would Prince George and Hannah really have selected the one family in London known to have the surname Rex, living right in the City too, to be foster-parents to their children if George, now King, were trying to disclaim their very existence!

This theory is, in any case, negated by the whole tenor of John Rex's will, showing as it does an extreme concern with the issue of his own body and his close blood relations. Had he been sheltering a pride of royal foundlings, they would surely have received handsome financial support from their royal father and have been in no need of the modest rents from the properties in Plaistow Marsh. Nor in that case would it have been likely that John Rex would have admitted any claim on their part to his inheritance in preference to his blood relations on his sister's side, or even to his stepson, Richard Perigoe, of whom he was obviously fond.

This also puts paid to another legend mentioned earlier, that John Rex junior, George's brother, assumed the name of Mackelcan and became a general in the British army.[32] John junior, after his father's death in 1792, continued to run the family business in

Druce Chr's Heirs
to
John Foster –
Bargain & Sale
Presentment of - „ —————— Do and each and every
' of them Doth Bargain Sell alien and Release unto the said
' John Foster and to his Heirs All those six acres and an
' half of Marsh Land (be the same more or less) called or
' known by the name of Bromley Field or Hog Hole formerly
" in the occupation of Joseph wells situate lying and being in
' New Marsh in Plaistow in the Parish of Westham in the .
' County of Essex And also all that piece or parcel of pasture .
' or Marsh Ground called Many Gates being an enclosed
' piece of Ground containing by Estimation two acres (be the
" same more or less) lying in New Marsh aforesaid in the
' parish of westham aforesaid in the said County of Essex and
" which said pieces or parcels of land were formerly in the occupation
' of John warren and   etc.   ¦   etc.

' assigns All those three acres and three Roods of land
' situate lying and being in Bromley Brook in the Parish
" of West Ham in the said County of Essex formerly in the
" tenure of John warren afterwards of Robert Hulme of
" Leadenhall Market Salesman afterwards of Thomas Harrison
" then of Thomas Hudson since of George Cole and now of
" the said Thomas wilkins and which said Copyhold land
" is delineated and shewn in the said Plan drawn in the
                etc.   ¦   etc.

Extract from the 'Bargain and Sale' record of the sale of lands in terms of the will of George Rex's sister, Sarah Rex of Bath. This mentions the 'three acres and three roods' of land in Plaistow Marsh detailed in her great-grandfather's, Thomas Hopkins', will. (By permission of the Essex Record Office. Ref. D/DPe M23)

The High Street, Whitechapel, London, in the mid-nineteenth century. (From the Grace Collection, by permission of the British Museum)

Wedgwood portrait medallion of King George III, re-modelled by William Hackwood, Josiah Wedgwood's top designer in the second half of the eighteenth century, from an earlier model he designed in 1775. This example is of excellent quality (Photo: Cloete Breytenbach)

A modern reproduction of the same medallion, made in the original mould which still exists in the Wedgwood potteries at Barlaston. (By permission of Josiah Wedgwood & Sons) partnership with his half-brother, Richard Perigoe. John had become a freeman of the Distillers' Company in 1795, but in January 1797, the minutes of the Court of the Company shows that he requested to be excused from taking up his Livery for the present as he was not in business for himself.[33] Presumably the firm of *Rex and Perigoe* was not too flourishing at this stage and John was not anxious to become involved in the additional expense inevitably following on election to the Distillers' Company. Almost certainly, in the years following his father's death, John would have continued to live with his widowed mother at 87 High Street, Whitechapel.

Richard Perigoe, who had initially been apprenticed to John Rex senior, his stepfather, but had become a freeman of the Distillers' Company in 1786,[34] died in March, 1795, leaving a small daughter, Maria, and a toddler son, Richard junior, in the care of his now elderly mother, Mrs. Sarah Rex. She was, incidentally, named as sole executrix in his will, which was proved on 2 November 1796.[35] Young Richard, aged only five, died tragically of burns in 1797[36] and some time between this event and Mrs. Sarah Rex's death from jaundice in 1803,[37] little Maria Perigoe went to live with her aunt, Miss Sarah Rex, who later lived in Bath and who corresponded so affectionately with her brother, George Rex, in South Africa.

On 25 December 1801, John Rex junior, bachelor, and Mary Goodeve, widow, were married in the parish of St. Catherine Coleman, Mary merely making her mark in lieu of signing her name.[38] Mrs. Mary Rex now became another important link in the chain connecting John, George and Sarah Rex. John and Mary had one daughter, Sophia.[39]

By 1802, probably because he was now married and wanted to be independent, John decided to establish his own business. From this year until 1820, he is shown in various London directories as having been in business as a wine and brandy merchant, first at 82 Fenchurch Street, then at Clare Street, Clare Market.[40] From the mention of property in Clare Street, Clare Market, in the will of John's sister, Sarah Rex, it can be inferred that this was family property, which John junior was allowed to use for as long as he needed it. The directories often did not eliminate 'dead addresses' for several years, so the fact that his name was still in the firm of *Rex and Perigoe* until 1805 is not necessarily contra-indication of his having set up his own business in Clare Market in 1802.[41]

Sometime before 1820 John became keeper of a public house called *The Castle,* in Highgate, in the Hornsey area. Here he died in December 1821, and was buried on the twenty-first of that month in the graveyard of St. Michael's parish church Highgate. There is no stone on his grave.[42]

Some speculation is aroused by the wording of an interesting document relating to the administration of his estate, the total value of which was £600. It reads: 'On the eleventh day Administrations of the Goods Chattels and Credits of John Rex late of Highgate in the County of Middlesex Victualler deceased was granted to James Flower, a Creditor of the said deceased, having been first sworn duly to administer Mary Rex Widow the Relict and Sophia Charrott (Wife of William Charrott) the natural and lawful Daughter and only Child and together the only Persons entitled in Distribution having first renounced the Letters of Administration of the Goods of the said deceased.[43]

James Flower, the main claimant on the insolvent estate, was entitled to recover what he could out of the wreck having first provided for the dead man's widow and child. Compared with his brother and sister, John Rex seems to have lived an undistinguished and none too prosperous life.

Fortunately the widow, Mary Rex, married again. On 1 March 1826, the marriage took place between Thomas Tingle, widower, and Mary Rex, both of the parish of St. Mary the Virgin, Alderman-bury, London.[44] This is the Mrs. Tingle – 'the Widow of my late Brother John' – who was a beneficiary in the next of the four vital documents, the will of Sarah Rex, sister of George and John. The daughter, Sophia Charrott, does not reappear in any other documents relating to the Rex family.

The will of Miss Sarah Rex, of 17 Henrietta Street, Bath, who died at her home on 17 August 1842, in her seventy-third year,[45] is an invaluable link in this chain of evidence which establishes the genealogy of the Rex family beyond doubt. The loving ties which existed between George Rex of Knysna and his sister, Sarah Rex, of Bath, the affectionate correspondence which passed between them, and the visit which young Caroline and Thomas Henry Duthie paid to this spinster aunt in the course of their long visit overseas, have never been denied. In the extensive literature on the subject of the Rex claims to royal connections, Sarah has always been acknowledged to be George's only sister.

Her will, signed on 23 March 1842, is in the probate records of the prerogative court of Canterbury. The terms, in a nutshell, are as follows: she appointed an old family friend, Charles Druce, and his two sons, Charles and John, as trustees and executors of her will. A freehold house and premises in Clare Street, Middlesex, on lease to Felix Booth, was to be held in trust and the rents paid to her friend,

Mrs. Elizabeth Liptrap and then to Mrs. Liptrap's daughter, Amelia Caroline. Amelia Caroline's brothers, Captain John Liptrap, in the service of the East India Company, and Samuel Davey Liptrap, are also beneficiaries under this will. The significance of the Liptrap connection as yet another corroboratory clue in the Rex saga will be explained shortly.

Then comes mention in the will of 'my freehold land and estate situate in Plaistow Marsh in the parish of Eastham in Essex in the occupation of Thomas Wilkins and . . . my freehold estate situate in Essex Street, Whitechapel, in the county of Middlesex, formerly Catherine Wheel Alley on lease to John Saunders but in the occupation of Robert Rea . . . and also my leasehold estates situate at or near Snaresbrook in the County of Essex' ('Eastham' was a slip on the part of the lawyer drawing up the will and this was corrected in the next document to be discussed. It should, of course, have read 'Westham'.)

These properties were to be sold and the moneys either held in trust for, or distributed to, various friends and relatives. 'I give to my nephews and nieces the children of my late brother, George Rex of the Cape of Good Hope deceased, the sum of one thousand pounds . . .' to be divided equally between them. To Caroline Duthie 'one of the daughters of my said brother, the wife of Thomas Henry Duthie,' the sum of £200 and, after some minor bequests to the Liptrap family, 'I give to Mrs. Tingle, the widow of my late brother John the sum of two hundred pounds . . .' Other legatees were Lieutenant Henry Lawless of the Royal Navy; William Thomson Esquire, of Bath; Mrs. Sollijma, of Bath, and Sarah Rex's servant, Ann Osborne, 'if in my service at the time of my decease.' The residue of her estate was to go to Charles Druce and his two sons.

Two points deserve mention here: John Rex's widow, now Mrs. Mary Tingle, as we have seen, was kindly remembered by her sister-in-law, and Caroline Duthie was the only member of the South African Rex family singled out for special mention, the one whom Sarah Rex had met and with whom she had established personal links.

The final document to be considered and the one which puts George, John's and Sarah's background beyond all question, is the record of a 'Bargain and sale' of 27 February 1843, between the Druces, who were discharging their duties as executors of Sarah's estate, and one John Foster.[46] Here it is recorded that the responsibility of disposing of certain freehold and copyhold lands rested upon them under the terms of Sarah's will, that this will had been proved in the prerogative court of Canterbury on 30 August 1842, and that when they had put up the land for sale at the Auction Mart in the City of London, the highest bid was made by John Foster. His bid was £850.

John Foster, incidentally, was probably an extremely shrewd man who saw the possibilities of this marsh land lying so close to the river on which London depended for her very existence, because it was only twelve years later that Plaistow Marsh came to form part of the land on which the Royal Victoria Docks was built. If he held the land until 1855 he would probably have had few financial cares thereafter.

The enrolment of the indenture of bargain and sale of the property is then described in detail – freehold and copyhold lands. The freehold property included about six and a half acres of marsh land called Bromley Field or Hog Hole in New Marsh, Plaistow, and also an enclosed piece of ground of about two acres, called Many Gates, 'formerly in the occupation of John Warren and now in the occupation of Thomas Wilkins'. Additional certainty in the identification of this plot of land with that which had been held by previous generations of the family, is provided by the record of the tenancies being taken back to John Warren, the occupant of this land when John Rex senior took possession in 1765.

The copyhold lands 'held on the Manor' were described as *'All those three acres and three roods of land situate lying and being in Bromley Brook in the parish of West Ham . . . formerly in the tenure of John Warren,* afterwards in the tenure of (naming four successive tenants) and now of Thomas Wilkins . . .' It is noted that Sarah Rex was admitted to these lands at a Manor Court on 8 October 1828.

The document is illustrated on two pages by diagrams showing the lands to be divided into two unequally shaped portions, both bordered on the west side by 'Dirty Lane – Leading to the Marshes.' It was not sufficiently valuable land to have enabled John Rex Senior to have raised himself into the class of the landed gentry, but it provided a little additional income to be added to his profits from the distilling business and a bequest to his daughter which in part enabled her to spend at least the latter part of her life in fashionable Bath.

It would be impossible to find more conclusive evidence than the passing of this parcel of lands down through four generations for more than 130 years – from Thomas Hopkins to his eldest daughter, Theodorus; from Theodorus to her only son John Rex; from John to his daughter Sarah, in succession to his wife. When Sarah died, the sale of these lands in the east end of London in part enabled the Druces to pay Sarah's bequests to George Rex's children in South Africa.

We are now able to fill in the few remaining gaps in Rex's life in London with greater accuracy. It is clear, for instance, that during the years he was establishing himself in Doctors' Commons, his life was punctuated by events of considerable significance. In 1792, his father, who must have been so proud of his son who had been made a proctor three years previously, died. Three years later his half-brother, Richard Perigoe who had been running the family business in partnership with young John Rex, died too.

Richards little girl, Maria Perigoe, was put in the charge of her father's half-sister, Miss Sarah Rex, when her grandmother, Mrs. Sarah Rex, died in 1803.[47] The old lady, incidentally, was buried in the graveyard of the church in which her husband had been baptised, in which she and John Rex senior had been married, in which all her children had been baptised, and in which her husband and her son by her first marriage were buried – St. Mary's, Whitechapel.[48]

Miss Sarah Rex, a lonely spinster, became extremely devoted to her niece, Maria, whom she cared for lovingly until the day in 1823 when Maria sailed for India to marry an old childhood friend, John Liptrap.

The friendship between the Rex and Liptrap families, a friendship which lasted between certain members for at least three generations, is of substantial significance in this story. It obviously accounts for the inclusion of four members of the Liptrap family – Mrs. Elizabeth Liptrap, her daughter, Amelia Caroline, and her two sons, John and Samuel Davey Liptrap – in the will of George Rex's sister, Sarah Rex, of Bath, and for the repeated references to the Liptraps in Sarah's letters to her brother in far-off South Africa. It may even have accounted for the seed of the Rex legend being sown, as will be seen presently.

Samuel Davey Liptrap senior, a prosperous distiller, and his wife were friendly with John and Sarah Rex senior. The Liptraps lived at Ducking Pond, Bethnal Green, an area not far north of Whitechapel and there was in all probability much visiting between the two families. Samuel Davey, then resident at Mile End, died in July 1789, leaving about £40 000 to his family.[49] His one son, Samuel Davey, married and had an only child, Amelia, whom he left well provided for when he died in 1836, according to Sarah Rex's letter to her brother, mentioned in the previous chapter. This daughter, Miss Amelia Liptrap, in 1840 married Lieutenant (later General Sir) Henry Charles Barnston Daubeny.[50]

Like his friend, John Rex senior, Samuel Davey Liptrap held successively important offices in the Distillers' Company, being finally elected Master of the Company in September 1788, ten months before he died.[51] His two sons likewise held increasingly responsible posts in the Company.

The elder son, John Liptrap, was taken into partnership with his father in the family business and was given £5 000 when this partnership came into effect. His father's capital of £30 000 was to remain in the business, which was to be carried on by his partner-son. John was promised a further £5 000 when he married. He married Elisabeth, daughter of James Hunt, of Union Hall, Middlesex.

A public-spirited and enterprising young man, John did not confine his interests to the business by any means, although he seems to have made a success of it. He founded, in 1793, the Bethnal Green Volunteers, later better known as the Mile End Volunteers, 'to protect the neighbourhood from the ruffian hands of interested depredators, and from the malicious schemes of disloyalty.'[52] Of this company, which numbered three hundred infantry by 1803, he became captain and then lieutenant-colonel.

John's enterprise even extended to horticulture, for he 'possessed a splendid collection of exotics' in his garden at Mile End and in 1800 was responsible for introducing the Eastern Cape cycad, *Zamia encephalartos horridus,* to Kew Gardens.[53] This is yet another link between the Liptrap and Rex families, as it is very probable that this extremely rare plant was sent to John by George Rex from the unique collection of plants at *Schoonder Zigt,* just at the time he was moving into his newly-acquired property. This cycad had also been cultivated in the famous Schoenbrun gardens in Vienna,[54] undoubtedly introduced there by Boos and Scholl from the same garden, when *Schoonder Zigt* belonged to Colonel Gordon.

John prospered in the family business and in time became sufficiently important to be elected one of the two sheriffs to the Lord Mayor of London. The handsome sum which he had inherited from his father was undoubtedly the silver spoon which accounted for his being in a position to undertake this term as sheriff, a position involving him in considerable expense. Each sheriff had to provide his own ceremonial coach and John Liptrap's was an outstandingly handsome affair elaborately decorated in blue and gold, the City Arms and Supporters displayed on it, the hammer-cloth of scarlet, richly trimmed with gold fringe and lace. His co-sheriff, Mr. Glode, also sported a fine state carriage, his liveries too being of blue and gold.[55] John would also have had to dress his own liveried attendants, to entertain lavishly and to meet all other costs attendant upon a public office of this nature.

John was a contemporary of George Rex and, as their parents were friendly, George, John and almost certainly sister Sarah, would have been drawn into some of the ceremonial celebrations connected with John Liptrap's duties as sheriff.

These sheriffs to the Lord Mayor were elected annually for the City and Middlesex and each was entitled to nominate his own under-sheriff, 'always a gentleman of the law'. During John Liptrap's term of office, 1795-96, one of his under sheriffs was Charles Druce, presumably the same Charles Claridge Druce who was chief executor of Sarah Rex's will and very likely also a legal colleague of George Rex. He would, of course, be a member of any gay party in which the Liptrap and Rex families were involved. This bond of friendship was to last a lifetime, with Charles Druce outliving all three Rexes and administering Sarah's will nearly fifty years later.

In the *Gentleman's Magazine* of May 1796, under the heading, *Births, April, 1796*, was a brief entry: 'To the Lady of Mr. Sheriff Liptrap – a son'.[56] This son was named John, after his father. The Sheriff's lady, Mrs. Elizabeth Liptrap, also bore a second son, named Samuel Davey after his grandfather and uncle, and a daughter, Amelia Caroline. All received bequests under the terms of Sarah Rex's will. These relationships can be clearly traced in the family tree. John and his wife later moved to Vansittart Terrace, Greenwich.

Young John Liptrap, the sheriff's son, left England in 1818, then aged twenty-two, went to India as a cadet in the service of the United East India Company and was soon commissioned as a lieutenant in the 2nd Battalion, 21st Regiment, Bengal Infantry.[57] His petition to the East India Company to be admitted as a cadet, his nomination by a director of the company, a copy of his baptismal certificate, some letters of recommendation and the sworn declaration which John himself completed in his own hand, are all in the military records of the India Office Library, London.*

Young Liptrap had, it seems, left his heart in Whitechapel, because on 1 September 1823, Lieutenant John Liptrap and Maria Perigoe, daughter of the late Richard Perigoe, were joined in holy matrimony in St. John's Cathedral, Calcutta.[58] Because of the extent to which the history of the Rex and Perigoe families is interwoven

*Appendix I

with that of the Liptraps, Maria and John would undoubtedly have known each other since childhood.

Because, too, of the close association over three generations of the Rex and Liptrap families, it is not surprising to find John's and Maria's names listed as sponsors at the baptism of George Rex's youngest daughter, Maria, at *Melkhout Kraal* in 1827.

Maria Liptrap, whose health had apparently been steadily declining ever since she had been in India, returned to her aunt, Miss Sarah Rex of Bath, after thirteen years of married life in India and it was at this relative's home, 17 Henrietta Street, Bath, that she died on 14 June 1838. Her epitaph is on one side of the tombstone, Sarah Rex's on the other, and so they lie side by side.

The widower, John Liptrap, became a distinguished general in the British army married twice more and died in London in September 1878 at the age of eighty-two.[59] His successful career and the intimate relationships between his wife and members of the Rex family may have, in a labyrinthine way, accounted for the germination of the legend that John Rex junior had become a general in the British army – General John Mackelcan – and died in London in his eighties.

The Liptrap story disposes of yet another legend – that the 'Maria' so affectionately mentioned in the letters which passed between George and Sarah Rex, might have been George's daughter by the Princess Amelia, youngest daughter of King George III.[60] As George Rex left England in the year in which the Princess turned fourteen, this fable does him no credit and is best forgotten. This is just one instance of many unlikely stories put into circulation with the intention of establishing his connection with the royal family but which, in fact, merely served to tarnish his remarkable record.*

The whole tenor of this book has been factual, the whole aim to discount the ill-founded, suggestive rumours and to tell a story based on firm evidence, but the temptation to put forward a new and light-hearted theory at this stage as to how George Rex's name came to be associated with royalty in the minds of certain of his contemporaries, is irresistible.

Robert Huish, that master of anecdotal, quasi-historical story-spinning, in 1831 gave a naughty account in his *Memoirs of George IV,* of a splendid dinner at which His Royal Highness, the Prince of Wales (Prinny), was an honoured quest. The Prince, according to Huish, was already heavily committed to Mrs. Fitzherbert when he 'received an invitation to dine with one of the Sheriffs

*Appendix J

184

of London, a celebrated distiller in Whitechapel'. The company was composed entirely of noblemen and gentlemen, the majority of whom were the intimate friends of His Royal Highness. 'The Sheriff's lady was one of the celebrated beauties of the east, being in her person of that *en bon point* which was so peculiarly the taste of His Royal Higness, and the features of her face were of that dignified and impressive cast, for which the Grecian beauties are so justly celebrated. Her eyes beamed with desire and passion, and her LIP was not the first TRAP which, by its lovely pouting, had ensnared the affection of the enamoured Prince. The lady left the table soon after dinner, and His Royal Highness felt a vacuum which could not be filled up by the coarser society of his companions. Feigning some excuse, he retired from the table, and the worthy Sheriff, fearing that the return of His Royal Higness might be delayed by indisposition, considered he should be wanting in respect if he did not hasten to make his personal inquiries respecting him.

There were several places in the house to which it was possible that the Prince had retired, but there was one, in particular, in which it was highly improbable that he should be found, and that was the bed-chamber of his lady. It was, therefore, the last which the worthy Sheriff visited – but, had he visited it the first it would have saved him a great deal of trouble, and calmed at once his anxiety for the safety of his royal guest. There, however, in reality, was the Prince found; and the Sheriff resolved on the most instantaneous punishment – he drew his sword – and England would, perhaps have had to mourn the loss of the heir apparent to her throne, had not prudence whispered to him to save himself by the most precipitate flight.

The darkness of the night favoured him, and he gained the garden; he heard his pursuers behind him, but no friendly door presented itself by which he could make his escape: in an instant he scaled the wall, and he now found the adage to be true, that a man should always look before he leaps. The Prince did not look; and therefore he leapt into as vile a compound of dirt and filth as ever received the body of a human being, much more that of a Prince, within its odoriferous bosom . . . In after years, his Royal Highness never heard the name of Liptrap mentioned, but he exclaimed, in the words of Shakespeare, 'Oh, but it has a rank, unearthly smell.'[61]

Huish, needless to say, had garnered the unlovely details of this amusing tale from a serving-man who had been in the employ of the Sheriff when the incident was supposed to have taken place.

Now supposing there to have been – as there often was in Huish's writing – a tiny kernel of truth at the centre of this fanciful story-weaving. It is more than likely that the Prince of Wales would have been a guest of honour at a banquet given by the wealthy distiller, one of the Lord Mayor's sheriffs, in view of the tremendous political importance of the livery companies and the City in general. The prince, whose roving eye was notorious, may even have flirted gallantly with his hostess.

The odds are better than even that George Rex, aged about thirty and a fully-qualified professional man at the time his friend, John Liptrap, took office as a sheriff, would have been at this sumptuous dinner party. In after life, what would have been more natural than that he should indulge in a bit of name-dropping and mention casually the occasion on which he had dined with the Prince of Wales. He may even have regaled his company with an amusing reminiscence on the lines of the anecdote quoted above.

Was there at any time, one wonders, any suggestion that the Liptrap baby born on 15 May 1796, had been fathered by the Prince? If the dinner party had been held roughly nine months previously (Huish is vague about dates), this rumour would inevitably have circulated vigorously. This child was our John Liptrap who was later sent to a distant land, married a half-niece of George Rex, and became a general in the British army. The well-shuffled ingredients of the later legends, including the one about John Rex having become General John Mackelcan, are all here. It is an interesting possibility. Although his age does not fit, a generation is often lost in the telling of such stories in after years.

Extravaganzas apart, readers should now be able to visualise this man of a vanished era, moving about in a solid world, with his parents, his brother and sister, his friends and his legal colleagues. Many writers have stated categorically that 'Little or nothing is known about George Rex's life before he arrived in South Africa', whereas a surprising amount is, in fact, known in view of the ordinariness of his home and upbringing. It is not the law-abiding citizen, setting up house, earning his living, making love, rearing a family and finally dying, who normally features in the history books. Had it not been for the claims to royal blood, it is unlikely that George Rex would have featured in one book, let alone several.

Thanks to Professor Christie's expertise in discovering the four vital documents discussed in this chapter, the mass of cobwebs which have for a century and a half effectively obscured Rex's origins, have now been dissipated.

It is possible now, not only to command the outline of his life, but to fill in that outline with what we know of his character and personality. We can see clearly how this ambitious man broke away from the family distilling business and, with the moral and financial support of his parents, qualified himself as a professional gentleman, moving steadily upwards in a world of rigid class distinction to a senior post in the Court of Vice-Admiralty and eventually to the position of *grand seigneur*, owner of vast tracts of land in an African garden of Eden. We can also appreciate the inevitable duality in his make-up resulting from these circumstances.

Professor Christie was, from the moment he learned of George Rex's history, sceptical about his alleged descent from Hannah Lightfoot; indeed about the whole Lightfoot legend. His first reaction was. 'Historians who have looked closely at George III regard this legend as utterly improbable, in view of what they know about the King's psychology during his years of early manhood ... He was, by the standards of his day, an extraordinarily straight-laced person. Those who know most about him are convinced that he would never have had any form of liaison outside wedlock. In this he was quite different from most of his contemporaries and several of his sons.'[62]

Having pointed out in subsequent letters that the early newspaper comments on Hannah were 'sheer malicious fabrications characteristic of the press at that time' and pertinently reminded this investigator that 'assertions, however often repeated, cannot be treated as evidence', this distinguished scholar continued: 'The absence of any mention of Hannah Lightfoot in the voluminous letters and diaries of the court gossip, Horace Walpole, is negative evidence supporting these conclusions. Walpole was uniquely placed to learn court secrets. In 1759 his favourite niece, with whom he was always on close terms, became the wife of the Earl Waldegrave, who had been Prince George's tutor for much of the past six years. Waldegrave died in 1763 and three years later she took as her second husband George III's favourite brother, William Henry, Duke of Gloucester. Walpole was also on intimate terms with various ministers and courtiers in high office during the 1760's. For political reasons Walpole became bitterly hostile to George III and lost no chance to report anything to his discredit. Any rumour of such a liaison would almost certainly have reached his ears and been recorded.'[63]

Nor did a whisper of the supposed affair come from the industrious pen of Fanny Burney, the novelist and diarist who became assistant Keeper of the Robes to Queen Charlotte and so lived in the closest daily contact for five years with all members of the royal household. Admittedly this was roughly a quarter of a century after the marriages were alleged to have taken place, but it is extremely unlikely that she would not have recorded – among the minutiae of the daily round which she *did* record – a hint, a rumour, a slip of the tongue pertaining to such an affair.

It is astonishing, in fact, to find how many well-read and rational people today, particularly in England, still cling tenaciously to the legend of George and Hannah having been married in 1759, in spite of the fact that every aspect of this King's life has now been examined in the minutest detail by his many biographers and that the registers of Kew Chapel, where the April 1759 marriage was supposed to have taken place, show no record of such an event.

There is a tiny loophole here for the would-be romanticists, thanks to the fact that the original registers of births, deaths and marriages recorded at Kew from 1714 onwards are not available today, but that these had been neatly copied – as was the custom – by an early rector of Kew into a vellum-bound book entitled: 'A Register of all the Marriages, Christenings and Burials which have been solemnized, had and performed in the Chapple of St. Anne's, Kew Green, and the Chapple Yard thereto belonging to the County of Surrey, beginning on Wednesday, 12 May 1714, being the day of the Consecration there of the Right Reverend Father-in-God, Jonathan, Lord Bishop of Winchester.'[64]

There is naturally no record of a marriage of George III's in this book, to Hannah Lightfoot or anyone else, but the legend believers continue to assert that it might have been in the original documents of 1759 and been purposely omitted from the copy in the book. This throws a nasty aspersion on the man of God who compiled the lists in the vellum-bound book.

There is another odd circumstance about the registers of this historic and charming little chapel; the registers from 1791 to 1845 were stolen on 22 February, 1845. If this theft was organised by someone hoping to find evidence of the royal marriage under discussion, then he – or she – must have been disappointed, as it would not have fallen into this period anyway. On the other hand, the motive may have been the very reverse of the one suggested; it may have been to remove the *absence* of proof that George III had married Hannah and the proof that *no* ceremony had been performed there by Dr. James Wilmot. The theft was widely publicised and a reward of £10 offered for the return of the registers, but with no success.

Mr. A. Lloyd-Taylor, whose forebears, the Taylors of Kew, were closely associated with the chapel from its inception and lived in several of the charming houses round the village green, believes that it was one of his ancestors, Henry Taylor, who organised the

188

theft of the registers, but at the instigation of some person unknown. It has always been assumed that Henry Taylor was substantially rewarded by someone who had an ulterior motive for removing evidence of some ceremony that had (or had not!) taken place in Kew Chapel.[65]

Six weeks after the theft of the registers, incidentally, the Churchwarden received a letter stating that the missing registers would be returned on payment of £50 to 'certain parties', provided no prosecution ensued. Who were the 'certain parties'? One woman in London, as we know, was at this time busy concocting evidence which would point to there having been a marriage between George III and Hannah; could she also have attempted to suppress negative evidence such as the absence of any record of the marriage in the Kew Chapel registers? The answer will probably never be known. No more was heard of the matter and the stolen registers were never recovered.

Any fantasy-weavers still reluctant to give up the legend of the secret marriage which was supposed to have resulted in the birth of George Rex – among others – must ponder the fact that Hannah Lightfoot has been dismissed in the past by such writers as Sir Charles Petrie, who does not mention her in *The Four Georges;* and Sir George Arthur, author of *Seven Heirs Apparent,* who points out that 'the document which set out that the Prince of Wales and Hannah Lightfoot were married in Kew Chapel in 1759, with William Pitt as a witness, was pronounced by the greatest legal authorities to be *a gross and rank forgery.*'[66]

Nor does Hannah earn a mention in the body of the text in either John Brooke's or Stanley Ayling's meticulously documented books on George III (both published in 1972). She is dismissed by both with brief notes appended to the text. Stanley Ayling writes: 'But the account by this author (B. Willson, *George III as Monarch, Man and Statesman*) and many others of the 'almost forgotten romance' between the Prince and Hannah Lightfoot is probably best forgotten altogether. It seems almost certainly not to have happened.'[67]

John Brooke's verdict is: 'There is no British King of modern times of whom so many legends exist as King George III. One of the most ridiculous is the story of his alleged marriage to Hannah Lightfoot, 'the fair Quaker . . .' Hannah Lightfoot certainly existed, but there is no evidence that the King so much as heard of her let alone married her. Royalty is peculiarly prone to legends of this nature, and there have always been people who profess to believe on the flimsiest evidence that they are descended from royalty.[68]

But these are erudite men looking at it all from the vantage point of the late twentieth century, when research techniques have improved immeasurably. It is possible now to sort out fact from fiction to a degree undreamed of fifty – let alone a hundred and fifty – years ago.

John Brooke, in the body of his book, points out that 'King George III had a claim to be considered the most cultured King ever to sit on the throne of Great Britain'; that he was the first King of Britain to study science as part of his education; that it was he who founded the King's excellent collection of scientific instruments in the Science Museum, London; who maintained his own astronomical observatory and patronised the greatest observational astronomer of all time (Herschel); he who founded the Royal Academy and paid the initial expenses out of his own private purse; and who purchased every book in the King's Library in the British Museum.'[69] He has been given little credit for these achievements in previous writings on his life.

This is the King, a prisoner at the bar of Time, who has stood accused for over two hundred years of fathering three children by Hannah Lightfoot and committing bigamy when he married Princess Charlotte, incidentally foisting a line of spurious sovereigns on the throne of Great Britain.

The defendant may now leave the court of History without a stain on his character.

10 The Aftermath

'The gap between the knowledge of the average man and woman and the knowledge of the scholar, in history as in science, is immense and is increasing year by year. Perhaps this does not matter in science but it does in history. It is the knowledge of the average man, not the knowledge of the scholar which determines the image of a nation's past and its hopes for the future.' (John Brooke)[1]

The verdict of the historians is loud and clear; George Rex was not a son, or even a relative, of King George III. This is one gap between the knowledge of the scholar and that of the average man which we contend has been closed. It remains now to recapitulate how and why the belief in Rex's royal paternity should have taken root during his lifetime and to try to evaluate the climate after his death in which it was possible for these beliefs to burgeon and multiply.

Many of the more exaggerated claims regarding the importance of Rex's position in the Vice-Admiralty Court, the handsome allowance which he received from England, the granting to him – by grace and favour – of huge tracts of land at Knysna and the grandeur of the *ménage* which he maintained at *Melkhout Kraal,* have been answered in the mere telling of the story of his life. Others need some elucidation.

According to John Lindsey – writing in 1939, the reader will remember – the earliest report of any connection between Rex and the King was contained in a complaint voiced by an obscure Government servant, Mr. Twistle, in 1801. He was supposed to have written a letter four years after Rex's arrival in the Colony, about Rex having 'been presented with one of the best positions in the Colony almost on arrival' and to have followed this up with further correspondence on the subject with his sister in England, a Mrs. Dacres.[2]

This letter of complaint was stated to have been addressed to the editor of *The Cape Post,* who did not publish it. But as this 'liverish gentleman's' remarks have been relied upon to back up the assertion that Rex was known from his earliest days in South Africa to have been related to the King, some pertinent comment has become necessary. In an appendix to Sanni Metelerkamp's book (in which, incidentally, Rex was elevated to the 'Vice-Admiraltyship')[3], Twistle's complaint was used as further proof of Rex's connection with the King and it was also accepted in effect by Arthur J. Rex Beddy in his *Genealogy of the Rex Family.*[4]

Apart from the fact that there is no record of Twistle's identity in documents relating to the first British occupation, at best he must have been unqualified and unimportant to have aspired to Rex's position. Secondly, there was no such publication as *The Cape Post* at that time according to D. McMurtrie's authoritative history, *The Introduction to Printing in South Africa,* and Dr. A. J. Boëseken's comprehensive *Nuusbode.* At the turn of the nineteenth century, a firm called Ritter and Smith had for a while been printing in a small way, confining themselves to Government notices, almanacs, handbills, notices of sale, catalogues, etc., but Sir George Yonge in 1800 arbitrarily transferred the monopoly in printing to Messrs. Walker and Robertson, of 35 Plein Street. This firm, it will be recalled, were merchants who had a finger in many pies and even engaged surreptitiously in a profitable slave trade as well.

On 16 August 1800, what is regarded as South Africa's first newspaper, the weekly *Cape Town Gazette and African Advertiser* appeared,[5] but by the end of that year, when Yonge had departed, the Government had taken over the printing press and placed it under the personal supervision of Mr. John Barrow himself, the Auditor of Accounts. Francis Dundas, then acting Governor for the second time, felt that Yonge's move – though sound in principle – had been premature in practice.

Politics were strictly barred in the *Cape Town Gazette* (as it was familiarly called), occasional paragraphs of news were permitted and 'constructive articles by Government officials' appeared from time to time. This must have been dry fare for George Rex, accustomed to the lively and many-facetted press of London.

After 1802, when the British had pulled out of the Cape, and it had reverted to the Dutch, the one and only printing plant was moved to the Castle and the Batavian Republic authorities brought out a journal every Saturday which was named the *Kaapsche Courant.*[6] So much for *The Cape Post.*

Lindsey writes that 'all attempts to get in touch with informants (about the identity of Mr. Twistle) have failed' and does not state where and by whom he was shown these significant items of correspondence. Twistle is also found, complaining in correspondence with his sister, that 'this so-called Rex is fêted and the recipient of so much honour on account of being the son of our King by a Quaker . . . before ever Queen Charlotte was thought of.'[7] It must be pointed out that these social highlights in George Rex's life seem completely to have escaped the notice of Lady Anne Barnard and others writing of the social and political scene at the Cape at that time.

Twistle, of whose existence there seems to be no proof, ostensibly wrote a letter, which was not seen by Lindsey, to an editor who did not publish it, of a newspaper which did not exist.

A significant comment on the subject made in Rex's lifetime, that of William Harrison, who later became an antiquary of some note, needs more serious examination. Harrison, to refresh the reader's memory, visited the Cape in 1830, stayed for a few days with the hospitable George Rex at Knysna, and in 1861 contributed to the correspondence still being carried on in *Notes and Queries*[8] on the subject of Hannah Lightfoot and George III and their putative issue. In a letter in which he recollected his impressions of this visit, he said about Rex 'I . . . should suppose that he was about sixty-eight years of age, of a strong robust appearance and the exact resemblance in features to George III.' Harrison was, although writing thirty-one years after the meeting took place, also able to quote from his journal in which he had recorded his impressions of his journey to South Africa. He was three years out in his estimate of Rex's age, which was not a bad guess.

Evidence of facial resemblances between the Rex clan and the house of Hanover has been commented on time and again, then and now, verbally and in print. It is a well-known psychological principle that we tend to see what we are predisposed to see in such matters. The comment, 'Anyone can see she is your daughter,' has repeatedly been made by casual acquaintances of the present writer apropos her younger stepdaughter.

Harrison undoubtedly knew all about the Lightfoot legend, was well aware that 'Rex' is the Latin for 'King' and saw that Rex was laird of an impressive domain. In the simple, bucolic community of that time, he appeared to live certainly in baronial, if not regal, style.

Harrison had also spent an evening with Captain Robert Harker, the Government Resident in Plettenberg Bay, and heard from him much of the local gossip surrounding the squire of Knysna. He learned that 'Rex was a Gentleman of good education and manners and had passed his early days much about the Court of St. James and was said to be a son of George III, to whom I had observed he bore a very strong resemblance.'[9] The visitor from

England was also told about Rex having occupied 'a high situation under the Colonial Government and having received a very extensive grant of land at the Knysna . . . where he continued to live like a Prince.' (Rex's appointment to the post of Marshal of the Vice-Admiralty Court was not, of course, a Colonial government appointment.)

There was no reason why Harrison should not have accepted Captain Harker's version of Rex's background. No attempt had been made to refute this. The Prince-and-Quaker legend was circulating merrily, if *sub rosa*, in the Colony, for here was a man whose very name and exceptional reticence, in addition to a certain amount of circumstantial evidence, indicated that he fitted admirably into the role of an offspring of this union. And the proliferation of paper impugning the royal family (put forth by Olivia Serres) was approaching a peak in London at this time. All such news and gossip from the capital was inevitably passed on to enliven the comparatively dull social life at the Cape.

If the idea that Rex was in some way connected with the King was rife in Cape Town in the early years of the century (and it would be surprising if it were not, in view of his well-known silence about his origins and background) then the monogram GR next to the Admiralty seal on official documents and elsewhere must have had a great deal to do with the fostering of the rumour. By the time Harrison visited South Africa 'GR' had for well over a hundred years indicated that a document had been signed by one of the four successive kings of England – all Georges. For over forty years at the Cape alone, Rex naturally had used these same initials with no intentional misrepresentation on his part, but this coincidence had its effect in stimulating a royal image.

Since Harrison's day the 'Hanoverian likeness' has been repeatedly commented upon and the suggestion made that the houses of Guelph and Rex shared a remote common root-stock. If the likeness had been remarked on nearly two centuries ago, the fact that it should have persisted to this day should occasion no surprise. If there were a similarity of feature then, the genes responsible for the predominant physical characteristics in the two families – unrelated by blood – in one generation will obviously persist in their parallel but separate channels to the next generation – and the next. New characteristics will, of course, be introduced too and old ones diminish or disappear with successive marriages.

A glance at the portraits of the four sovereigns who ruled Britain during George Rex's lifetime (frontispiece) indicates a substantial divergence of physical characteristics between these three

194

men and the woman, who were closely related. There are those who are not convinced that the existing photographs of George Rex's sons and daughters strongly reflect the fair hair and rather bulbous blue eyes of George III. In any case, likeness is one thing, proof is another. Resemblance is far from being conclusive evidence of relationship. Familial likenesses have been strongly preserved among Rex descendants to this day, largely because of the proportion of cousinly marriages which have taken place between them.

By the time Rex died in 1839, the legend was sufficiently well-established for the following extract to appear in a newspaper of the day within a few weeks of his passing: 'This month there died at Knysna, South Africa, a mysterious person known as George Rex, believed to be a morganatic son of the late King George the Third, and a lovely Quakeress, Hannah Lightfoot. He was sent out to South Africa in the early part of the century and received large grants of land in the beautiful wooded lake district of the Cape Colony; he was also given the post of Marshal to the Admiralty in Cape Town; a great many relics of our late monarch remain in the possession of the family, for George Rex had many children.

'He was buried on a portion of his estate which he had specially chosen for the purpose, on a day of wild wind and rain, and the whole population of Knysna paid tribute to the founder of their town, recalling his dignity; his regal bearing; his reputation as a family man and squire, and the manner in which he ruled over his vast estate. Of him it can be truly said – *he left no enemy behind.*'[10]

If he had tried to scotch the rumours about his elevated origins which had been put around during his lifetime, he obviously had not succeeded. The Rex legend had now received its first public airing in print in South Africa.

George Rex is reputed to have made two last requests on his death bed; one, that the royal crest be obliterated from the silver and cutlery which, according to family tradition bore it; the second, that under no circumstances should his body be taken to England for burial.[11] There is, of course, no documentary evidence of these requests; they, like many other such stories, have been handed down by word of mouth. Examining them from this distance in time, it is only necessary to point out, with regard to the first, that not one of the many travellers who called at *Melkhout Kraal*, from Lord Charles Somerset (a ducal scion himself) to itinerant artists, from missionaries to merchants, made any mention of silver bearing the royal coat of arms, although many of them, as has been seen, made detailed observations on most aspects of the way of life at *Melkhout Kraal* and such blazonry would surely not go unnoticed.

Also, it is not unknown for articles emblazoned with a royal ciper, crest, or coat of arms to be inherited, received as gifts or even bought as collectors' pieces, without any personal association or claim to royal descent being made by their owners. A case in point is a magnificent solid silver meat-cover bearing the crest of King William IV, which is in the possession of a well-known Johannesburg doctor who firmly disclaims any connection with royalty.

If the second request were indeed made, it was not necessarily portentous. The noble Lady Anne Barnard, for instance, was satisfied to leave the bones of her beloved Andrew, who had lived in South Africa for only a short time compared with George Rex, buried in Cape Town and to have him described on his tombstone as 'an Afrikaner' signifying 'one who desired the welfare of your country and loved its inhabitants'. Besides, Rex's mother and father, his brother and most of his relatives and friends in England were long dead. Only his sixty-nine-year-old sister, Sarah, who was to outlive him by three years, would have been there and it would have been no kindness to have sent his body to Bath for her to attend to the lonely obsequies.

Knysna was the spot where had had made his mark, *Melkhout Kraal* was the fulfilment of his dream; it was only proper that he should lie right there, where members of his large and closely-knit family and friends could pay their last respects to him.

William Harrison would probably have seen, during his three-day visit to *Melkhout Kraal*, the mace of Admiralty and the beautiful Wedgwood portrait medallion of George III, if on display. He would also have been shown, in view of his special interest in antiques and *objets d'art*, some of the many other souvenirs stated to have been given to Rex by the King at the alleged last interview, including the gold signet ring engraved with the initials 'GR', the gold locket containing a lock of 'His Majesty's hair, auburn touched with grey', a cornelian seal for a watch-chain, set in gold and engraved with the words 'Though lost to sight to memory dear' and the 'massive pinchbeck watch'.

The significance of the mace has been dealt with in an earlier chapter. Displayed with the mace today as another of Rex's 'instruments of office' is a seal-stamp with the monogram 'GR' in the centre, encircled with the words, 'Cape of Good Hope'.[12] It may have been the official seal used on Admiralty documents, though this is unlikely as one would then expect it to be surmounted by a crown or some such symbol of authority. A rather more prosaic explanation put forward by a Rex descendant is that this stamp may indeed have been an 'instrument of office', the stamp used by Rex

196

before 1820 (when George III died) for sealing mailbags. It will be remembered that he was in charge of postal matters at Knysna from 1810 onwards.

There is no shred of evidence of the last interview between George Rex and the King. The 'GR' engraved on a signet ring indicated simply that this ring belonged to a man with these initials, as it certainly did. The cornelian seal engraved with the words, 'Though lost to sight to memory dear', could have been given to George Rex by any friend or member of his family when he left England for good.

A chronicler who saw 'the massive pinchbeck watch' in the possession of a Rex descendant in the nineteen-forties, described it as follows: 'an old watch of a brass-like metal in a round detachable case (described to me as Pinchbeck) by Morris Tobias, given to George Rex (junior) by his father.'[13] This was undoubtedly the old Rex's own watch and does not sound as if it were nearly valuable enough to have ever been taken seriously as a gift from the King. Pinchbeck, an alloy of zinc and copper, is used in making cheap jewellery.

As for the locket, George Rex himself is described as having auburn hair, so this was probably a familial characteristic. The lock of hair contained in it may have been his mother's, his sister's or that of any dear friend of his. Indeed, if there is any foundation for the surmise (mentioned in Chapter 4) that he may have been married before he left England, then any or all these personal mementoes could have been given him by his wife.

Of all the 'royal' relics, the Wedgwood portrait medallion of George III has carried most weight and has greatly influenced thinking towards acceptance of the theory that there was a special relationship between the King and Rex. This particular medallion, modelled originally in 1775 by William Hackwood (one of Josiah Wedgwood's top designers) from a wax portrait by Isaac Grosset and re-modelled again by Hackwood in 1776, was made in considerable quantities for public sale and might therefore have been the property of anyone from the King to the least of his subjects. In the absence of documentary evidence, however, there is no reason to suppose that this particular piece was ever in the King's possession.[14]

The excellent quality of the glaze and the rather unusual frame do indicate that this particular version was made for a special purpose or an esteemed customer. It is a highly desirable collector's item. George III and Queen Charlotte, especially the latter, were most appreciative of Wedgwood's pottery, his jasperware in particular, and undoubtedly owned quantities of his products. The usual procedure was for Josiah Wedgwood to present copies of his royal medallion portraits to the King and Queen, whose permission he had to obtain anyway before the portraits of members of the royal family were put on public sale.

There were various medallions of George III produced by Wedgwood, however, and even the one in question was remodelled. As the original mould still exists at the Wedgwood potteries, reproductions can be made from it today.[15]

William Hackwood, who had been an engraver of transfer prints for the painted enamel trade, joined Wedgwood and became his chief staff modeller in bas-relief. Some of Hackwood's plaques are equal in quality to those designed by some of the most eminent sculptors of the period. Wedgwood once said of him 'We want half-a-dozen more Hackwoods.' This artist's excellent profile portraits include, apart from the ones of George III, those of Queen Charlotte, Josiah Wedgwood himself, David Garrick, Admiral Keppel, Dr. Priestly, Louis XVI and an old bricklayer employed on the Etruria pottery kilns.[16]

Featured on medallions by other designers, apart from members of the royal family and the aristocracy, were Pitt and Fox, among the politicians; Captain Cook, the explorer; Sir William Herschel, noted scientist; Garrick, the actor and Mrs. Siddons, actress; Shakespeare and Dr. Johnson, Voltaire and Rousseau.[17] More than seventy independent designers and modellers were employed by Wedgwood in the last quarter of the eighteenth century. Wedgwood had his finger on the public pulse and showed unusual ingenuity in commemorating people and events of the day in his ceramics. Any customer could order a personal portrait to be modelled. An idea of the cost of such an enterprise is obtained from a Wedgwood catalogue notice of the day: ' . . . A model of a portrait from wax, when it is of a proper size for a seal, ring or bracelet, will cost about *three* guineas, and a portrait from three to six inches in diameter, *three, four* or *five* guineas. Any number of portraits in the same material, from three to six inches in diameter, not fewer than ten, at 10s 6d. each.'[18]

In view of the high quality and unusual surround of the portrait medallion of George III now in the possession of a descendant at Knysna, one may speculate as to how George Rex came to own it. As it was first cast in 1775, when he was a boy of ten, it is unlikely that he had anything to do with its purchase. It is more likely that George's father, John Rex, then a highly-respected office-bearer in the Distillers' Company, one of the old Guilds of London Town, was presented with it in the course of his civic duties, or he may simply have bought it. Such a possession would have been treasured in the family until after John Rex's death and possibly given to his son when he left England in 1797.

As ten different portraits of George III were cast by the Wedgwood potteries over the years, a noteworthy one being that of 1789 commemorating the King's recovery from his first illness,[19] it is pertinent to observe here that it is unlikely that George Rex, during his proctorship at Doctors' Commons or on his departure from England, would have been presented with the particular model under discussion, then more than twenty years old.

Sanni Metelerkamp, in *George Rex of Knysna*, writes: 'Among the most valuable and valued of the heirlooms are a necklace, a work-box and a 'Lady's companion' that are said to have belonged to Hannah Lightfoot.'

'According to tradition' the necklace was given to Hannah by George III when Prince of Wales and inherited by their only daughter, Sarah Rex, of Bath.[20] As with all these relics, the verdict regarding their origin is, of course, *not proven*, but in this case, as the necklace was said to date from about 1700, it is not impossible that the heirloom may have been handed down in the Rex family to the eldest daughter in succeeding generations from George's and Sarah's great-grandparents, Thomas and Prudence Hopkins of Stepney. It was this comparatively affluent couple, it will be remembered, who bequeathed the original Plaistow lands which also came down through three generations to Sarah Rex, George's sister.

The work-box and 'Lady's companion' were given in 1833 to Caroline Duthie by her aunt, Sarah, when the young Duthies visited her in Bath. The old lady told Caroline that these treasured possessions had belonged to her mother. In terms of semantics, her statement was accurate, her mother being Mrs. Sarah Rex, of Whitechapel.

Among latter-day acquisitions that in time came to be looked upon as tacit proof of royal connections, were a heavy muzzle-loader, specially designed for shooting elephants or other big game, and a gold hunting-watch. The muzzle-loader has been described by one chronicler as 'a fine specimen of a period sporting gun of large calibre with a gold plate bearing the Royal crest set in the walnut stock'[21] and by George Rex's biographer, Miss Metelerkamp, as '. . . a lordly weapon with gold mountings, and a crown and an oval gold shield, the latter bearing a griffin or boar's head, surrounded by the motto *Fortiter et Prudenter*.'[22]

This brings us to an event which took place well after Rex's death, but which some writers, who have thrown recorded history to the winds in their enthusiasm for forging one spurious link after another between George III and George Rex, have rashly stated as having taken place in the latter's lifetime. All in the cause of a good story! This was the visit to Knysna in 1867, twenty-eight years after Rex died, of His Royal Highness Alfred, the youthful Duke of Edinburgh, Queen Victoria's second son.

He had ostensibly come to shoot an elephant, but it was common talk in Knysna, said the family chronicler, that everyone realised 'it was, in fact, to see the Rexes'.

One of Mary Pendered's correspondents (already quoted in Chapter 2) who had stayed at Knysna and heard all the rumours, wrote that 'The late Duke of Edinburgh, when visiting the Colony, stayed with the head of the family, and on leaving, presented him with a gold watch.[23] John Lindsey, in *The Lovely Quaker*, went further and claimed that the young Duke of Edinburgh 'stayed several weeks with George Rex' (long-departed) 'and treated him with the courtesy due to a relative'.[24]

A fascinating book could be written about this episode alone – Prince Alfred's visit to Knysna. The elephant hunt does, in fact, feature prominently in *The Cruise of the H.M.S. Galatea in 1867-68*, a journal written by the Reverend John Milner and Mr. Oswald Brierly, who accompanied the Duke from England and on the whole triumphal tour through the Cape Colony. Brierly was, *inter alia*, the official artist of the party and his sketches of the hunt were reproduced in *The Illustrated London News* of the day.

A valuable insertion in their book is the letter which Prince Alfred wrote to his elder brother, the Prince of Wales, giving an exuberant first-hand account of the shooting of the beast.

The party consisted of Sir Philip Wodehouse, Governor of the Colony, his military secretary, his private secretary, and the Colonial aide-de-camp, while in the Duke's 'own especial portion of the party' were 'my two especial friends at the Cape, Sir Walter Currie and General Bisset'; Captain Gordon, commander of *The Petrel* (in which the visiting party had entered the Knysna harbour), and Dr. O'Malley, 'a very Irish surgeon of the same ship'.

The Duke described how they landed at the tentative little town of Knysna and 'remained at a small inn for the night'. (This was Thomas Horn's *St. George's Tavern*, which had never seen such glory as it did that night.) Some of the farmers of the district – including George Rex junior ('head man of the hunt'), Thomas Rex (the 'baby' born in 1834) Archibald Hamilton Duthie (Thomas Henry's son), George Atkinson (who was married to one of George Rex's daughters) and Thomas Charles Bain, the brilliant engineer of the recently completed spectacular pass over the Outeniqua Mountains, which the Duke graciously consented to have named after him – Prince Alfred's Pass – had assembled to give the royal party the benefit of their experience of the local forests and of the near-mammoths inhabiting them.

Two of 'the native huntsmen', both Stroebels (grandsons of old Gert Stroebel) were well to the fore in beating up the elephants and driving them in the direction in which it would be feasible for the Duke to bring one of the great pachyderms down. The Duke's letter to his brother gives a vivid and genuinely exciting account of the progress of the hunt and his eventual dropping of one of the strange, ferocious giants of the forest. (To catch a glimpse of a Knysna elephant today, by the way, is a rare phenomenon, as there are reported to be only ten left of the hundreds which once roamed this vast expanse of forest).

After his return to England, the Duke sent each member of the hunting party, including the Stroebels, a souvenir of his visit. George Rex junior received a silver tankard and a gold hunting-watch (the one which is listed among the family relics); Thomas Rex received a gold signet ring engraved with his initials; Archibald Duthie was given a gold watch-guard and George Atkinson a gold ring, suitably inscribed. Thomas Bain's gift was a gold pen and pencil set, which was forwarded to him by Sir Philip Wodehouse. From Mr. Brierly, of the Duke of Edinburgh's staff, Bain also received an especial letter, written on board the *H.M.S. Galatea*, reading, in part: 'His Royal Highness desires me to thank you for the trouble you have taken, and is much pleased to have so admireble a record of his Knysna Expedition.' This was in appreciation of a valuable detailed chart of the progress of the hunt which the outstanding road engineer had thoughtfully prepared for the Duke.[25]

The gold hunting-watch in the possession of a Rex descendant is now accounted for. It is also conceivable that the large-bore gun, once so proudly displayed, may date from this historic hunt too, but there is another possible and more mundane explanation of how this weapon may have come into the possession of the family at a much earlier date.

On 24 November 1799, Major General Francis Dundas, acting Governor of the Colony, wrote to London 're the presentation of an English musket apiece to be presented (to the Commandants of the Militia) in His Majesty's name'. These were to be given to the Commandants 'for services done to the British Government' and the requirements were set out in exact detail. One was to be 'double-barrel, with several sights, very large bore, calculated for killing elephants – long and strengthened at the stock' and the other 'single-barrel, very large in the bore and very long for killing elephants or rhinoceroses'. Both were to have a suitable brass plate on the case.[26]

It is quite likely that George Rex may have received a similar gun 'for services to His Majesty's Government' or have acquired it by purchase from one of the original owners, especially as Sanni Metelerkamp states that this weighty gun was accompanied by a pamphlet entitled, 'The Report of the Society for the Encouragement of Arts, Manufactures and Commerce, 1802', in which the gun was described as 'A New Invention'. This would link it approximately to the time at which the dissolution of the Vice-Admiralty Court was looming on the horizon and George was planning to move into elephant country.

Credence has been given to the various versions of the origins of the articles described above, and the very fact of their possession by members of the family has done much to substantiate the belief that George Rex – whether the son of the King or not – and members of his family were indeed the recipients of several handsome gifts with a regal aura surrounding them.

More subtle in their effect and more difficult to evaluate are nebulous, sometimes patently inaccurate, rumours which proliferated after Rex's death. The exercise of categorising and attempting to analyse them has been rather like trying to come to grips with ectoplasm, which is only seen or felt by believers.

A number of the semi-secret family anecdotes which alluded to George Rex's early life in England are highly sentimental and rather unctuous. 'Yes, dear, the story is true. Your great-grandfather was the son of King George III and Hannah Lightfoot, the beautiful Quakeress; but he never spoke of it and we must not either.'[27] (A reported conversation between mother and daughter.)

Some rely heavily on verisimilitude to influence the reader. For instance, in *George Rex of Knysna*, Miss Metelerkamp wrote:

'He (Rex) and the younger Pitt were contemporaries, Pitt being the elder by a couple of years; and it is known that when George Rex received the news of that statesman's death he went into retirement for several days, seeing no one, but keeping to his study and taking solitary walks over the hills. As young men they had no doubt shared many an escapade together and would have confided their hopes and ambitions to each other –

hoped and ambitions which in the one case bore abundant fruit, and in the other were withered in the bud.'[28]

The younger Pitt, born in 1759, became Prime Minister in 1783 – at the age of twenty-four – when George Rex had been for three years articled to Edward Cooper, the notary public in whose office he qualified.

Another example:

'Mrs. Rex (wife of George Rex junior) believes that her husband never told her all he knew about his father. She remembers his saying that when his father took him to Cape Town with him he always first visited a titled old lady and kissed her, the only person outside the family that young George ever saw his father kiss. Her husband seemed to know absolutely that his father was the son of George and Hannah. He advised her not to reply to enquiries on the subject.'[29]

(The 'titled old lady' could quite possibly have been the wife of Baron von Ludwig.)

There are also occasions on which – to use Professor Christie's phrase – 'assumption slides into assertion'. Rex's biographer, having discussed a family tradition that Rex had lived for a time at George III's court and had a love affair with one of the princesses (who would have been his half-sister, had the royal parentage story been true), continues:

'Whether this was so, who can say today? Not a scrap of evidence exists, yet it has been a fixed tradition for a hundred and fifty years.'
'If true, it must naturally have caused consternation in royal circles – as it is said to have done – *and immediate steps were taken to hush it up*.'[30]

The last sentence contains a definite assertion. The reader of the biography also had to contend with the cumulative effect of a hundred such phrases as: 'It is known from tradition and hearsay; tradition asserts that; these traditions have been believed and handed down in the Rex family from the beginning; there is the fact that; a tradition firmly believed; the background that has been traditionally ascribed to him; he is said to have been *persona grata* at the English Court; it seems certain that; tradition says; there was evidently some close connection between the two; we must accept the persistent tradition; it has been common knowledge in the family for generations; it has always been firmly held that . . .'

And so on. The reiteration of these and similar introductions to assertions on page after page had an almost subliminal effect and few persons who read this book (and it had a wide circulation) could have doubted Rex's royal connections by the time they came to the end.

To take a final example of the type of presentation of material which so effectively mingled fact and fiction in the readers' minds:

'Putting aside the date of George Rex's birth fourteen months after the alleged marriage of George to Hannah (this would be 1760, the reader will remember), there is the tradition held from the earliest time that they had three children – two sons and a daughter – and that George Rex was the eldest of them. There is the fact that he was sent out to the Cape at the very time when, had the story of an *affaire* with one of the Princesses been true, it was desirable to get rid of him.'*

'There are the two promises demanded of him: the destruction of all documentary evidence (Church registers etc.) in various parts of England that might have confirmed the traditions. There is his own silence as to his origin, and there is the burning of his papers so that 'His secret' might die with him.'

'Then there is his remarkable likeness to George III and the likenesses of his descendants to the Hanoverians – so striking that he would never allow any pictures of them to be made. There are, too, the mementoes and relics handed down in the family . . .'[31]

And so it goes on.

It would be a clear and strong-minded reader indeed who was not persuaded of the connection between George III and George Rex after being exposed to three hundred pages of this treatment. This book represents the distillation of the Rex family's sincerely-held beliefs in their own partly-blue blood.

The mention in the last quotation of 'the destruction of Church registers etc.' probably refers to the registers stolen from the Chapel of St. Anne at Kew in February 1845,[32] an episode already dealt with in Chapter 9.

Regarding the inventory of fine furniture and objets d'art – Chinese vases, a Wedgwood jug, copper coffee urn, Sheffield plate tea caddies, blue china soup tureen, wine funnel and so on – these may well have been brought out from England by Rex in 1797 or have been acquired in Cape Town, especially at the end of the first

*Appendix J

204

British occupation when so many British subjects were selling out and returning to their home country.

The diaspora of the estates was rapid and relentless following Rex's death. Some writers have attributed this to the theory that the Crown grant of £1000 'went out with him', but the explanation was simpler than that. He had been the sturdy support on which all the large family had leaned. Without him, the organisation ground slowly to a standstill. Caroline and Frederick were both married, but there were eleven sons and daughters left behind at Knysna, four of them minors and the youngest, Thomas, only five years of age. It was beyond the ability of the three eldest sons to maintain the family in the manner to which they had been accustomed; difficult for them even to continue to earn a living for all of them out of the soil, the forest, the stores and the trading.

Early in 1840, almost a year after the father's death, an advertisement appeared in a Cape newspaper giving notice of the sale of the furniture and effects of *Melkhout Kraal*. The 'many fine pieces of furniture', the silver, glassware, cutlery, ornaments, books and bric-a-brac, the livestock and horses, the contents of the blacksmith's shop and the dairy, were all listed in some detail. Three score years and ten had passed since Stephanus Terblans had settled on his idyllic spot: Rex had spent half this period there and now its glory was departing, never to return.

Part of the explanation for the rapid dispersion of the grandeur lies in the terms of Rex's will,[33] which – in the spirit of the country's Roman-Dutch law – directed that 'all my lands and places held on Quitrent or otherwise, Houses and Buildings and also my real and personal Estate and Effects, of what nature or kind so ever and wheresoever which I shall or may be possessed of, or entitled to at the time of my Decease shall be sold and disposed of at the Discretion of my Executors here after named, and that the money arising from the sale thereof (after payment of my just Debts; Funeral Expenses I hope there will be none) shall be divided into sixteen equal parts or shares . . .'

Of these sixteen equal shares, Carolina Margaretha (Mrs. Rex II) was to be entitled to three 'for her own sole and separate Use and Benefit' and one share was to go to each of the thirteen children; meticulously listed in his legal way.

There are three features of this document which should be remarked upon. Firstly, in the opening sentences he scrupulously describes himself as 'I George Rex residing at the Knysna in the District of George, Cape of Good Hope (not having submitted myself to the matrimonial Laws of this Colony) . . .' and mentions

ANNA ROSINA (deceased) with whom I formerly lived and cohabited' and CAROLINA MARGARETHA, with whom I have since lived and cohabitted'. He seemed anxious to make it impossible for any misinterpretation to be placed on his position and that of the two Mrs. Rexes.

He, as a lawyer, was well aware that under the circumstances he had to ensure the legal rights of Carolina Margaretha, her children, and his children by Johanna Rosina, in regard to their inheritance.

Secondly, he makes a point of his 'having excluded as I do hereby shut out and totally exclude, from all Interference with my Estate and Effects the Master of the Supreme Court of this Colony and all other official Persons and Magistrates who by virtue of their Office might or could interfere therewith, hereby revoking and making void all former Wills by me at any time heretofore made and declaring this paperwriting, all written with my own hand to be and contain my only last Will and Testament . . .'

Thirdly, he appointed his sons Edward and John, together with Carolina Margaretha, as executors of his estate and nominated Carolina Margaretha as the 'Guardian of my aforesaid minor children during their minority . . .' Altogether an interesting document, simple and to the point, the purpose of which was not open to any misinterpretation.

He had made this will on 8 April, 1837, two years before his death, and deposited it in a closed packet 'sealed with a seal in three distinct places' with John Barker, notary public, in Cape Town.

As could be expected, the major load of responsibility in winding up the father's affairs fell on John's capable shoulders and he is found in Cape Town in 1841, two years after George's death, spending some weeks consulting lawyers and, at the same time, carrying on the family business, arranging for cargoes to be loaded, timber to be delivered and so on. In a letter to Carolina Margaretha at this time, he mentioned that Thomas Henry Duthie had paid the last instalment of £750 for the Westford and Portland properties on 28 October.[34]

There had been two sales held of the furniture and effects (some of them being bought in by the family), but the lands were advertised widely and repeatedly for sale without a bid being received. These were difficult years, because there were a great many heirs involved and, until the properties could be sold, very little capital on which to live. Anne was by now dead and Frederick, the surveyor, had drawn so heavily on his share of the inheritance in his father's lifetime that he actually owed the estate money. There were still the 'widow' and eleven children, however, and in order to wind up the estate it was eventually decided that they should take it over for the sum of £3 000, each paying an equal share of £250. With the exception of Caroline, now married and living at Belvidere, they all continued to live at *Melkhout Kraal* as before.

Five and a half anxious years passed after Rex's death before the *deus ex machina* who was to solve the family's problems appeared on the horizon.[35] This was a wealthy Anglo-Indian, Lieutenant-Colonel John Sutherland of the 2nd Bombay Cavalry and of the East India Company. On a visit to the Cape, he heard the story of the famed Rex estates lying waiting for a purchaser, came to inspect them forthwith, but decided to look at other properties inland before making up his mind.

He announced his decision to buy the Knysna properties in a letter to Thomas Henry Duthie, who had been appointed Inspector of Forests in the year George Rex died, and was now a man of substance, owner of considerable stretches of land, and able in many ways to advise and assist the widow and younger offspring. It is clear that the family relied heavily on the able Scot, now nearly forty. Duthie, immediately on receipt of the Colonel's letter, wrote enthusiastically to Mrs. Rex outlining the terms of the offer.

These were: to buy part of *Melkhout Kraal,* including the area on which the homestead and outbuildings stood, for £3 000; The *Eastford* property, excluding the forty morgen which had been ceded for naval purposes, for £1 000, and *Westford,* Duthie's own property, for £2 000.

This was extremely satisfactory and on 18 December, 1844, the following document was drawn up: 'We the Undersigned Proprietors of the Perpetual Quitrent Place or Farm named *Melkhout Kraal,* situated on the Eastern Bank of the River Knysna, do hereby Acknowledge and declare that we have sold, and disposed of, to and in favour of Lieut. Colonel John Sutherland, H.C.S., a certain extent or part of the abovementioned Farm of *Melkhout Kraal* being on the northern side of a division line . . . reserving only one morgen of land near the Village of Melville which the late Proprietor had given for the building of a Church or place of worship, for the sum of Three Thousand Pounds Sterling.'[36]

With the prospect of having to move out of *Melkhout Kraal* eventually, the Rexes had been preparing a home at what they called New Place (on what was later to be called Rexford) and in June 1845, a letter arrived from John – again in Cape Town on business – warning the family that it would be advisable to vacate *Melkhout Kraal* and move to New Place as expeditiously as possible, because the Sutherland party, which included the Colonel's brother and sister, three sons and several friends, was about to sail from Cape Town for the Knysna. When they arrived, Thomas Duthie reported in a letter to his brother ' . . . such a cavalcade and such profusion never has been seen in these parts before.'[37]

It seemed as if the successful drama of the splendid days of *Melkhout Kraal* was about to be replayed with a new cast.

Having installed his eldest son at *Melkhout Kraal* and organised everything to his satisfaction, the Colonel left for India in December 1845, intending to return to South Africa within five years to settle permanently at Knysna. His dream was not to be realised, however, and he died in India in June, 1848. His son, John, was left to carry out as many as he could of the sound schemes his father had had for the improvement of the properties, among others the dividing up into small plots of about fifty-seven hectares excised from the *Melkhout Kraal* property. Within ten years, forty of these were sold and most built on and so the village of Newhaven, the eastern half of the present town of Knysna, came into being.

But the Sutherland fortunes crashed dramatically about ten years after the purchase of *Melkhout Kraal;* the family dispersed, leaving only the second son, Eric Sutherland, earning his living as the first teacher appointed to the first public school in Knysna. *Sic transit gloria mundi. Melkhout Kraal* was repeatedly advertised for sale by them, but without success, the last time being in 1872.

And today?

Mention the name *Melkhout Kraal* or *Old Place* to a dyed-in-the-wool Knysna man and the name 'Stroebel' rather than 'Rex' will spring to his lips, because in this century the Stroebel family has owned this land for as long as anyone can remember. In recent years, however, a quick succession of recent deaths in both branches of the family which inherited the land – mainly in two separate portions – has resulted in the direct line of descent being broken.

Time has not stood still here any more than it has in any other part of the world. On the left hand side of the national road as the traveller heads east towards Plettenberg Bay, the picturesque little Coloured cottages which have been dotted over the slopes for generations are being pulled down ('demolished' is too strong a word for these gimcrack little huts) following the dictates of the Group Areas Act, and modern, much grander 'White' houses are marching up the hill, spreading eastward from the borders of the Hospital grounds.

On the right-hand side, where once the homestead and out-buildings stood, the prospect is strictly utilitarian. It is just possible to trace out on the ground the ruined foundations of the spacious-roomed house of *Melkhout Kraal* and to imagine, as one stands at the end of the lane of spreading oaks which once led up to the hospitable front door, the arrival of the many travellers who came this way.

But now, within thirty-five metres of what was the front wall of the house, where Rex must so often have gazed from the windows across the cultivated lands to the tranquil lake beyond, is the border of a new industrial township – *No. 6 – Stroebel Land*. Plots have been marked out for factory sites and general industrial development. Stalking across the landscape to these plots are the pi-shaped transmission pylons of ESCOM (Electricity Supply Commission), bringing high-voltage power to be tamed for distribution to the Knysna and Plettenberg Bay districts.

Fortunately a buffer strip of public land has been left between the national road and the industrial area and in this green belt, sheltered by tall pines, within a few metres of the giant transformer station, is the stone-walled enclosure in which George Rex is buried. Here he will continue to lie undisturbed, while power undreamed of in his lifetime brings progress to the very threshold of his old home and to his last resting-place.

*   *   *

To return to the Rex family in the middle of the last century. The various members continued their busy lives, united and well disposed to one another, as evidenced by the many affectionate letters which passed between them. They still owned *Springfield*, as well as the section of *Melkhout Kraal* which had been divided up into three farms, so there was land in plenty and, although the superabundance of undeveloped land had not proved to be a ready asset once the gifted hand at the helm was taken away, at least this meant that as each son in turn married there were spacious grounds in which he could set up his own home.

John, the first to marry after his father's death, actually chose to build his house in Melville (the first portion of the embryonic Knysna town). Here he and his wife, Susanna, kept open house and maintained the tradition of hospitality instilled in all the Rex offspring by their father. Frederick, who had been the first of the sons to marry, was also the first to die. He passed away in Bloemfontein in 1850, aged only thirty-nine, and there he was buried.

The eldest son, Edward, and the youngest, Tom, never married, but Jacob Govert and George Junior in time followed their brother John's example, Jacob Govert and his wife settling at Woodbourne (the portion of the *Melkhout Kraal* lands nearest the Knysna Heads) and Georgie at *Hunters Home* (the portion nearest the original home). In between these two areas, was *New Place*, run as competently by Carolina Margaretha as she had run the old homestead. From this time *Melkhout Kraal* began to be referred to as *Old Place*, or *Ouplaas*, a name which is still in use today for the area which made up the grounds surrounding the original homestead.

Of the remaining daughters all married except the eldest, Betsy, the one who had been born at *Schoonder Zigt* in Cape Town early in the century. In time Carolina Margaretha was left at *New Place* with Betsy and the two unmarried sons, the four of them joined later by Christina, when her husband, Coenraad Nelson, died. The two youngest daughters, Sarah and Maria, married respectively Robert Cholmondeley Atkinson and Captain John Fisher Sewell, and the two couples settled on farms in the vicinity of Plettenberg Bay.

None of the family – with the exception of Frederick, whose work took him travelling widely in South Africa, and Louisa, who went overseas with her husband, and never returned to South Africa – moved very far away from their old home.

Christina and her husband, when first married, moved into a little thatched cottage in Melville where, in March 1854, they rented out a room with kitchen to the brilliant young Swedish naturalist and artist, Johan Fredrik Victorin, for six shillings a month. Victorin's summing up of the family's situation at this time was, 'All the farms mentioned have been cut off from the large farm and must have brought in a considerable sum of money, but in spite of that the whole family is very poor.'[38] He was noting this fact more sympathetically than critically, as he had become friendly with John Rex, whom he found to be extremely knowledgeable about the local flora and fauna.

Without wishing to dwell unduly on the decline in the fortunes of the Rex family, it must be appreciated that this history would lack integrity if it were not pointed out that it seems that it was in this atmosphere, in these straitened circumstances, in this isolated and sparsely populated spot, that the remaining members of the family began to speculate ever more imaginatively on the validity of their father's claims to royal connections. They had a number of apparently significant relics and documents and they had their happy memories of a glamorous past of dances, picnics, grand dinner parties, distinguished house guests and the visits of dashing young Anglo-Indian Officers. It all contrasted so vividly with the humdrum daily round and common task of their present. They must have felt that the disparity was too great to be accounted for by their father's death alone, had he been an ordinary commoner.

210

Within the family circle rumours and ideas were developed and the foundations of the family traditions laid. From the backwater of Knysna, they would hardly know how to set about checking or verifying the emergent traditions. In any case, as Professor Christie has pointed out, 'until recently this task would technically have been so burdensome as to be virtually impossible!' What has made it possible now is the enormous development of the British system of archive repositories and elaborate improvements in research facilities.

Christina Nelson, widowed, childless, known to be rather a busybody – almost certainly had something to do with laying the foundations of the later legends. It was she, it will be remembered, who wrote to Mrs. Lavinia Ryves in December 1866, stating confidently that her father was a son of George III and Hannah Lightfoot. Carolina Margaretha had died in April of that year, at almost the exact time that Mrs. Ryves brought her case to court, and it is probable that with her going the last vestige of parental control over prying into the Rex parents' backgrounds had been removed. Carolina Margaretha would have respected her husband's reserve on the subject of his early life, as she had respected his wishes throughout her life, and likewise would not have encouraged discussion about her own origins.

It is possible that the brothers and sisters – their security badly shaken by the traumatic changes which had taken place since their father's death – may, in psychological terms, have had a subconscious tendency to over-compensate for their now comparatively humble circumstances by over-romanticising the glamorous past. This they probably did by building on to the whispers and gossip about George Rex and by adducing evidence of royalty from such heirlooms as the Marshal's mace of the Vice-Admiralty Court.

Certainly it seems significant that eight months after Carolina Margaretha's death, when Christina had had ample opportunity of examining all the letters, documents and relics around the house, that she responded to Lavinia Ryves' request for information on the subject of the Prince George-Hannah Lightfoot romance. One is also entitled to speculate as to who censored the documents and excised certain vital fragments – dates, names and so on – from the letters.

It seems unlikely that George Rex himself was responsible, as he – a lawyer – surely would have destroyed completely any evidence he wished to suppress and not spent his time snipping little bits out of his correspondence to leave posterity to puzzle over the reasons for the excisions.

What people throw away or ignore, as well as what they treasure, is a direct revelation of their characters.

To later generations the enormous gaps in the story were more thought-provoking than the actual contents of the documents available to them. It was inevitable that some of these gaps would be filled by conjecture. To some extent it is understandable that many descendants were inclined to believe that every blank space was evidence of some vital link with the royal family, that every omission was a confirmatory clue to their father's real and regal identity, and, in such a frame of mind, alternative, less romantically-attractive explanations were overlooked.

The probable reason for Rex's well-known reticence about his early life – his reluctance to admit to a comparatively humble background of the liquor trade once he had raised himself into the class of a professional gentleman – was most understandable. Rigid class distinction had an unhealthy stranglehold on society. Because his consort and his children, however, had known him only in his heyday – an affluent member of the landed gentry – it was the one reason for his reserve which would never have occurred to them. Such frailty – if frailty it be – never entered their minds.

Ironically, it has been these very claims to an exalted background which have resulted in the family's true origins being investigated in extraordinary detail and led to the consequent dé-'nouement.

With each passing decade, as the events which formed the bases of the legend receded ever further into the mists of time and the likelihood of arriving at the truth receded with them, the belief in Rex's connection with the house of Hanover seems to have grown stronger. To many members of the family, to believe in their royal descent had become an act of faith. The fact that the contentious matter of the relationship of the family to the Crown of Britain has never before been authoritatively rebutted has tended to leave each generation unassailed, believing implicitly in what they had been told by their kinsmen. Royal protocol, of course, demands that pretenders – and there have been many of them – are ignored.

Upright and honest parents have passed on the story of George Rex's supposed origins, as they had received it, to their children and they, in turn, handed it on in all sincerity to their offspring. This unquestioning acceptance of the legend of their part-royal ancestry has perhaps not been such a bad thing. It has engendered a certain spirit of *noblesse oblige* which is reflected in the courteous demeanour and innate good manners of all Rex descendants; standards which the founder of their family himself set.

212

Abraham Lincoln once said, 'I don't know who my grandfather was; I am much more concerned to know what his grandson will be.' Mr. Douglas F. Rex, an outstanding descendant of the founder of Knysna, unwittingly echoed this wise sentiment when he wrote recently: 'I have always resisted temptation to bask in the glory of an illustrious past, and have taught my sons that their own contribution to the world around them during their lifetime is of far greater importance than their genealogy.'

Appendices

Appendix A

PORPHYRIA

If it could have been proved that some of the descendants of both George Rex and King George III had suffered from the comparatively rare inheritable metabolic disorder known as porphyria, this would have strongly favoured the Rex family being of royal descent.

There is some evidence, strongly put forward by Doctors Ida Macalpine and her son, Richard Hunter, in *George III and the Mad Business* (published in 1969), that the King did suffer from porphyria and that this accounted for his recurring bouts of physical and mental illness. This is a view supported by some leading doctors and psychiatrists. As H.R.H. Prince Charles commented in his foreword to John Brooke's *King George III* (1972): 'there has been long and furious argument amongst the medical and historical professions on the controversial subject of porphyria . . . It does indeed fit the symptoms, but the evidence is only suggestive, not conclusive.'

Dr. J.G.K. Dean, in his book, *The Porphyrias: a Story of Inheritance and Environment* (2nd edition, 1971), deals extensively with the occurrence of *variegate* porphyria in South Africa and does not agree with Drs. Macalpine and Hunter. This latter disorder, fairly common in certain South African families, differs so radically from the malady from which King George III suffered, that it may be a different disease altogether, in spite of the name.

It is of interest to note that a serious attack of variegate porphyria will be precipitated in sufferers (otherwise apparently healthy) by the administration of a barbiturate drug.

Dean's work on variegate porphyria indicates that this disease has not been identified among descendants of the Rex family – any more than has porphyria proper. South African sufferers from variegate porphyria, mostly to be found in the Eastern Province of the Cape, are all directly descended from a late seventeenth century immigrant source.

It is thus clear that any attempt to link Knysna and Windsor genetically on these lines would be fruitless.

Appendix B

A ROMANTIC TALE

Of the scores of variations of this story, the following, which appeared in *The Daily Dispatch*, East London, South Africa, on 9 January 1931, is probably the most entertaining. Having mentioned 'the several sensational repercussions and political

214

agitations' which resulted from the romance of Prince George and Hannah, the writer, Mr. Luhis, continued:

'The brothers Rex were the children of George III (then Prince of Wales) and the beautiful young Quaker girl, Hannah Lightfoot, whose father kept a haberdasher's shop in the Haymarket. In driving to and from St. James's Palace young George often saw her and became enamoured. With the help of one of the maids of honour, one Elizabeth Chudleigh (afterwards the notorious Duchess of Kingston) George was enabled to meet her at the house of one of her friends, where she was visiting; but the courtship did not thrive. The little Quaker girl remained obdurate, and nothing but marriage would satisfy her.

'Her father also proved very hostile, and in order to put an end to the intrigue he betrothed his daughter to the son of a prominent grocer in the City, a highly respected member of the Guild of Grocers, and a prospective alderman.

'Hannah, although no doubt in her heart unwilling to obey the mandate of her stern Quaker father, was at last compelled to comply with his wishes, and the marriage was arranged to take place. But George – as the sequel showed – had not been idle. On the eve of the wedding, when all the guests were assembled at the house of the future father-in-law drinking the healths of the bride and bridegroom-to-be, a coach drove up to the door, and when, in answer to a peremptory knock, the door was opened, a number of masked men rushed in and forcibly bore Hannah away from amidst the wedding guests.

'An outcry naturally followed, but the masked men, keeping the crowd off at the point of their swords, bundled the screaming bride into the coach and the furiously lashed horses galloped away at a desperate speed. Hannah was gone, no one knew where.

'But this arbitrary and illegal proceeding by no means ended the matter. The whole City was aroused as one man. At the Guildhall, the Mansion House and on 'Change meetings of protest were held. The apprentices, with cries of 'Clubs! Clubs! rushed from their shops and paraded the streets shouting, 'Privilege, Privilege! redress! *Habeas Corpus!* Our liberties are outraged! Clubs! Clubs!' The City Train-bands were called out. The Lord Mayor and Councillors, Aldermen and Sheriffs walked in procession to the Guildhall and demanded justice, and rioting broke out in all parts of the City. The doors and windows of the house occupied by officers of the Crown were demolished, barricades of paving-stones were thrown up at Temple Bar and other gates, and everything pointed to a first-rate riot.

'Nothing would pacify the citizens. The cry of *Habeas Corpus* was heard everywhere as they demanded that Hannah Lightfoot's body should be produced in Court, where a charge of criminal abduction was to be laid against the Prince of Wales.

'George II became alarmed. He was an old man now and nearing the end of his reign. He therefore gave orders that Hannah should be produced in Court. This satisfied the citizens for the time, and the riots ceased.

'But they reckoned without the lady, for when the law officers arrived at the secluded retreat of the bride she absolutely refused to comply with their wishes, stating that she was there of her own free will, and had in no way been coerced. No charge could therefore be laid against His Royal Highness, and as Hannah was presumably of age, even her father was powerless to enforce his action.

'The citizens simmered down after this, and the cobble-stones were replaced in Fleet Street. The cage in which George kept his little bird was situated at Hackney, north-east suburb of London – a house surrounded by a high wall enclosing a well-kept garden and orchard. Here her two sons were born and she continued to reside there for many years, being well looked after and provided for by George III, who had in the meantime (1760) succeeded his father 'that snuffy old drone from a German throne" as a contemporary critc labelled him.'

Appendix C

BIOGRAPHICAL SKETCH OF WILLIAM HARRISON (1802-1884).

William Harrison's account of his visit to the Cape in 1830-31 is now in the MSS collection of the South African Pub.ic Library. The following details of his life are summarised from an account by Peter Crail, in an article in the *Quarterly Bulletin of the South African Library,* Vol. 13.

Harrison, the son of Isaac Harrison, a hat manufacturer, was born at Salford, near Manchester, in 1802, was educated at the Moravian school at Fairfield at which Mary Smith, later the wife of Dr. Robert Moffat, was also educated. In his earlier years was engaged in shipping and commerce and in July 1830, left Manchester for the Cape. In his introductory remarks to the 357-page journal, *Minutes of a Voyage to the Cape of Good Hope and a Journey into the Interior of South Africa in the Years 1830-31,* he states that, although he kept a proper journal on his voyage out to the Cape, the account of both his residence in Cape Town and his journey to the Eastern Cape was written up afterwards from pencilled notes which he had jotted down at the time. His contribution to *Notes and Queries,* in which he commented on George Rex's resemblance to George III (already out of the public eye for fifty years), was made in 1861, some twenty-two years after Rex's death.

On 26 November 1830, Harrison set out for the Eastern Cape on horseback from the residence of Dirk Van Reenen (owner of the Newlands Brewery) together with a young Dutch-speaking companion, Jacob Deneys. He listed his kit meticulously, from '2 nightcaps' to 'Canvas bag of money, chiefly Silver' and gives several entertaining sidelights to the general progress of the journey. The early part of the trip has no relevance here. From George, a 'small place built chiefly on both sides of a long street', they continued their way through 'scenery romantic in the extreme' to Knysna. They arrived that night at *Melkhout Kraal,* where they spent three pleasant days exploring the estates, the harbour and the surrounding countryside, as guests of Mr. George Rex. Harrison's description of the subsequent precipitous journey over the Paardekop to the Long Kloof, where they finally arrived at the hospitable abode of Mr. Zondagh, who had 'a large place and numerous sheep', makes vivid reading.

On Christmas Day, almost a month after they had set out, they were in Grahamstown, where Harrison was at last able to call on Lieutenant Duthie (Thomas Henry) whom they had just missed at the Knysna. 'I had a long and interesting chat with him about his journey up from the Cape. He is much of the same opinion as myself that there is much sameness in the country and once seeing is quite sufficient.'

A year after his return to England in 1831, Harrison married Mary Sefton Beck at Prestbury, Cheshire. About ten years later, he retired from business and settled on the Isle of Man. He was a member of the House of Keys from 1856-1867, was a foundation member of the Manx Society, and became an antiquarian of some note. He died at Rockmount, Kirk German, Isle of Man, on 22 November 1884.

ROBERT JACOB GORDON – A REMARKABLE DUTCHMAN (1743-1795)

The illustrious owner of *Schoonder Zigt*, five years before George Rex bought it, was Colonel Robert Jacob Gordon. This versatile and gifted Dutchman, of Scots descent, was born in Doesburg in Gelderland in 1743. He became a captain in the foreign Scots Brigarde in Holland, a regiment of which his father, also certainly of Dutch parentage, was a Major-General.

Robert Jacob first came to the Cape on furlough in 1773 and travelled extensively, probably as far as the Great Fish River. From a subsequent remark written on a map about five years later, it appears that he may have been to Plettenberg Bay in 1773. He also spent a week on foot exploring the mountains 'between the Cape and False Bay' with the botanists, C.P.Thunberg and F.Masson.

In 1777 Gordon again arrived at the Cape as military captain of the garrison there. Three years later he was promoted to be its Commander. Details and discussion of his journeys, maps, drawings and notes have been comprehensively chronicled by Professor Vernon S.Forbes in his *Pioneer Travellers in South Africa*. Gordon is, of course, well known in school histories for his naming the Orange River in honour of the Prince of Orange, to whom he was greatly devoted. Not so well known is a comment he made on his Drawing no. 37 of Plettenberg Bay on 14 February 1778, to the effect that he had named this bay after the Governor some eight months previously.

Map 3 of the Gordon Collection in the Rijksmuseum, Amsterdam, which 'he drew up or caused to be drawn up . . . sums up more geographical knowledge of South Africa in a single sheet than any similar work of similar compass available up to the end of the eighteenth century.' Gordon's maps are supplemented by some 400 drawings showing scenery, the native inhabitants, fauna and flora of the Cape. One panorama of the Cape is about eight metres long. His records have been summed up as 'an unrivalled treasure of pictorial information of the highest value not only to geographers, but also to historians, ethnologists, zoologists and botanists.'

He and his wife had six sons and a daughter, but only four of the boys were alive at the time of their father's death. The youngest child, James Carel Gerhard, was baptised after the family had moved into *Schoonder Zigt*.

Schoonder Zigt was a haven for foreign visitors. Here guests met a courteous, cultured and entertaining host, who spoke a number of languages, including a knowledge of Hottentot and Gaelic. He was tall and robust, 'a very fine, jovial fellow and most agreeable companion as can be'. But emotional upheaval, when the Cape was surrendered to the Dutch on the instructions of the Prince of Orange, so that his personal loyalty became split between the Stadtholder and the new Republic, was said to have caused his conduct to be irresolute in the extreme. Insulted by his own soldiers, in addition weakened by illness and possibly unhappy in his domestic life, this remarkable Dutchman tragically ended his life in 1795 by shooting himself at his home, *Schoonder Zigt*.

Nine years after his death, his widow wrote from Switzerland to try – without success – to persuade the British government to purchase Gordon's valuable papers, maps and drawings. After being in the hands of several owners for over a century, these documents were eventually bought by the Rijksmuseum, Amsterdam.

REFERENCES

Vernon S. Forbes, Pioneer Travellers in South Africa (1965);
Archives Year Book of South Africa History (1950) vol. I;
A. Gordon Brown's, Pictorial Art in South Africa during Three Centuries to 1875 (1952).

Appendix E

COMPOSITION OF THE VICE-ADMIRALTY COURT ABOUT 1800

The full list of the personnel of the Court is as follows:

John Holland Esq.,	– Judge
John Holland Esq.,	– Register
B. W. Rouviere Esq.,	– Deputy Register and Actuary
George Rex Esq.,	– Marshal
Thomas Wittenoon Esq.,	– King's Proctor
Peter Mosse Esq.,	– Advocate
Thomas Rowles Esq.,	– Examiner
Mr. E.B. Ziervogel	– Translator
Mr. Alex Tennant	– Vendue Master
Messrs. Wm Menzies	– Register's Clerks
Joseph Rankin	
Edward Halloran	– Messenger and Crier

Appendix F

SOME CAPE TOWN RESIDENTS IN 1800

The names of some residents of Cape Town, listed in *The Cape Directory, 1800,* whom Rex may have known:

Johan(n) Diederik Ungerer, a gunner from Welzheim, Germany, was living – probably boarding – at 23 Burg Street with Nicolaas Gulde and his wife.

Samuel Frederick Ungerer, also of Welzheim (married to Anna Elisabeth Bergh), living at 76 Loop Street.

Johanna Rosina van Coeverden (widow, formerly Greyling), at 71 Long Street, in the same house at a Pieter Kacobus (sic) van Coeverden.

Carolus Augustus Freislich (married to Elisabeth Geertruyda Minne), at 11 Castle Street.

Jan Freislich, a warden of the Lutheran Church (married to Anna Maria Minne), at 21 Bree Street.

Johannes Gerhardus Freislich (possibly a son of the above) is shown as boarding at 21 Bree Street.

Francois de Necker, a fire-master (married to Jacoba Freislich) at 35 Bree Street.

Mrs. C.A. Freislich (widow, formerly Johanna Margaretha van der Stap) and
  Johannes Gerhardus Freislich (possibly her son) living on the *Tuyn Schoonderzigt.*
Alexander Tennant, Vendue Master of the Vice-Admiralty Court (married to Cor-
  nelia Agatha Sannenberg), at 16 Berg Street.
Egedius Benedictus Ziervogel, translator of the same Court (married to Beatrix Auret)
  at the Quipage near the docks.
Pieter van Wyngaarden, of Amsterdam (married to Christina Elisabeth Bussinger), at
  3 Mosselsteeg (Mossel Lane).

Appendix G

JAMES CALLANDER – MAN OF THE SEA

James Callander, according to some writers, was well connected with the nobility of
Scotland, claiming kinship with the Grahams, Campbells, Buchanans, MacFarlanes,
Stuarts and MacGregors. He was born about 1757. In 1772 a relative, Sir Lawrence
Dundas, obtained employment for him in the service of the English East India
Company and Callander's first voyage was to China. Two years later, when his ship,
The Prime, under the command of another relative, James Dundas, had to leave for
the East at short notice, Callander switched ships and sailed to the West Indies in
The Thames. Later he was serving on a ship carrying army supplies to Boston, which
arrived just in time for him 'to see the first battle fought in October, 1775 in the
American War of Independence.'

During the following seven or eight years he was on the warship, *Ramillies,*
(seventy-four guns) and 'fought some very hard battles with the French and
Spaniards', as he put it. He saw service in the vicinity of New York, in the West
Indies and was at Gibraltar when the Spaniards assaulted it. At some stage he was
promoted to lieutenant.

When hostilities ceased he returned to service in the East India Company and
during 1784-1793 undertook extensive trading voyages to the Far East 'command-
ing several fine ships . . . in the merchant service principally, from Bombay to
China, but frequently to Bengal, Madras and other ports.' At this time he claimed to
have prospered and to have owned three ships by 1793. French privateers from
Mauritius, however, captured two of them, with their valuable cargoes and Callander reputedly lost £14 000. He had perforce to dispose of the third ship as he was
not insured for such a contingency, being unaware that war had broken out again.
He returned to England in 1797.

During 1798 he skippered a brig for John Murray, merchant and trader,
between Cape Town and Mossel Bay. Towards the end of the year, possibly
through the patronage of General Dundas, he was commissioned to examine and
report on all relevant features of the coastal regions between Mossel Bay and Algoa
Bay. He sailed to Plettenberg Bay and travelled overland to Knysna, accompanied
by an experienced ship's carpenter, who was to investigate the various kinds of
timber growing in the area. Many years later, in 1817, Callander rather surprisingly
complained that he had himself paid for sending the boat by sea from the Cape to
Plettenberg Bay.

At Knysna he must have obtained permission from Johann von Lindenbaum,
then owner of *Melkhout Kraal,* to build a small wooden house at The Heads. One
map shows that he first lived at the eastern head and later moved further inland to

the area now known as *Woodbourne*. There is also a belief that he may have had some sort of dwelling at Plettenberg Bay as well.

This rumbustious sailor, now in his forties, proceeded to survey and chart the lagoon. He never got around to examining the rest of the coast eastwards towards Algoa Bay, but seemingly concentrated on the great potential of the Knysna lagoon and environs. On 4 August 1799, when the Kaffirs and Hottentots were on the rampage, he appealed to the authorities in Cape Town for powder for the inhabitants of the Knysna-Plettenberg Bay area. Again in 1800 and 1802 the area was raided and his little dwelling *(and Melkhout Kraal)* suffered from the depredations of the savages. As no help resulted from his appeal for assistance, except being adjured to stand firm, this seasoned salt no doubt took appropriate tactical action whenever danger threatened, returning each time to repair the damage done. John Barrow's story of 'boors' being responsible on one occasion for his house being robbed and devastated is, by some historians, not believed to be correct.

Governor Janssens, accompanied by Captain Paravicini di Capelli, a surgeon, Dirk Gysbert van Reenen (of Papenboom, also called the Brewery, at Newlands) van Reenen's son, Daniel, and others spent most of Friday, 22 April 1803, at Knysna and met this 'courteous Englishman' (according to di Capelli). This 'English gentleman' (van Reenen's version) presented the Governor with a map of the bay and the river, showing all nautical features. His enthusiastic recommendation of the lagoon as a possible harbour, was not appreciated by van Reenen, who considered the narrow passage between The Heads very dangerous.

Callander recounted the damage done to his property by the raiders and the Governor promised to give consideration to this matter on his return to Cape Town provided 'Callander got on with the job of surveying the approach to the Knysna accurately and reported his findings in detail'.

Commissary-General de Mist and the famous German scientist, Henry Lichtenstein, visited Knysna in December 1803. Lichtenstein refers to Holiday as the owner and Callander as 'the present possessor (not owner) of *Melkhout Kraal*'. He was well aware of Callander's projects, but does not mention having met him. Neither did Robert Semple, who so much enjoyed the von Lindenbaum family's hospitality at this farm in 1801. Possibly Callander was away at the Cape or elsewhere on Admiralty business at the time.

From October 1804, British subjects – with certain exceptions – were compelled to reside in Stellenbosch in a type of gentlemany confinement and James Callander was one of those he described as 'prisoners at large'. During this enforced nine-month pause from his naval activities, he took the opportunity of marrying an Afrikaans woman, Catharina Sandenbergh, in the Dutch Church in Stellenbosch on 7 April 1805. He then settled in Cape Town, where he owned property and where two children were born of the marriage in 1810 and 1815. Mrs. Callander died in December 1817.

Throughout the years Callander maintained an interest in Knysna and in August 1817, a few months before his wife's death, he wrote a memorandum recounting his own earlier findings and recommendations regarding a possible harbour at Knysna, spurred on by a recent survey made by Captain Wallis, of the sloop-of-war, *Podargus*. Callander also suggested in this memorandum that his 'local knowledge of the country and the people and his perfect knowledge of the river may be an inducement to his being placed as resident there. No more was heard of this, however, and three years later, at the age of about sixty-three, he was in Uitenhage 'confined to bed with a serious ashmatic complaint'. He made his will there on 1 August, 1820, and a little over a month later he was dead. His will was registered on 22 September. In his testament a considerable estate, the existence of two illegitimate sons, as well as some brothers and sisters living in Scotland, are recorded. James Callander's descendants are today mainly Afrikaans-speaking.

REFERENCES:
J. A. Wiid, *James Callander: 'n Romantiese Loopbaan*, Die Huisgenoot, 28.1.1928; *D. G. van Reenen se Joernaal*, Van Riebeeck Society, (18) p. 65 & footnote; G. M. Theal, *History of the Cape Colony, 1795-1828*, p. 252; G. M. Theal, *Records of the Cape Colony*, XI, pp. 374-375; Cape Archives, Map B.R. 52, p. 803; John Barrow, *Travels in Southern Africa* (1st Ed.) pp. 76 and 131; Cape Archives, *Andrew Barnards Official Diary;* Paravicini di Capelli, *Reize in de Binnenlanden* (Van Riebeeck Society, vol. 46), pp. 38n, 39 and 39n; H. Lichtenstein, *Travels in South Africa in the Years* 1803 etc. (Van Riebeeck Society, vol. 10) pp. 199 and 245.

Appendix H

COPYHOLD LAND

Unlike the title of Freehold land which, as the name indicates, refers to estate owned without limitation to any particular class of heirs, the title of copyhold land was held by a manorial court which kept the 'copy' containing the admissions of tenants to such land. In the case of the 'three acres and three roods lying at Bromley Brook in Plaistow Marsh', the title was held by the Manor Court of West Ham Burnells. It was the system by which copyholders were empowered to grant leases of up to thirty-one years to a tenant without fine to the lord of the manor, i.e. a sum of money paid by the incoming tenant in consideration of a small rent. If a longer lease were granted, the copyholder paid the penalty of forfeiture of the copyhold.

The copyhold system was widespread in east London and it was in this way that 'St. George in the East, Stepney, Spitalfields, Ratcliffe, Limehouse, Wapping, Shadwell, Mile End Old Town, Bethnal Green and Wapping (close to Plaistow) were developed or allowed to fill out in that straggling confused manner, without plan or purpose, so thoroughly deplored by Defoe in his description of London in 1724.' (George Rudé, *Hanoverian London*, p 11).

Appendix I

JOHN LIPTRAP'S CAREER

Liptrap, John (1796-1878) General 45th N.I. born London 15 April 1796; Cadet 1817. Admitted 5 September 1818; Ensign (21 April 1818) 30 August 1818; Lieutenant 4 November 1818; Captain 19 June 1831; Major 17 February 1850; Lieut. Colonel 7 May 1855; Bt. Colonel 20 June 1857; Major General 22 August 1865; Lieut. General 8 March 1873; General 1 October 1877.

Died Kensington Gate, London, 21 September 1878. Baptised St. Dunstan's Stepney, 21 June 1796. Son of John Liptrap of 6 Vansittart Terrace, Greenwich and his wife, Elizabeth, daughter of James Hunt of Union Hall, Middlesex.

Married, 1st, St. John's, Calcutta, 1 September 1823, Miss M. Perigoe

       2nd. Eliza, widow of William Cook Wallace. (She died Surbiton, 26 February 1850)

       3rd. In Calcutta, 2 January 1854, Emma, daughter of William Jell and widow of – Nash.

(List of Services follow)

from:
Officers of the Bengal Army
by Major V. C. P. Hodson. Vol. 3, (1946)
(War Office Library)

Appendix J

HALF-BAKED HISTORY

Many of the stories which were circulated about George Rex were silly, some unpleasant to the point of viciousness. Typical is the following, which was handed down by word of mouth, recorded by Peter MacOwan from information which he received from S. A. Deacon, an old resident of Concordia, Knysna, in June, 1891:

'GEORGE REX Son of George IV (III?) by Hannah Lightfoot, the Quakeress. Knysna is full of his progeny by a slave-wife or concubine. Strange stories at Knysna. He is stated to have been sent out to Knysna with honor and title of Admiral of the Colony, to have had a grant of land 'as far as he could see from a certain spot!' Certainly he lived in great state and owned all the land around the harbour of Knysna, which to this day (1891) is in the hands of his grandchildren 'Rex'. Hannah Lightfoot is said to have had two sons by George IV, (III) one being the Knysna Rex and the other being spirited away to America and reported to have been drowned. George Rex of Knysna is said to have received a large pension terminable in case he should marry, and thus raise legitimate heirs. Took a slave woman by whom he raised a dusky brood, and subsequently increased his tribe by cohabiting with this woman's daughter by another man, previous to the connection with Rex.

The local story is that he was brought up at Court and his expatriation was in consequence of some incestuous intercourse with a step-sister, a legitimate child of George IV (III).'

Sources

PREFACE
1. Marion Scott, *Beethoven* (Master Musician Series, London, 1934) p. 12

CHAPTER 1
1. Sanni Metelerkamp, *George Rex of Knysna: the Authentic Story* (Cape Town, 1955)
2. Ibid p. 41
3. British Museum *Notes and Queries* (First Series) vol. viii p. 87
4. A composite story, derived originally from correspondence in *The Monthly Magazine* No. 355, Vol. 51 pp. 493-588, No. 356 Supp. to 51 pp. 589-662, No. 358 Vol. 52 pp. 97-192, No. 359, Vol. 52 pp. 193-288, 1821, and repeated in various publications ever since
5. *Notes and Queries* (First Series) vol. viii p. 87
6. *The Registers of Mayfair Chapel*, 9 Dec. 1750 – 25 March 1754: The Bishop of London's Registry
7. British Museum *The Monthly Magazine*, No. 355, vol. 51 pp. 493-588, No. 356 (Suppl. no. to vol. 51) pp. 589-662 No. 358, vol. 52 pp. 97-192, No. 359, vol. 52 pp. 193-288. Variations of the story appeared later in *The New Monthly Magazine, Notes and Queries* and *The Farthing Journal*
8. In the library, Friends House, Euston Road, London
9. *The Fair Quaker, Hannah Lightfoot, and Her Relations with George III* (London, 1910)
10. *The Monthly Magazine*, pp. 97-192, No. 358 vol. 52 (Pearne's will was proved in April 1757)
11. Charles Bradlaugh, *The Impeachment of the House of Brunswick* (London, 6th ed. 1877)
12. Published Great Britain, 1972
13. John Brooke, pp. 42-43
14. James Earl Waldegrave, K.G., Governor to the Prince of Wales, afterwards George III, *Memoirs from 1754-1758* (London, 1821) p. 8
15. Sir Lewis Namier, *England in the Age of the American Revolution* (London, 2nd edition, 1961) p. 84
16. Brooke, p. 51
17. Metelerkamp, p. 35
18. *Letters from George III to Lord Bute, 1756-1766*, ed. Romney Sedgwick. London, 1939) Letter 46, p. 37
19. Ibid, No. 47, p. 38
20. Ibid, p. 39
21. Egerton MSS, 1719, fo. 81, British Museum (Information via Prof. Christie from Mrs. Marie Peters)
22. Letter from Prof. Christie, 22.5.1973

23. Ian R. Christie, *Myth & Reality in Late 18th Century British Politics,* (London, 1970) p. 323
24. *The Monthly Magazine,* No. 352, April 1, 1821 (3 of vol. 51)
25. Ibid No. 355 vol. 51, p. 532
26. Ibid
27. Ibid No. 359 vol. 52, p. 197
28. Ibid
29. *An Historical Fragment,* pp. 44-45
30. John Heneage Jesse, *Memoirs of the Life & Reign of George the Third,* (London, 2nd ed. 1867) p. 32
31. Metelerkamp, p. 30
32. Attributed to Lady Anne Hamilton, Lady-in-Waiting to Queen Caroline
33. *Anonymous Authentic Records of the Court of England,* (1831-'32) pp. 2–7
34. *The Secret History of the Court of England* pub. by William Henry Stevenson, London 1832, pp. 27/28
35. A Gordon Brown, *Pictorial Art in South Africa during Three Centuries,* (London, 1952) p. 118
36. *The Royal Academy of Arts, A Complete Dictionary of Contributors, 1769-1904* compiled by Algernon Graves, vol. 4 (republished 1970) Entry under Serres, J.T.
37. Gordon Brown, p. 18
38. Mary L. Pendered & Justinian Mallett, *Princess or Pretender ?* (London, 1939)

CHAPTER 2

1. The account which follows of the Ryves Trial, is drawn from Pendered & Mallett's *Princess or Pretender ?* and from the documents of the trial, in the Public Record Office, London. Ref. J.77, 44 R.31
2. Most of this *Appeal* had appeared in *The Morning Post,* 26 May – 16 Sept. 1848
3. Romney Sedgwick, *William Pitt & Lord Bute: an Intrigue of 1755-1758, History Today* series (London, October 1956) p. 653
4. *Letters from George III to Lord Bute* (ed. Romney Sedgwick) Letter 57, p. 45
5. In Public Record Office, London
6. South African Library, Rex MSS
7. Ibid
8. Heneage Jesse, pp. 30-36
9. Many sources, from *The Monthly Magazine,* October, 1821, to a summary in M.L. Pendered's *The Fair Quaker,* pp. 288-298
10. South African Library, MSS Collection, *Minutes of a Voyage to the Cape of Good Hope and a Journey into the Interior of South Africa in the Years 1830-'31,* p. 181
11. Unpublished diary, pp 79/80, In the possession of Mrs. I. Rosenbrock-Drège, Port Elizabeth
12. H. Barton Baker, *The Streets of London* (London, 1899) p. 360
13. *The Fair Quaker and Her Relations with George III*
14. Ibid, p. 288
15. Ibid, p. 277
16. Ibid, pp. 278-279
17. Ibid, pp. 299-301

18. Nom de plume of John Saint Clair Muriel, (Published London, 1939)
19. *The Lovely Quaker,* pp. 296-302
20. Ibid, p. 297
21. In *People and Places* (Cape Town, 1944)
22. In *The Daily Dispatch,* East London, 9.1.1931 (Contributor Luhis)
23. Three editions, 3rd. 1955
24. Johannesburg 1961. Further editions 1963, 1967 and 1973
25. Cape Town, 1971

CHAPTER 3

1. Lambeth Palace Library, Faculty Office Fiats F 11/1787
2. Lambeth Palace Library, Court of Arches Records, Admissions KKK
3. Charles Lamb, *Essays: The Superannuated Man*
4. W.S. Holdsworth, *A History of the English Law,* vol. IV, p. 236
5. Faculty Office, London, quoted in Metelerkamp, p. 46
6. Pendered & Mallett, Appendix D. p. 256
7. *Boyle's City Companion,* 1798, part II, p. 112
8. Holdsworth, vol IV. p. 236
9. Pendered & Mallett, p. 257
10. Holdsworth, vol. IV, p. 237
11. Charles Dickens, *David Copperfield,* Chap. XXIII
12. *David Copperfield,* Chap. XXIII
13. Holdsworth, vol. XII, p. 50
14. Christopher Hibbert, London: *The Biography of a City* (London, 1969) p. 104 et seq.
15. Burton, Elizabeth, *The Georgians at Home* (London 1967) p. 289
16. M.S. Geen, *The Making of South Africa* (Cape Town, 1958) p. 44
17. M. Whiting Spilhaus, *South Africa in the Making,* (Cape Town, 1966) p. 212
18. Public Record Office, London, Administrations 2/1065 pp. 404/405
19. Public Record Office, London, Administrations Index 4828, Promiscuous 44

CHAPTER 4

1. G. McCall Theal, *Records of the Cape Colony,* 1796-1799, vol. II, p. 220
2. Cape Archives, B.O. 160 (Old reference B.O. 56)
3. Theal, *Records . . .* vol. II, pp. 34/35
4. *South Africa a Century Ago, Letters Written from the Cape of Good Hope, 1797-1801, by the Lady Anne Barnard,* ed. memoir & notes by W.H. Wilkins, Johannesburg Public Library
5. *Diary of Eusebius Hudson* (Manuscript, Part I) Johannesburg Public Library
6. Geen, p. 41
7. *South Africa a Century Ago,* p. 45
8. Ibid, p. 146
9. Geen, p. 42
10. Theal, *Records . . .* vol. II, p. 151
11. Ibid, pp. 110/111
12. Vernon S. Forbes, *Pioneer Travellers of South Africa* (Cape Town, 1956) p. 132

13. The Library of the University of the Witwatersrand, No. 127 of the Papers of Earl Macartney, Collection No. 88
14. Theal, *Records* . . . vol. II, pp. 22-28
15. Public Record Office, London, Adm. 2/1065 pp. 404/405
16. Vice-Admiralty Proceedings, Cape of Good Hope Muniment Book, p. 39, H.C.A. 49/38/1
17. Cape Town, 1971
18. Ralph Kilpin, *The Old Cape House* (Cape Town, 1918) p. 38
19. The following history of maces is based on information in *Oar Maces of Admiralty*, National Maritime Museum, Her Majesty's Stationery Office, 1966
20. Eric Walker, *A History of South Africa* (Cape Town, 1928) p. 170
21. *South Africa a Century Ago*, pp. 148-154
22. Theal, *Records* . . . vol. II, pp. 134/135
23. Ibid, p. 241
24. C. Graham Botha, *Social Life in the Cape Colony*, 2nd ed. (Cape Town, 1970) p. 34
25. Cape Archives, B.O. 160 (B.O. 56/172 – old reference – is the number given for these appointments in Miss Metelerkamp's book, but as this file was being bound in Pretoria and unobtainable for inspection throughout the many months this present book was being written, it has been impossible to check these statements.
26. Metelerkamp p. 49
27. *South Africa a Century Ago*, p. 140
28. Theal, *Records* . . . vol. II, p. 160
29. Ibid, passim
30. *South Africa a Century Ago;* p. 187
31. Theal, *Records* . . . vol. II, pp. 234-237
32. Ibid, p. 300
33. Madeleine Masson, *Lady Anne Barnard* (London, 1948) p. 233
34. Theal, *Records* . . . vol. II, p. 304
35. Ibid, pp. 304/305
36. Ibid, pp. 329-333
37. Ibid, p. 333
38. Ibid, pp. 323-328
39. Ibid, pp. 408/409
40. Ibid, p. 477
41. Ibid, pp. 314/315
42. *South Africa a Century Ago*, p. 263
43. M. Whiting Spilhaus, pp. 273/274
44. Cape Archives, B.O. 9 (1800-1801) p. 100
45. H.W.J. Picard, *Gentleman's Walk*, (Cape Town, 1968) p. 142

CHAPTER 5

1. Deeds Office, Deed of Transfer No. 51 1/1788
2. Information from Dr. Mary Cook
3. Deeds Office, Deed of Transfer No. 51 1/1788
4. Forbes p. 93
5. C.J. Barnard, *R.J. Gordon se Loopbaan Aan die Kaap* (in Archives Year Book of South African History, 1950, vol. I) p. 365

6. Ibid, p. 384
7. Deeds Office, Deed of Transfer No. 82
8. Deeds Office, Deed of Transfer No. 79
9. Deeds Office, Deed of Transfer No. 372
10. Beddy p. ix
11. Cape Archives, MOOC 6/9/16 No. 3452
12. G. T. Nurse, Letter of 18/6/1973
13. A. J. Böeseken, *Simon van der Stel en sy Kinders* (Cape Town, 1964) Inleeding
14. G. T. Nurse, letter of 18/6/1973
15. Jenkins & Nurse, *Blood Group Gene Frequencies, S.A. Mediese Tydskrif,* 29/4/1972, p. 560
16. Beddy, p. I
17. Ibid, p. ix
18. S. Metelerkamp, letter to Madge Beddy, 1936 (In possession of A. J. R. Beddy)
19. Cape Archives, MOOC 6/9/115 no. 2661 (filed May, 1866)
20. Cape Archives DN 3119 (filed 17/1/1839)
21. Beddy, p. xi
22. Compiled by A. N. Berner (Cape Town, 1969)
23. South African Library Crail cards, Reference given, N. 92 no. 596
24. South African Library Crail cards, Reference given, B.O. 42/761 (old ref.)
25. South African Library Crail cards, Reference given, N. 86, Nos. 921, 835, 836 and 837
26. Spilhaus, p. 26
27. Beddy, pp. x & xi
28. South African Library Crail cards, Ref. given Vrybrief 23/12/1801
29. Cape Archives B.O. 9(1800-1801) pp. 98-104
30. Cape Directory of 1800
31. Cape Archives B.O. 10(1801) p. 79
32. Cape Archives B.O. 80 (old reference)
33. Theal, *Records* . . . vol. III pp. 125-127
34. Ibid, vol. IV, p. 266
35. Ibid, vol. III p. 458
36. Beddy, p. I
37. Theal, *Records* . . . vol. IV pp. 205/206
38. Ibid, pp. 74/75
39. Theal, *History of S. Africa, 1795-1828,* p. 91
40. Theal, *Records* . . . vol. iv, pp. 216/217
41. J. A. Wiid, *'n Romantiese Loopbaan,* in *Die Huisgenoot,* January, 1939, p. 33
42. Spilhaus p. 332
43. Theal, *Records* . . . vol. XI, pp. 374/375 (Memorandum by Mr. James Callander, August, 1817)
44. *Dirk G. van Reenen se Joernaal,* 1803, Van Riebeeck Society, vol. 18, (Cape Town, 1937) pp. 11-13
45. Theal, *Records* . . . vol. II, p. 498
46. Metelerkamp, p. 72
47. Theal, *Records* . . . vol. IV, p. 447
48. Ibid, vol. V, p. 163
49. Theal, *Records* . . . vol. V, pp. 191/192
50. Ibid pp. 206/207
51. Metelerkamp, p. 53
52. Beddy, p. I

53. Deeds Office, Deed of Transfer No. 309, 27/9/1804
54. Beddy p. I
55. Cape Archives, BR. 60 pp 65/66
56. Theal, *History of S. Africa*, pp. 153/154
57. Cape Archives, BR. 60, pp. 65/66
58. Theal, *History of S. Africa*, p. 135
59. Cape Archives, BR. 9, p. 3825
60. Paravicini di Capelli, *Reizen in de Binnenlanden*, V.R.S. vol. 46 (Cape Town 1965) p. 34
61. *D.G. van Reenen se Joernaal*, pp. 11-13
62. Ibid pp. 65-67
63. Cape Archives, B.R. 9, p. 3825
64. Ibid
65. Graham Botha, *Social Life in the Cape Colony*, p. 52

CHAPTER 6

1. J. Phillippe Augusta De Mist, *Diary of a Journey to the Cape of Good Hope and the Interior in 1802 and 1803* (C. Town, 1954) p. 44
2. C. I. Latrobe, *Journal of a Visit to South Africa in 1815 and 1816* (London, 1818) p. 169
3. Published Cape Town, 1965
4. Francis Masson, *An Account of Three Journeys from the Cape Town* (London, 1776) p. 169
5. Ibid p. 291
6. Forbes, p. 30
7. Karl Peter Thunberg, *Travels in Europe, Africa & Asia made Between the Years 1776 and 1779*, 2nd ed. (London, 1795) vol. I, p. 181
8. The information on early land tenure in the Cape is condensed from: C. Graham Botha, Collected Works II, *Cape Law, Medicine & Place Names, Early Cape Land Tenure*, pp. 81-98; John Noble, *The Cape Colony & Its Resources*, (Cape Town, 1875) p. 243; C. Graham Botha, *Social Life in the Cape Colony* (2nd ed. Cape Town, 1970) pp. 66-68
9. J. St. L. Chase, *The Cape of Good Hope and the Eastern Province* (London, 1843) p. 132
10. Cape Archives, RLR 21/2 p. 108
11. Cape Archives, M3/36, *Nieuwe Kaart van den Zuydelyker Oever van Afrika*, 1790
12. Godee-Molesbergen, E.C. *Reizen in Zuid-Afrika in de Hollandse tijd . . .* vol. IV (Nijhoff, 1932) p. 55 et seq.
13. Ibid
14. *Die Duminy Dagboeke*, Van Riebeeck Society, vol. 19, (Cape Town, 1938) p. 13
15. Paravicini di Capelli, *Reizen in de Binnenlanden* (V.R.S. vol. 46, 1965) p. 34n
16. Robert Semple, *Walks and Sketches* (London, 1803) p. 159
17. Cape Archives, BR. 60 pp. 65/66
18. Di Capelli, p. 39
19. Henry Lichtenstein, *Travels in S. Africa in the years, 1803, 1804, 1805 and 1806* (from the German) (V.R.S. vol. 10, 1903) pp. 242/243
20. Theal, *History of S. Africa, 1795-1828* (London, 1903) pp. 251/252

CHAPTER 7

1. *Outeniqualand: The George-Knysna area,* ed. Peter Tyson, published by S.A. Geographical Society (1971) pp. 11-14
2. Ibid p. 22
3. Katharine Newdigate, *Honey, Silk & Cider* (Cape Town, 1956)
4. South African Library, Rex MSS
5. Metelerkamp, p. 81
6. Latrobe, p. 159
7. Beddy, p. I
8. Cape Archives, RLR 27/3, p. 149 (Original grant to Stephanus Ter Blanche 13/10/1780)
9. Theal, *History of South Africa,* p. 251
10. Deeds Office, Diagram No. 433 (In George Quitrents, vol. I, No. 40)
11. Cape Archives, RLR 32, p. 138, Original grant to Stephanus Wyers, 26/10/1784
12. Cape Archives, RLR 23/2, p. 181, Original grant to Hendrik Barnard, 12/1/1775
13. Andrew Steedman, *Wanderings and Adventures in the Interior of Southern Africa* (London, 1835) p. 319
14. South African Library, Rex MSS
15. Deeds Office, Diagram 254/1816 (In George Quitrents, vol. I, No. 41)
16. Cape Archives, B.O. 60, pp. 63/64 (old reference)
17. Cape Archives, RLR 90 No. 92, p. 213
18. South African Library, Rex MSS
19. Metelerkamp, p. 81
20. Theal, *Records . . .* vol. VI, p. 371
21. Henry Raikes (editor) *Memoir of the Life and Services of Vice-Admiral Sir Jahleel Brenton, baronet* (London, 1846) p. 491
22. Theal, *History of South Africa* pp. 221/222
23. South African Library, Rex MSS
24. Cape Archives, C.O. 122 No. 14
25. Cape Archives, C.O. 4843, pp. 74-76
26. Metelerkamp p. 113
27. *The Historical Monuments of South Africa* ed. J.J. Oberholster (Cape Town, 1972) p. 126
28. James Holman, *A Voyage Round the World, including travels in Africa, Asia,* etc. *1827-1832* (London, 1840) vol. 2, p. 186
29. Cowper Rose, *Four Years in Southern Africa* (London, 1829) p. 269
30. *Historical Monuments of S. Africa* p. 34
31. Steedman, p. 320
32. John Croumbie Brown, *Crown Forests at the Cape of Good Hope* (London, 1887) p. 8 et seq.
33. Theal, *History of South Africa,* pp. 251/252
34. Cape Archives, C.O. 2604 (Opgaaf)
35. South African Library, Rex MSS
36. In the possession of the Rev. A. Rex Beddy
37. Capt. A.F. Jones Report of 1/11/1812, quoted in Croumbie Brown, p. 15
38. South African Library, Rex MSS

CHAPTER 8

1. Beddy, p. I
2. *Doopregister* van die Ned. Geref. Kerk, George, 21/3/1809
3. Unpublished diary of Carl Drège
4. Gordon Brown, *An Artist's Journey along the Old Cape Post Road, 1832-'33,* (Cape Town, 1972)
5. J.F. Victorin, *Travels in the Cape, 1853-1855* (Translated from the Swedish) (Cape Town, 1968) p. 72
6. Cape Archives, Opgaaf 1.6.1812
7. Beddy, p. I
8. *Doopregister* van die Ned. Geref. Kerk, George, 1813-1827, Ref. G9-3/1
9. Details of life at *Melkhout Kraal,* unless otherwise indicated, are drawn from this diary
10. South African Library, Rex MSS
11. Ibid
12. Thelma Gutsche, *The Bishop's Lady* (Cape Town, 1970) p. 162
13. Metelerkamp, p. 35
14. Ibid p. 149
15. South African Library, Rex MSS
16. Robert & Annie Hart, *A Memoir of the Rev. A.G. Duthie & of W.H.M. Duthie* (Oxford, 1934) p. I
17. A.F. Hattersley, *An Illustrated Social History of South Africa* (Cape Town, 1969) p. 67
18. Ibid p. 168
19. South African Library/Duthie Letters and Journals
20. R. & A. Hart, Memoir, p. 4
21. Metelerkamp, pp. 224-233
22. George Rex's Diary, 1833-'34
23. Latrobe, pp. 158-163
24. James Bowie, *Diary of Travels in South Africa, 1816-1823* Quoted in J. Hutchinson's *A Botanist in Southern Africa* (London 1946) pp. 623-4
25. George Thompson, *Travels & Adventures in Southern Africa* (London, 1827) p. 7
26. Cowper Rose, p. 268
27. Holman, pp. 186/187
28. Steedman, pp. 319-321
29. Frank Bradlow, *Baron Von Ludwig and the Ludwig's-Burg Gardens* (Cape Town, 1965) passim.
30. James Backhouse, *Narrative of a Visit to the Mauritius & South Africa* (London 1844) p. 131
31. O. Spohr, *Travel Journal of Ferdinand Krauss* (Translated from the German) (Cape Town, 1974)
32. Cape Archives, MOOC 6/2/p.213
33. Cape Archives, MOOC 6/2/p. 283
34. Cape Archives, MOOC 6/9/14/3119
35. Deeds Office, Erf. 2081, Transfer 1/7/1851
36. Cape Archives, C.O. 2609, no. 16
37. *Doopregister* van die Ned. Geref. Kerk, George, 24/2/1822
38. Cape Archives MOOC 6/9/3/573
39. South African Library, Rex MSS
40. Metelerkamp, pp. 223-233

41. Public Record Office, London, PROB 11/1967
42. Metelerkamp p. 239
43. South African Library, *Cape of Good Hope Commercial Advertiser*, cutting in Rex MSS, undated.

CHAPTER 9

1. Beddy, p. xiv and letter dated 30.4.1973
2. Cape Archives MOOC 6/9/16 No. 3452
3. South African Library, Duthie Letters, Folder 1
4. Metelerkamp p. 238
5. *Baptismal Register* of St. Mary, Newington, 1707-1777, Ref. p. 92/MRY/8 p. 266
6. Pendered & Mallett, p. 254
7. Ibid
8. Greater London Record Office P93/MRY1/28 p. 98
9. Essex Record Office, D/DPe, M5
10. County Hall Record Office, P. 98, MRY 1.10, Mar.1758-Oct. 1774
11. Essex Record Office D/DPe, M5
12. Information received from Prof. Christie, letter 29/11/1972
13. Pendered & Mallett, p. 255
14. Burton, p. 254
15. George Rudé, *Hanoverian London* (London, 1971) p.85
16. *Baptismal Register* of St. Mary, Whitechapel, P93/MRY/7 R. 728 p. 141
17. Guildhall Library, London, MS 6207/1 (not foliated)
18. Information from Prof. Christie, letter 2/4/1973
19. Guildhall Library, London, MS 6207/2
20. Towers Hamlet Central Library, London, Location B.R.A. 984
21. London merchant directories; information from Prof. Christie, letter 29/11/72
22. Rudé, pp. 7/8 and 96
23. The Metropolitan Borough of Stepney; *Official Guide* (8th ed. 1958) p. 94
24. H.V. Morton, *Ghosts of London* (London 1952) p. 133
25. Essex Record Office D/DPe, M5
26. Ibid
27. *Burial Register* of St. Mary's, Whitechapel, P93/MRY.1/64 (not paginated)
28. Public Record Office, London, PROB. 11/1229
29. Guildhall Library, London, *Minute Book of the Court of the Distillers Company* MS. 6207/1 (not paginated)
30. Information from Prof. Christie, letter 27/11/1972
31. Metelerkamp, p. 300 Note X
32. Lindsey, Chap. XVII
33. Guildhall Library, London, *Minute Book of the Distillers Company, 1779-1809* MS. 6207/2 p. 154
34. Ibid, pp. 50/51
35. Public Record Office, London PROB. 11/1281 f. 572
36. *Burial Register* of St. Mary's, Whitechapel. P93/MRY.1/64. Burials in Oct. 1797
37. Ibid. Burials in December, 1803
38. *St. Catherine Coleman Marriage Register, 1800-1812.* No. 10 (unfol.)
39. Public Record Office, London, PROB. 6/198 Administrations March, 1822
40. *Westminster Poll Book* 1818 p. 153, *Kent's Original London Directory* 1815 p. 274 and Thomas Underhill, *Triennial Directory* 1817-'19 (not paginated)

41. Information from Prof. Christie, letter 15/1/1973
42. *Register of Burials at Highgate in the Parish of Hornsey in the County of Middlesex in the year 1821*, p. 30 – No. 236, 'John Rex, Highgate, Dec. 21, 50 years, by S. Mence'
43. Public Record Office, London PROB 6/198 Administrations March 1822
44. *The Register of St. Mary the Virgin, Aldermanbury, London:* Transcribed and edited by A. W. Hughes Clarke (Pub. of the Harleian Soc.) vol. lxv, 1935, part III, p. 144
45. Public Record Office, London PROB. 11/1967
46. Essex Record Office D/DPe M23
47. *Burial Register of St. Mary's Whitechapel* P93/MRY.1/64. Burials in Dec. 1803 No. 9
48. Public Record Office, London, PROB 11/1182 f. 432
49. *Gentleman's Magazine,* June 1840, New series, xiii p. 646
50. Guildhall Library, *Freedom, Livery, Stewards & Assistants of the Distillers' Company,* MS. 6212 (not paginated)
51. Public Record Office, London PROB. 11/1182 f. 432
52. Tower Hamlets Central Library, Bancroft Road, London: *Bethnal Green Extracts Book* (not paginated)
53. *Hortus Kewensis* or a Catalogue of the plants cultivated at the Royal Botanic Garden at Kew, 2nd. ed. enlarged by William T. Aiton. vol. V (London, 1813) p. 411. Information from Mary Gunn.
54. *The Cyclopaedia* or *Universal Dictionary of Art, Sciences and Literature,* by Abraham Rees DD. vol. 39 (London, 1819) p. 2
55. *Gentleman's Magazine,* Sept. 1795, p. 788
56. Ibid No. lxvi p. 437
57. India Office Library, London. *Military Records* L/MIL/9/130 (Cadet papers 101-200, 1817)
58. War Office Library/Major V.C.P. Hodson, *Officers of the Bengal Army.* (1946) vol. 3
59. India Office Library, London, L/MIL/9/130
60. Metelerkamp p. 234
61. *Memoirs of George IV* (London, 1831) pp. 138/139
62. Information from Prof. Christie, letter 2/4/1973
63. Ibid
64. In Kew Chapel
65. *The Taylors of Kew* (published privately, London, 1973) p. 24
66. (London, 1937), p. 146
67. Stanley Ayling, *George the Third* (London 1972) p. 36n
68. Brooke, p. 389
69. Ibid, p. xv

CHAPTER 10

1. Brooke p. xvii
2. Lindsey, p. 296
3. Metelerkamp, p. 299 (Note X)
4. Beddy, p. xiii
5. Theo E.G. Cutten, *A History of the Press in S. Africa* (1935) p. 6
6. Ibid p. 7
7. Lindsey, p. 297

8. 10 Feb. 1861
9. South African Library, MSS Collection/W. Harrison, *Minutes of a Voyage to the Cape of Good Hope and a Journey into the Interior of S. Africa in the Years 1830-'31*, p. 181
10. The similarity in the wording of the last sentences suggests that the Obituary quoted in Chap. 8 emanated from the same pen as this one.
11. Metelerkamp p. 240
12. Beddy, facing p. xiv
13. N. Napier Devitt, in *People and Places*, p. 178
14. Information from Robin Reilly, letter 26/2/1973
15. Ibid, letter 11/4/1973
16. G. Bernard Hughes, *English & Scottish Earthenware*, 1660-1860 (London, 1961) p. 97
17. Alison Kelly, *Canals, Clay and Causes* (Britain, 1962) p. 41
18. Bernard Hughes, p. 96
19. Letter from Robin Reilly, 26/2/1973
20. Metelerkamp p. 257
21. Napier Devitt, pp. 177/178
22. Metelerkamp, p. 260
23. Pendered, p. 301
24. Lindsey, p. 301
25. Information and xerox copies of these documents from Miss M.H. Lister, a grand-daughter of Thomas Bain.
26. Theal, *Records . . .* vol. 2, p. 503
27. Metelerkamp, p. 266
28. Ibid, p. 222
29. Ibid, p. 278
30. Ibid, p. 40
31. Ibid, p. 35
32. Ibid, p. 155
33. Cape Archives MOOC 7/1/151
34. Cape Archives MOOC 7/1/151
34. Ibid
35. Metelerkamp, p. 246 et seq.
36. South African Library, Rex MSS (This document unsigned, but accompanying Agreement of Sale signed by John Rex, as Executor, on behalf of his co-Executors)
37. Metelerkamp, p. 251 et seq.
38. Victorin, p.72.

Index

235

236

238

TREE SHOWING LIPTRAP CONNECTION

SAMUEL DAVEY LIPTRAP
(d. 1789)

(——
1st. wif

*ELIZABETH = JOHN L.   SAMUEL DAVEY L.= ——
(d. 1836)

—— = AMELIA

(WM. PERIGOE =) (THOM. RASHDALL =)
(d. 1757)   (d. 1762)
1st. Husband   2nd. Husband

(C

RICHARD PERIGOE = ——
(1750 – 1795)

*AMELIA CAROLINE   *SAMUEL DAVEY L.   JOHN L. = MARIA
(1796 – 1878)   (1791 – 1838)

Johanna Rosina van der Caap   GEORGE REX = Carolina Ma
(C. 1772 ? – 1812 ?)   1st.   (1765 – 1839)   (C. 1792 – 1

*Edward R.   *John R.   *Elizabeth   *Jacob Govert R.   Anne   *Fre
(1801 – 1879) (1802 – 1858) Caroline   (1805 – 1882)   (1809 – 1839)   (18
                m.   (1804 – 1877)   m.
            S.M.C. Müller   F.A. Wentworth   J

*Sarah Rex of Bath and
Names underlined indicate

C.D.S.